£28.00

# Our countryside: the future

## A fair deal for rural England

*Presented to Parliament by
the Deputy Prime Minister and Secretary of State for the Environment, Transport and the Regions,
and the Minister of Agriculture, Fisheries and Food
by Command of Her Majesty
November 2000*

Cm 4909

Learning Resources
Centre

Department of the Environment, Transport and the Regions
Eland House
Bressenden Place
London SW1E 5DU
Telephone 020 7944 3000
Internet service http:/www.detr.gov.uk

Printed in Great Britain. Text and cover on material containing 75% post-consumer waste and 25% ECF pulp.

November 2000

# contents

## foreword by Rt Hon John Prescott, Deputy Prime Minister and Rt Hon Nick Brown, Minister of Agriculture Fisheries and Food

How we live our lives is shaped by where we live our lives.

But wherever people live, we believe they want the same basic things: jobs, a healthy economy, a stable and safe society, good public services – opportunity for all. North or south, urban or rural, the parts of our country – though different – are inextricably intertwined and interdependent. People also want to have a say in what happens in their community and to shape their own future.

The character, vitality and beauty of our countryside are important to all of us. But many rural communities are going through difficult changes. Basic services have become over-stretched. In traditional industries, such as farming, incomes are falling and jobs are disappearing. There has been pressure for unwelcome development. Wildlife diversity has declined. Previous Governments have failed to tackle these problems. Over the past 20 years we have seen post offices disappearing, council houses sold off, rural schools closed, building on green fields and village bus services cut.

We are beginning to turn this round. There have been real improvements over the the past three years. We have stemmed the closure of rural schools and we are introducing measures to reduce closures of post offices in rural areas. We are working to help farmers through very difficult times, providing millions of pounds in additional support and a new direction in agricultural policy. We are recruiting extra police officers in rural areas and, as part of our 10-Year Transport Plan, have begun investing more in rural bus and train services.

We know, however, that there is much more to do.

Our vision is of a living, working, protected and vibrant countryside. Not an outdated, picture-postcard version, but one where people have access to the jobs and services they require. We want to give a fair deal in public services, to support a diverse and successful rural economy, and to protect and enhance the environment. We want a countryside which can shape its own future, with its voice heard by Government at all levels.

Above all, we believe in a countryside for everyone. We have listened to the whole range of needs and concerns expressed by people living in the countryside. It is clear that our rural areas have a diverse set of problems and interests. This paper addresses the real needs of people in the countryside. It is also clear that in the past some rural voices have been louder than others. Government must listen to everyone.

In future we want decisions to be taken with the active participation of local people, and to develop new partnerships in delivering change. Government's role is to provide the framework and support for rural communities to succeed.

Some people want to drive a wedge between town and country. While we recognise what makes our countryside special, we also believe that rural and urban areas are interdependent. Our aim is to deliver an improved quality of life for everyone in the countryside – as well as in cities and towns. This White Paper sets out how we can achieve that.

John Prescott

Nick Brown

# ten ways we will
## make a difference

Our **vision** is of:

- a **living** countryside, with thriving rural communities and access to high quality public services;
- a **working** countryside, with a diverse economy giving high and stable levels of employment;
- a **protected** countryside in which the environment is sustained and enhanced, and which all can enjoy;
- a **vibrant** countryside which can shape its own future and with its voice heard by Government at all levels.

Our **aim** is to sustain and enhance the distinctive environment, economy and social fabric of the English countryside for the benefit of all.

To deliver this we will ensure that our main programmes on health, education, housing and transport achieve real improvements for rural communities. In addition we are allocating **£1bn over the next 3 years on rural programmes, in addition to increased agriculture support, and the £1.6bn (7 year) England Rural Development Programme.**

## A LIVING COUNTRYSIDE

We will give rural communities **a Fair Deal on services**. For the first time we are publishing a **Rural Service Standard** setting out what rural users can expect, with an annual independent audit.

### 1. Support vital village services

We want everyone to have the basic services they need – shops, health and education – close at hand. To support services at the heart of village life we will:

- take forward, in the light of consultation, our proposals for 50% mandatory rate relief to **help village shops, pubs and garages** which offer a community benefit;
- retain and **renew the rural Post Office network** and make banking, internet, pensions, benefits, prescriptions, health and other services available from rural post offices;
- create a new **'Community Service Fund'** to support local enterprise and enable key services to be re-established (£15m).
- continue the presumption against closure of **rural schools;** invest to improve facilities; connect all rural schools to the Internet by 2002;

- **reduce the rate of VAT** on repairs and maintenance for listed **churches** – subject to EC approval.

### 2. Modernise rural services

We will use new technology to give rural areas the benefits and opportunities of the digital age – on lifelong learning, skills, job search, health and other public services. We will:

- improve GP services through mobile service delivery units and new **primary care one stop** Centres with internet and tele-links to local hospitals in over 100 rural communities (£100m);
- provide 100 **Internet Learning and Access Points** in rural areas by the end of 2000;
- increase resources for **rural policing**.

### 3. Provide affordable homes

We want young families to be able to live in the communities where they grew up. We will:

- double the Housing Corporation programme by 2003-04 which, with local authority investment and use of planning powers, we expect to provide a total of **3,000 affordable homes a year in small rural settlements** and a total of around **9000 homes** a year across all rural districts (£300m);
- make **better use of the planning system** to secure a higher proportion of affordable homes, in mixed developments in market towns and villages;
- consult on a proposal to allow local authorities **to charge the full council tax on second homes** and to use the revenues to alleviate local housing shortage.

### 4. Deliver local transport solutions

We want to improve transport for all in rural areas making best use of car, bus, rail and community transport. We will:

- **reduce taxation for motorists** as announced in the Pre-Budget Report to help those who rely on the car.
- increase by a third the number of rural households with a **regular bus service** within 10 minutes walk by 2010;
- promote flexible transport including car clubs, car-sharing, dial-a-ride, taxi and minibus schemes through 500 more **Rural Transport Partnership** projects and by providing **parishes** with up to a £10,000 grant to develop tailor-made community based solutions.

### 5. Rejuvenate market towns and a thriving local economy

We want a diverse rural economy that attracts new businesses which fit with their surroundings, and provides opportunities for all. We will:

- increase funding for **market town regeneration** by £37m to strengthen their role as a focal point for economic opportunity, transport links, leisure and services through a £100m programme for 100 towns;
- establish a new remit on **rural regeneration** for **Regional Development Agencies,** sharing in a £500m budget increase by 2003;
- improve **business support** and invest in ICT and transport infrastructure.

### 6. Set a new direction for farming

We want to help farming and related industries become more competitive, diverse, modern and sustainable. We will:

- seek reform of the Common Agricultural Policy (CAP) which will reduce the role of production subsidies and increase the funds available for **rural development** including environment, whilst reducing the burden on consumers and taxpayers;
- build on the opportunities being provided through the **£1.6bn England Rural Development Programme** (ERDP) for farmers to develop new business and benefit from support for conserving and enhancing the countryside;
- help farmers by additional help for **small abattoirs,** by regulating only when it is necessary, by providing business support, and by helping farm **diversification** through better operation of the planning system and by consulting on rate relief.

### 7. Preserve what makes rural England special

We want to look after, restore and conserve the landscape, wildlife, architecture and traditions that make our countryside special. We will:

- **reduce development pressure** through our policies for successful cities and by targeting development on brownfield sites;
- strengthen **management** of the best countryside;

- develop a more holistic approach which takes better account of all **landscapes** in national best practice guidance;
- reverse the decline in farmland birds, restore threatened **habitats** such as lowland heath and increase funding to maintain biodiversity.

### 8. Ensure everyone can enjoy an accessible countryside

People of all backgrounds should be able to enjoy attractive and accessible countryside. We will:

- modernise **the rights of way system** through new legislation and additional (£46m) finance;
- **open up access** to commons, heath, mountain, and moorland by end 2005;
- launch a new initiative to enhance and restore the **countryside around towns**.

### 9. Give local power to country towns and Villages

We will help Town and Parish councils develop a new role and give communities the opportunity to help shape their future. We will:

- fund a new programme of **town and village plans**, to help 1,000 communities map and safeguard their most valued features and influence future development plans;
- enable **Quality Town and Parish Councils** to play a greater role in managing local facilities in partnership with Counties and Districts, subject to Best Value;
- equip every Parish and Town Council with an **internet** link and strengthen their role as the voice of the local community.

### 10. Think rural

We want to ensure that rural needs are taken into account. We will:

- establish a **rural proofing mechanism** to ensure that all major policies are assessed for their rural impact
- establish a **national and regional rural stakeholder panels** informed by independent assessment of Government's performance on rural issues.
- report on a **new set of countryside indicators**.

**Explanatory Notes**

1  **Consultation with the devolved administrations.** This White Paper applies to England but some of the legislation and measures referred to are UK wide or shared between England and Wales. Where these matters are devolved, we are consulting the devolved administrations as appropriate on how initiatives in these areas will be taken forward. In some cases measures have already been taken by one or more of the devolved administrations, for example on giving local authorities discretion to end the council tax discount on second homes in Wales, which we propose to extend in England. In other cases there will be initiatives in the White Paper which the devolved administrations will want to consider further before forming a view and for some – for example in relation to many agriculture measures – it is important to proceed on a UK wide basis. We will want to remain in close contact with the devolved administrations to consider what may be appropriate in each case.

2  **The public expenditure** tables shown as an annex to each part cover only a small proportion of total public expenditure in rural areas. Rural and urban areas benefit alike from the main central and local government expenditure programmes. For the purposes of this exercise, we have not attempted to carve up the major programmes between urban and rural, not least because in many cases public services will be provided through towns and cities, for rural as well as urban dwellers. However, a number of programmes are specifically targeted at rural areas or needs, including a substantial part of the MAFF budget. The tables, one for each main section in the Rural White Paper, give an indication of the total value of such programmes, alongside the share of certain national programmes where the portion spent in rural local authority districts can be identified. Figures for 1996–97 are given only when comparable information is available. Some figures for 2003–04 represent projected expenditure in cases where plans are not yet finished.

3  **The quotations** in this paper are taken from *Living in the Countryside*, a report by Alan Hedges for the Countryside Agency, based on interviews with rural residents of different age groups and social groups in Buckinghamshire, Cumbria, Lincolnshire, Dorset, Somerset and Derbyshire.

4  **Full details** of publications referred to in italics in the text can be found in the bibliography at the back.

# introduction
## the countryside –
## the challenge

**1.1.**  The countryside is important to all of us. Town and country are interdependent and the needs of both have to be addressed together. But there are special problems in rural areas which require a direct response and that is the focus of this paper.

**1.2.**  The challenge for rural communities is clear. Basic services in rural areas are overstretched. Farming has been hit hard by change. Development pressures are considerable. The environment has suffered.

**1.3.**  Change in the countryside is nothing new, but, over the last 20 years, the pressures have become acute. Many rural areas are prosperous but elsewhere there is real loss. For example farm incomes having risen steeply in the early 1990s have fallen by 60% in the last five years, as a result of global competition, exchange rates and the effects of BSE. It is a diverse picture in which there is hardship as well as success.

---

**Long term trends in rural services**

In rural counties monitored between 1965 and 1990, each year 1 or 2% of small settlements experienced closure of **their last general store or food shop**, representing a loss for around 15% of rural communities over this period. Between 1991 and 1997 a total of 4000 food shops closed in rural areas. Closures of **rural schools** increased in the 1970s to reach a peak of 127 in 1983 continuing at around 30 a year up to 1997 and declining to 2 in 1999. Provision of village halls and community centres has increased. The National Federation of Women's Institutes 1999 survey "The Changing Village" showed that 90% of communities now have a hall compared with only 54% in 1950. **Rural pubs** increased in number in the 1980's but have declined since the early 1990's – with current estimates of 3 closing in each county each year. On transport the picture is mixed. The 1990's surveys of rural parishes showed a 3% decrease between 1991 and 1997 in the number of parishes with a daily bus service, but many new services have been introduced in the last 3 years and community transport has expanded significantly.

---

The key challenges include:

**1.4.  housing and migration**

A hundred years ago, the countryside suffered from depopulation as younger families left rural poverty for better opportunity in the cities. Rural areas were seen as in need of new development and diversification. Nowadays, due to in-migration, the population of rural districts is growing twice as fast as the national average. But many of the newcomers are older and wealthier and can outbid rural residents, with their lower than average incomes, in the competition to buy homes. With less social housing available as right to buy has taken effect younger people have less opportunity to find affordable housing. These trends are changing the character of communities in some parts of the country – leading to polarisation and social exclusion. In the Cotswolds District Council area, for example, one third of households have annual incomes below £7,000.

**1.5.  community strength and services**

The community strength of rural England is an important part of the character of the countryside. Many communities are strong, remoteness often fostering self-reliance. But many more could have active parish councils positively seeking out initiatives to meet the needs of local people. Rural services are increasingly difficult to find locally, as village post offices find it harder to keep going, and rural bank branches, pubs and village shops close. Traffic casualties are reducing more slowly on rural than urban roads. Income levels for less well off rural residents are not keeping up with inflation. On the other hand, opportunities for education and training are improving, and very few rural schools are closing. After a period of decline bus services have improved in the last few years. The health of rural residents is as good or better than the national average, in terms of birth weight, incidence of long-term illness and longevity, but there is often difficulty in accessing more specialised hospital services. There is greater access to childcare but provision in rural areas is still patchy. Despite perceptions, the incidence of crime in rural areas is still very much less than in towns and cities.

**Save Stanhope Post Office**
Credit: Philip Wolmuth

traffic growth bring more noise and intrusion into tranquil areas each year. As a recreational resource the countryside is highly valued by most rural residents and visitors.

**Closed public house**
Credit: The Countryside Agency, A Seth

## 1.6. economy

The economy in rural areas offers a mixed picture. Employment and self-employment are higher than in urban areas and claimant unemployment is lower. But average earnings are lower and rural jobs are more likely to be casual or seasonal, than jobs in urban areas. The nature of employment is changing, with fewer jobs in primary industries such as farming, and other jobs moving to edge of town locations. Home based working is on the increase. Business health is hard to judge, but three quarters of rural districts have business registration rates below their regional average. Transport difficulties can prevent people competing for jobs. In-migration, on the other hand, is generating new jobs (1.7 full-time jobs for each self employed urban to rural mover). Businesses in rural areas are gaining access to ICT, but more slowly than urban areas, due to delays in providing infrastructure. Farming is in crisis, affecting many related businesses though it accounts for only about 4% of GDP in rural areas. Where market town prosperity is declining, as services and industry are rationalised, this has a consequent effect on the surrounding rural areas.

## 1.7. countryside environment

The environment is one of the things rural people value most. Agricultural intensification and homogenous development have diluted countryside character, eroding the diversity that makes rural England so special. Too few new houses are built in materials and styles that respect local qualities. The decline in farm and woodland bird populations indicates a wider decline in wildlife and countryside biodiversity, partly as a result of changes in farming practices. Rivers are getting cleaner, but they are suffering from increases in abstraction and modification of watercourses. Air quality in the countryside is improving in most respects, although increasing road and air

## 1.8. regional variation

It is dangerous to generalise about the countryside, since different areas face different problems. The things that concern those who live in Alton, a market town in Hampshire, will be very different from those of concern in Alston, a market town in Cumbria. The contribution of land based businesses to the economy of the Home Counties is limited and farmers struggle to manage land in the green belts around major cities, where their holdings are fragmented by urban service infrastructure and subject to vandalism. Remote counties such as Shropshire, Lincolnshire and Cumbria suffer more from declining farm incomes. In the south west and along the east coast fishing remains a vital industry. In the remoter areas the local and health authorities find it hard to provide services, such as meals-on-wheels and clinics. Other areas of countryside are suffering from structural change due to coalfield closures. As the Forest of Dean has showed, this type of change can take a generation to tackle. Counties like Durham, Nottinghamshire and South Yorkshire face considerable physical and community decline.

## 1.9. public concern

Public concern for the countryside remains at a high level. The greatest concern is development. Even so, most people view it as a good place that they would like to move to, mainly because they believe it provides a healthier environment. There is also a very high concern about modern methods of farming. Yet few discriminate in their purchasing of food or travel in a way that would directly sustain the landscapes and biodiversity they value. As an analysis of the 1998 Social Attitudes Survey, *Rural spaces and urban jams,* has shown, high levels of public concern about the environment co-exist with a deep seated reluctance to support measures to reduce the impact of their own lifestyles on environmental quality.

# the countryside – our commitment

**1.10.** We can and will respond to this challenge. We want to help build prosperous, sustainable and inclusive rural communities. We are addressing the needs of all who live and work in rural areas. We will maintain and improve basic local services. We will help farmers and businesses adapt to change and support new enterprise. We will give local communities the chance to shape their own future.

**1.11.** People in rural areas want the same opportunities as everyone else: employment opportunities, decent public services, affordable homes, good schools and the ability to enjoy life. Yet they also value the special qualities the countryside provides: a sense of space; of independence; of not living on top of each other. Remoteness makes services expensive to provide and some will never reach every rural dwelling. Those who live in the country accept that as part of rural life.

## Diversity and local choice

**1.12.** We need to give rural communities a fair deal but to do so in a way which does not undermine the qualities that make the countryside special. We need to get the balance right. And so we recognise the diversity and local distinctiveness of the countryside. We do not expect the same approach to work everywhere. This White Paper sets out a toolkit of measures which local communities can apply to meet their priorities and concerns.

## Commitment to the countryside

**1.13.** Government's role is to provide the framework and support within which people can succeed and the flexibility to develop appropriate local solutions. We are making **a new commitment** to rural communities that sets out what they can expect, what Government will do, and the tools that are available to help them succeed.

- We will ensure that rural areas get **a fair deal in public services** by taking better account of rural needs in the way we plan and allocate services, safeguarding the local delivery of basic services, making clear for each service what rural users can expect and by giving rural users a role in how services are assessed and improved;

- We will **help rural communities make the character of the countryside an economic as well as an environmental asset**. We will support farmers and rural businesses in developing rural products, such as speciality foods and tourism enterprises. We will work with local people to maintain and regenerate special countryside features – landscapes, wildlife and buildings – so that they become a business strength;

- We will **empower local communities**, so that decisions are taken with their active participation and ownership. We will help communities map out how they would like their town or village to evolve and let them take on more responsibility for managing their own affairs;

- We will ensure that our rural **policies are joined-up**, recognising the inter-relation of economic, environmental and social factors in the countryside, and also the interdependence of town and country.

## Rural England – what we want to see

**1.14.** Change will continue. Population change and economic growth, new technology and new patterns of travel, leisure and consumer taste will have as much impact in rural as in urban areas. Our goal is to help people in rural areas to manage change, exploit the opportunities it brings, and enable them to create a more sustainable future.

**1.15.** Everyone who lives in, works in, uses or cares about the countryside needs to see how they fit into the wider picture and how change and external pressures on rural England have to be directed in a way which benefits the countryside as a whole.

**1.16.** The role of central and local government is to provide the framework and public services (including infrastructure) for business and individuals to thrive, to deliver macro-economic stability, to raise educational standards, make work pay, assist people with their job search, ensure that the basic services which rural communities need can be provided, and that the environmental regulatory framework can respond to today's pressures and enable everyone to enjoy the benefits which that environment provides.

**1.17.** In 1999 the Government completed an extensive analysis of the rural policy framework in the PIU study *Rural Economies* (many of its recommendations are referred to in this report), followed by an Interdepartmental Cross Cutting Review of Rural Policy to inform the Comprehensive Spending Review 2000. This agreed an **overall aim to sustain and enhance the distinctive environment, economy and social fabric of the English countryside for the benefit of all** and high level objectives to provide a framework for rural and countryside policy:

## The Government's Rural Policy Objectives

> **Objective 1** To facilitate the development of dynamic, competitive and sustainable economies in the countryside, tackling poverty in rural areas.
>
> - helping rural businesses to succeed through improved skills, business support and better infrastructure (Chapters 7 and 8);
>
> - helping farmers to restructure, become more competitive and consumer oriented and to develop speciality products, with reduced reliance on production subsidies, and reduced regulatory burdens and better advice and support;
>
> - targeted support for deprived rural areas (Chapter 7);
>
> - better rural services which combat poverty and social exclusion (Chapter 4);
>
> - a planning system which encourages business growth, for example on farm diversification (Chapter 8) and provision of housing (Chapter 5) while meeting broad objectives to protect the rural environment;
>
> - support to develop the potential of Market Towns for their economic role (including leisure and tourism) and as service centres.

> **Objective 2** To maintain and stimulate communities, and secure access to services which is equitable in all the circumstances, for those who live or work in the countryside.
>
> - retain basic local services such as the Post Office (Chapter 3);
>
> - provide modern rural services using ICT and flexible delivery (Chapter 4);
>
> - more flexible and demand responsive local transport (Chapter 6);
>
> - increased provision of social and affordable housing in order to sustain balanced communities.

> **Objective 3** To conserve and enhance rural landscapes and the diversity and abundance of wildlife (including the habitats on which it depends).
>
> - a vigorous and strong policy of protecting the countryside through redirecting new housebuilding pressure away from greenfield sites and maintaining the quality of valued landscapes while meeting the needs of rural communities (Chapter 9);
>
> - implementing a new direction for agriculture support which takes full account of the environment benefits which farming provides (Chapter 10);
>
> - a holistic approach for assessing landscape value (Chapter 9).

**Farming has shaped our valued landscapes**
Credit: The Countryside Agency, Harold Turek

**Objective 4** To increase opportunities for people to get enjoyment from the countryside. To open up public access to mountain, moor, heath and down and registered common land by the end of 2005.

- increasing access to land as set out in the *Countryside and Rights of Way Bill*;

- improving management and recreational potential of land on the urban fringe (Chapter 9).

**Objective 5** To promote government responsiveness to rural communities through better working together between central departments, local government, and government agencies and better co-operation with non government bodies.

- a stronger role for Town and Parish Councils which meet the Quality Test (improved consultation) and better recognition of rural issues in central and local government policy making (Chapter 12);

- rural assessment of policy making and implementation (Chapter 13).

**1.18.** These objectives build on the policy evaluation set out in the PIU report and will be taken forward in Departmental Public Service Agreement targets and their subsidiary *Service Delivery agreements*. They underpin the new initiatives to benefit rural communities made possible by the Spending Review 2000 and have informed the approach to rural policy set out in this White Paper.

**1.19.** In developing this rural policy framework, we have **consulted and listened** to rural communities. Over 2,000 individuals and rural community groups responded to our consultation document on *Rural England* published in 1998 and subsequently. They have given us a wide range of views and priorities. Some of these are reflected in the quotations used in this paper taken from interviews with a cross section of rural people in Cumbria, Lincolnshire, Derbyshire, Somerset, Dorset and Buckinghamshire. We have considered the recommendations of the House of Commons Environment Transport and Regional Affairs Select Committee (to which our response is published separately). This White Paper has also been informed by preparatory discussion with a group of rural stakeholders meeting with DETR and MAFF Ministers (The Rural White Paper Sounding Board).

Churches in rural areas are a community base as well as part of the historic fabric
St Mary's Church, Ewelme, Oxfordshire
Credit: The Countryside Agency, Graham Wiltshire

**Rural White Paper Sounding Board**
The Sounding Board was created as an informal advisory forum to stimulate discussion on key themes for the Rural White Paper and included the following members.

**Joint Chairmen**

| | |
|---|---|
| Michael Meacher and | DETR |
| Elliot Morley | MAFF |

**Members**

| | |
|---|---|
| Chris Baines | Environmental advisor |
| Anthony Bosanquet | President, Country Landowners Association |
| Helen Browning | Vice President, Soil Association |
| Tony Burton | Assistant Director (Policy), Council for the Protection of Rural England |
| Moira Constable | Chief Executive, the Rural Housing Trust |
| Michael Gwilliam | Director, Civic Trust |
| Lord Haskins | Chairman, Northern Foods plc |
| Steven Joseph | Director, Transport 2000 |
| Barry Leathwood | National Secretary, Rural, Agricultural and Allied Workers |
| Jonathan Porritt | Chairman, Sustainable Dervelopment Commission |
| Hugh Raven | Green Globe Task Force |
| The Earl of Selborne | Blackmoor Estate |
| Richard Wakeford | Chief Executive, Countryside Agency |
| Baroness Young of Old Scone | Chairman, English Nature |

A protected countryside in which the environment is sustained
Mitchell Field, Peak District, Derbyshire
Credit: The Countryside Agency, Mike Williams

A working countryside with a diverse economy
Market Road, Tavistock
Credit: The Countryside Agency, Graham Parish

**1.20.** Our approach recognises **different regional priorities**. It is far from that of 'one size fits all'. Just as the English countryside itself varies dramatically in its landscapes and character, so priorities and issues will vary strongly between and within regions. We have developed an approach within which Government can work with rural partners at all levels, regional, area, and parish, to draw on the most relevant policies, and which gives flexibility and discretion to those partners in developing solutions for their areas.

**1.21.** For this reason the Government has given the **Regional Development Agencies** a strong rural focus reflected in Regional Economic Strategies and the Rural Priority Areas. Similarly there is a strong regional focus for the **England Rural Development Programme** which sets a more collaborative basis for encouraging rural regeneration and environmental improvement, for example through agri-environment schemes, and enterprise in the farming, food, and forestry sectors. Bringing together the full range of countryside issues, the Government has created a specialist adviser **The Countryside Agency,** to advise it and all public bodies and to research, highlight and pilot best practice on a living, working and accessible countryside. Each of these and their local partners will play a key role in taking foward the policies set out in this White Paper.

## the countryside – our vision

**1.22.** So our vision is of:

* A **living** countryside, with thriving rural communities and access for all to high quality public services

* A **working** countryside, with a diverse economy giving high and stable levels of employment

* A **protected** countryside in which the environment is sustained and enhanced, and which all can enjoy

* A **vibrant** countryside which can shape its own future and whose voice is heard by Government at all levels

# Part 1

# a *living* countryside

*We want to see a living countryside, with thriving rural communities, and access to high quality public services*

# a new standard for
## rural services

## 2.1. Setting out what rural people can expect

**2.1.1.** Basic information about what people can expect from services is a fundamental need, but it is often hard to find out what level of service is on offer – leading some people in remote areas to think they may be out of reach.

- We are making clear for the first time how we will deliver equitable access to the everyday public services which rural people need;

- We will ensure that existing access to services is monitored and maintained, and a range of measures in this paper sets out how it will improve.

**2.1.2.** The table on pages 19–22 sets out minimum standards and targets covering access to and the delivery of public services in rural areas. This Rural Services Standard shows how we are working towards giving people living in the country more choice about how they access the services they need, and better understanding of what they can expect to get. It sets out new, upgraded and existing commitments to rural access to services, where they are additional or different to national commitments, or especially significant to people living in rural areas. It explains how national or local entitlements to services apply in rural areas, and refers to charters of rights to services.

**2.1.3.** The standards will be updated as our modernisation of our public services proceeds and we improve access to services in rural areas.

- We will **review this Rural Services Standard annually** through the Cabinet Committee on Rural Affairs, in the light of advice from the Countryside Agency and the national and regional panels of rural stakeholders as described in Chapter 13.

## The Rural Services Standard

### Explanation and key

**Presumption against closures:**
Protecting the existing network of schools and post offices is essential to the viability of local rural communities. We have strengthened our policy of presumption against the closure of schools. We have also strengthened our commitment to avoiding closure of post offices. Their unparalleled reach into rural settlements will be exploited through better community access to schools and the development of post offices as access points for a wide range of government services.

**Indicators of access levels:**
We don't have firm access standards for these, but by committing ourselves to monitor levels of access using surveys, we will be able to identify problems and set targets for improvement to deliver more equitable outcomes for access to public transport, social services and other services. Rural dwellers may access some types of services less than urban dwellers, for a variety of reasons including convenience of access. Information on levels of access will help identify these reasons and (where necessary) develop responses.

**Geographic access standards:**
Sometimes a benchmark standard can usefully be set, giving the maximum distance or time which people should be expected to travel to reach a service outlet.

**Response time targets:**
For some services having a speedy response is critical. We are introducing new national target response times for ambulances. These targets will be monitored and reported on.

**Telephone services:**
Information and advice over the telephone can often replace the need to travel to consult service providers or perform basic transactions.

**On line access:**
Access over the internet will increasingly be used to provide convenient information and advice in rural areas, under our commitment to make all public services available on line by 2005. The provision of information and communication technology (ICT) access points through schools, libraries and (in the future) post offices will provide assisted and convenient access in rural areas.

**Help with fares:**
Financial help is made available to users of services such as job centres who are especially disadvantaged.

| Service | Service provider | | Requirement, indicator, standard or target |
|---|---|---|---|
| **General** | All | | **All Government services to be available on line by 2005.** This will be particularly helpful in rural areas, and a series of initiatives will enable all people to learn to use the internet, such as putting all public libraries on line, and the development of post offices as internet learning and access points. Access will also be provided through local authority information kiosks. |
| **Education** | | | |
| Access to Primary and Secondary Schools | LEAs | | **Presumption against closure of rural schools;** published guidance requires that the need to preserve access to a local school for rural communities is taken into account in considering closure proposals. |
| | | | **Local education authorities (LEAs) must provide free transport** if they consider it necessary to enable a pupil to attend school, and they may help other pupils with their fares. Free transport is always necessary for a pupil of compulsory school age (5-16) who attends the nearest suitable school if it is beyond the statutory walking distance of two miles for children under eight years and three for children aged eight and above. This ensures that education for compulsory school age pupils is accessible to rural communities. |
| Schools' access to learning material | LEAs | | All schools to be linked to the **National Grid for Learning** by 2002 – especially important for small rural schools. |
| Further Education Colleges | | | Entitlement to **assistance with access/travel costs** (from FE Access Fund). Childcare and residential costs may also be supported. |
| **Childcare** | LEAs, local authorities, private and voluntary sectors | | The Countryside Agency is developing an indicator of likely need against formal public and private sector childcare provision. This information will enable more equitable access standards to be developed. |
| | | | Online information on childcare providers and vacancies in your area is available from the childcare website at: http://212.53.85.14/ |
| **Post offices** | The Post Office | | Formal **requirement on the Post Office to maintain the rural network** of post offices and to prevent any avoidable closures of rural post offices. |
| | | | Introduction of Horizon network will enable **all post offices to provide on-line banking services,** greatly increasing access to financial services and providing access to universal banking facilities through post offices. |
| | | | The Postal Services Act for the first time makes legal provision for a **universal delivery service,** at a uniform national price, to all addresses. |
| **Transport** | | | |
| Access to bus services | Local authorities | | We have set a **target for the proportion of the rural population living within about 10 minutes' walk of an hourly** or better bus service to increase from 37% to 50% by 2010, with an intermediate milestone of 42% by 2004. |

19

| Service | Service provider | | Requirement, indicator, standard or target |
|---|---|---|---|
| Rural rail services | Train operating companies | | The level of franchised passenger services on rural lines is protected by the Passenger Service Requirement (PSR). The Strategic Rail Authority (SRA) has announced that a requirement of replacement franchises will be to meet at least the existing PSR. This means that people living in rural areas will have the **security of knowing that their trains are protected:** operators can run more trains, but they cannot run less than set out in the PSR. |
| Libraries | Local Authorities | | **National standards for library services,** to be introduced in April 2001, are likely to cover access (ie location and opening hours) to mobile as well as branch libraries. |
| | | | All **public libraries to be on-line by 2002** with trained staff to support public use of information and communications technology (ICT). |
| ICT Learning Centres | Various | | Network of 700 **learning centres** in England aimed at improving access to ICT and ICT-based learning for adults in disadvantaged communities. Rural needs recognised in guidance. |
| **Health/care services** | | | |
| Access to GP and other primary care services | Health Authorities Primary Care Groups (PCG) and Primary Care Trusts (PCT) | | Guaranteed access to a primary care professional within 24 hours and to a doctor within 48 hours, to be achieved nationally by 2004. The Countryside Agency will **monitor average population distance from GPs and dentists.** |
| Access to advice about healthcare | Health Authorities | | NHS Direct provides nurse based health advice by phone 24 hours a day, 7 days a week. **Service now available countrywide.** It is also available online at www.nhsdirect.nhs.uk. 100% **pre-booking** of outpatient appointments and inpatient admissions by 2005. |
| **Social care** | LA Social Services Departments | | The national charter *Better Care, Higher Standards*, a joint initiative between the Department of Health and DETR, tells anyone who needs care or support over the longer term what they can expect from local housing, health and social services and what to do if things go wrong. Local charters published in June 2000 set out standards and targets to be achieved through joint working between local authorities (housing and social services) and health authorities, in partnership with users and carers. **The local charters will be regularly monitored to** improve service delivery. |
| | | | The Department of Health publish a wide range of indicators on social services, such as numbers in receipt of intensive home care, and of older people (aged 65 or over) helped to live at home: **these will enable us to review rural levels of support,** by comparing boroughs and shire counties which broadly represent 'urban' and 'rural' local authorities. |

| Service | Service provider | | Requirement, indicator, standard or target |
|---|---|---|---|
| **Emergency services** | | | |
| Ambulance services | NHS Ambulance Trusts | 🕐 | The NHS ambulance service is setting **targets to respond to life threatening calls** within 8 minutes in 75% of cases by March 2001 and to other 999 ambulance calls in rural areas within 19 minutes in 95% of cases (compared with 14 minutes in urban areas) |
| Police | Police Forces | 🕐 | Each police force sets **target times for responding to urgent incidents** in rural areas, under Best Value. These are monitored as a key element in police performance and published by Police Authorities. |
| Fire | Fire Brigades | 🕐 | The national standards of fire cover are based on **set response times** according to the category of fire risk. In most rural areas the standard is to reach a fire within 20 minutes. The fire service maintains a high level of performance in meeting the standards (96% on average in 1998-99). |
| **Community legal service** | Local authorities, Legal Services Commission (LSC), Citizen's Advice Bureaux etc. | 📊 | The LSC is forming community legal services partnerships (CLSPs) to deliver local networks of legal services, based on local needs. **Target is for 90% of the population to be covered by spring 2002.** |
| | | 💻 | CLSPs will use innovative methods such as the online directory Just Ask! and kiosks to **deliver better access in rural areas.** |
| **Access to courts** | Courts Service, Magistrates Courts Committees (MCCs) | 💻 | We are **reducing the need for travel to courts by exploiting IT.** piloting the use of video-conferencing, including facilities for witnesses to give evidence in Crown Court trials; and providing information through touch screen kiosks for county courts. |
| **Access to benefits** | | | |
| Benefit Agency Offices | Benefits Agency | 🚌 | Claimants can **claim travel costs of attending benefit offices** (on those occasions where a visit is unavoidable the guideline is that customers should incur travelling costs of no more than 80 pence per week). |
| Online Information | Benefits Agency | 💻 | The Department of Social Security (DSS) web-site contains general and technical information on BA benefits and services, and **allows customers to correspond by e-mail.** Localised web-sites are being developed in 9 pilot areas. Local authority information kiosks will also provide – in partnership with the BA – online information from the DSS website. |
| Benefit payment | Benefits Agency | | We have pledged that all benefit recipients who wish to do so will **continue to be able to access their benefits in cash at a post office counter** both before and after the changeover to payment by automated credit transfer. |

| Service | Service provider | | Requirement, indicator, standard or target |
|---------|------------------|---|--------------------------------------------|
| **Employment** <br> Job centres | Employment Service | | **Job Centre vacancies** available via Employment Service Direct for the cost of a local phone call. |
| Online information | Employment Service | | From this autumn **vacancy information will be available on the internet** and via computerised job points at conveniently located public places. ICT Learning Centres will give access to Employment Service Direct and the Employment Service (ES) Learning and Workbank. This will increase the availability of access to jobsearch facilities and help for those people in isolated rural areas. |
| New Deal Schemes | Employment Service | | Commitment to **providing customers with individual help** to overcome transport difficulties in accessing employment opportunities. <br><br> New Deal for Lone Parents scheme also provides **help in locating and paying for childcare.** |
| Action Teams for Jobs | Employment Service | | Action Teams for Jobs in some areas of labour market disadvantage (such as Cornwall) will work closely with local employers and **tackle transport to jobs issues**. This could include help with individual fares or involvement in new community transport services. |
| Job seeker's Allowance | Employment Service | | Special **arrangements apply for people with poor public transport access to job centres, allowing them to attend less frequently**. Round trip or one way public transport travel time thresholds apply. In the case of journeys involving being away from home for 8 hours, advisory interviews are arranged in the claimant's home area. <br><br> **Financial help available to meet public transport costs of travelling to interviews** |

# vital village
## services

**3**

## The issues

- Around a third of all villages have no shop and the loss of banks, garages and pubs in rural areas has continued. To remain viable, village enterprise needs to exploit new technology, offer a wider range of services and share facilities.
- People in villages increasingly rely on travelling to meet their everyday needs. Loss of services can threaten the viability of communities and affects some severely – particularly the low paid and unemployed, young people and the elderly.

## The future – what we want to see

- Diversified, village community-backed enterprise offering a wide range of products and services, using new technology and good business skills.
- Public service providers retaining and improving essential village services which are well-used and at the heart of the community. Using new technology, post offices will offer local access to banking and a wide range of services.
- Community initiative to share use of village facilities, such as the church, school, hall or pub, and to re-establish basic services.

---

### Summary of measures

- Extension of mandatory rate relief for village shops, pubs and garages which offer community benefit – subject to consultation;
- reduced rate of VAT on repairs and maintenance for listed churches – subject to EC approval;
- A new £15m Community Service Fund to help safeguard or re-establish community backed basic services in small settlements;
- Maintaining the Post Office network;
- New services available at village post offices including banking;
- Further safeguards against the closure of village schools;
- Increased funding for rural schools and access to internet for all rural schools by 2002;
- New childcare and early education provision in rural communities.

# 3

## Contents

## 3.1. Introduction

We want villages to be active, living communities, where people are also able to meet their essential needs and with opportunities for both old and young.

## 3.2. Supporting basic local services

**3.2.1.** The most basic community service for most rural communities is the **local shop (often combined with a post office)**. We want to support the retention of shops in small settlements, offering a wider range of products and services – and combining with post offices, garages, pubs and other facilities.

*"There's too much temptation to get in the car and go to Sainsbury's or Somerfields"*

*"We'll use it every now and again. It's good for when we run out and we think it's not worth going into town and you don't mind the price you pay down at the shop"*

### Trends in village services

- The decline in village shops was steady in the 1970s but has slowed since then – the number of parishes with a permanent shop (of any kind) fell by 1% to 58% between 1991 and 1997.

- On average 77 schools closed a year in the 1970s; between 1983 and 1997 around 30 schools a year were closing. Last year the number was 2.

- A *NFWI survey* in 1999 showed the number of villages with a post office had declined from 85% to 75% since 1950. But much of the decline was in the last 10 years.

*"Use it or lose it applies, it's only at the last minute when it was closing up the whole village seems to be able to get together and do something about keeping it open"*

### Case study – revived village shop

The revival of the shop in the village of Harting, Hampshire was a partnership arrangement between the Harting village shop association and the shopkeeper who pays a rent for shop and living accommodation. The shop has gone from strength to strength providing services such as fresh on-site baking, specialist foods and local produce.

Harting Village shop, Hampshire – supported by the local community
Credit: Harting and District Village Shop Association

## Village shops

**3.2.2.** That means encouraging new and co-operative ways of providing the services people want, and removing any constraints which stand in the way of community action to address these needs. It also means reviewing the financial support that is available, and ensuring that it is effective. The **village shop rate relief scheme** offers mandatory 50% rate relief to sole shops and post offices in settlements under 3,000 in designated rural areas with a rateable value of less than £6,000. Local authorities can also give support to a wider range of rural businesses in small settlements. We propose to extend that support:

- We are consulting in our Green Paper *Modernising Local Government Finance* on an **expansion of the village shop rate relief scheme**. This would offer mandatory rate relief to 2nd or 3rd food shops;

- We are enabling the Countryside Agency to **expand their support for village shops** to help retailers become more viable.

---

### Village retail partnership

Large retailers can play a vital role in sustaining village services either through trading partnerships with small shops, business support or by making goods available via remote ordering on internet links at community service points.

Sainsbury's SAVE scheme which allows village stores to stock selected own brand produce, is being expanded – to 200 stores by end 2000. Somerfields Village Link offers free delivery of groceries and fresh produce to village stores – initially within 10 minutes of a Somerfield main store – but this will be expanded later. Other larger retailers are helping by seconding an experienced manager to work with small rural enterprises sharing business expertise and acting as a mentor.

---

## Pubs, garages and other rural businesses

**3.2.3.** It is not just shops which provide a vital community role in small settlements – pubs, garages and other businesses can all play a valuable role, by providing a range of other services alongside their main business such as cashback facilities, internet access or acting as a collection or ordering point for more distant businesses.

- We are consulting in our Green Paper *Modernising Local Government Finance* on **extending rate relief to pubs and garages which offer community facilities**. We have proposed that mandatory 50% rate relief would be given in settlements of less than 3,000 population in designated rural areas to:

  - any **singly owned pub** which is the sole remaining retail outlet in the village or is the sole pub and provides a defined community facility or service (eg cash machine, cashback facility, meeting room for local community or public information and communication technology access point) and which has a rateable value of less than £6,000.

  - **singly owned garages** offering community benefits such as a cash machine or cashback facility in a village where there is no post office and with a rateable value of less than £6,000. Small garages in rural areas offer a wide range of other benefits to the community, and in the light of our consultation, we will look at whether all singly owned garages in this category should get relief.

---

### Community service points – village internet access

We will promote the concept of 'community service points', offering ICT access at local level in rural areas. Different organisations, from the Post Office to schools and parish councils, will help deliver a comprehensive network of outlets offering internet access – rural local authorities will have a particular interest in delivering local internet access and many are already establishing networks. An example is: **Linnet Local**, set up by Lincolnshire Libraries Authority with other partners and funders, has put computer-based library facilities in pubs, post offices, village shops, village halls, church halls, doctors' surgeries, a hospital and an opticians. Each Linnet Local is a fully functional PC with internet access to training, community and other information.

---

**Linnet Local in the Fox & Hounds, Willington-by-Stow**
Credit: Lincolnshire County Council

**3.2.4. Joint use of a wide range of premises** – from the village hall to the pub – can help deliver community facilities at village level. The role of the **churches** – often the last remaining public building in many rural communities – has been highlighted under the £7.5m initiative 'Rural Churches in Community Service' which has received a £2.5m lottery grant and which aims to complete 100 projects by the end of the year, providing new facilities in churches of different denominations for activities such as:

- Mother and Toddler groups
- Playgroups
- After school and holiday clubs
- Youth drop-ins
- Drop-ins for older people
- Luncheon clubs
- Day care centres (for frail older people)
- Employment and training advice
- Training
- School use for curriculum studies, music, performance, PE
- Library services
- Alcoholics Anonymous groups

There are 9,000 parish churches in rural areas which are listed buildings for which the repair costs are largely borne by the congregation

- We are acting to support the community role of churches in rural areas. In the Pre-Budget Report 2000, we have announced that we will seek European Commission agreement to our proposal to **reduce the rate of VAT (from 17½% to 5%) payable for repairs and maintenance on listed buildings which are also places of worship.**

### Community operated services

**3.2.5.** Communities have often taken the lead in safeguarding or re-establishing basic services in villages and small settlements – community based shops, social facilities, basic banking. We want to encourage and support this.

- We will establish **a new Community Service Fund of £15m over three years**, operated by the Countryside Agency, to help communities sustain or re-establish basic village services. This will be open to a wide range of organisations including parish councils, churches and community groups.

## 3.3. Maintaining and modernising the rural post office network

**3.3.1.** Post offices are the most visible, and often the only, commercial outlets in many rural communities. 99% of people in rural areas live within three miles of a post office. But the network has been slowly declining, and changes will occur in some areas of existing post office work, such as from the switch to bank credit transfer of benefits payments and new means of delivering public services. We have, however, given a commitment that any pension or benefit recipient who wants to collect their payment in cash at a post office counter will continue to be able to do so, in full and weekly. We have also asked the Post Office to develop new business opportunities, and pledged to underpin the rural network and support its modernisation by firm commitments about its future, in close consultation with the National Federation of Subpostmasters. For example, the Post Office is piloting a scheme in 1,000 offices in the south west in which customers can nominate their local office as a **collection point** for parcels, packages and items needing a signature.

*"They're closing the banks slowly. … But then the post office is tending to take a lot on. And while the post office is available in these little rural areas – I think that's very important again, that there is a post office."*

- We have accepted all 24 of the **recommendations** in the Performance and Innovation Unit (PIU) report *Counter Revolution: Modernising the Post Office Network*;

- Ring-fenced funding was set aside in the Spending Review for **new investment of £270m over the next three years** to start the implementation of the PIU recommendations for maintaining, modernising and improving the post office network in both urban and rural areas. **We have also made clear that we are prepared to add significantly to this investment over the next few years, subject to satisfactory business plans and pilot trials.**

- We are placing **a formal requirement on the Post Office to maintain the rural network**, and to prevent any avoidable closures of rural post offices. In the first instance this requirement will apply up to 2006;

- The **Postal Services Commission will monitor and report annually** to Government on the shape of the rural network, the services offered and whether these meet the needs of rural communities.

## New business for the Post Office

**3.3.2.** To allow post offices to develop new business we have acted to ensure that by April 2001 all rural post offices will have networked IT capabilities. This will allow them to introduce a wide range of new or improved services, including banking and financial services. Access to other services can be greatly improved if a broader range of transactions can be delivered through post offices.

- We have enabled the Post Office to pilot programmes from Spring 2001 to develop post offices as **one stop shops for access to a wide range of central and local government services** and related voluntary sector activities and as Internet learning and access points (see box). People should be able to rely on their local post office as a major source of information and independent advice for a vast range of needs – including access to electronic government services for those without internet access. The **England pilot** will operate at 283 post offices throughout the county of Leicestershire.

### New business for the Post Office
The pilot will give older people, families and children a specially tailored information and transactions service in their local post offices, not only by face to face access across the counter, but also using internet kiosks, web phones, telephone links, help-lines and surgeries. These will provide new health services, and general community and educational information. There will be a package of training for sub-postmasters. Depending on the results of the pilot, we will consider the case for full roll-out which could offer a comprehensive range of other services such as:
- Application for education courses and grants;
- Ordering a library card and books;
- Business services such as notifying job vacancies to the Employment Service, and tax, employee and VAT returns;
- Notification of property crimes and payment of parking and court fines;
- Community consultation and voter registration;
- Registration of births, marriages and deaths;
- Application for travel passes, stakeholder pension and other services for older people.

Over the counter service
Credit: The Post Office

*"They've just given us a cashpoint, which is a life-saver, we didn't have one, and then we've had one now for like about the last 8 months."*

## Post offices and banking

**3.3.3.** Banking and other financial services are a key area of development for the Post Office, using the investment in the new computer network as a platform for 'universal banking' and other banking services. Telephone and internet banking and cashpoints can substitute for some services but many people still want to carry out their banking person to person. There are more rural post offices than rural branches of all the banks combined, so post offices are well placed to provide banking services; access to banking in rural areas is improving as more banks turn to the post office to provide their customers with convenient access. The Post Office are developing plans, in discussion with the banks and government, to reduce financial exclusion and to extend access to banking services to those currently without bank accounts, either through a Post Office-based simple banking facility or new basic accounts introduced by the banks and accessible at post offices. **The Government is strongly supporting the Post Office in this work and has made clear that it is prepared to provide funding for 'universal banking' on the basis of a robust business case.** The Post Office's IT capability will, in addition, allow it to extend its existing network banking arrangements with Lloyds TSB, Barclays, Alliance & Leicester Girobank and the Co-operative Bank to others.

## 3.4. Supporting local schools

*"I think that's where a strong sense of community is in there, and if you've got children going through the school system then it's a focus for parents – and you meet a lot of parents that way, you get to know a lot of people."*

**3.4.1.** Local schools are at the heart of many rural communities, and a school closure in a rural area can have effects well beyond the schooling of the community's children. This is why we have included in our statutory guidance to local School Organisation Committees and Adjudicators a presumption against closure of rural schools. We have thereby dramatically reduced the closure of village schools. Between 1983 and 1997 around 30 schools a year were closing. Last year the number was two.

### Action to support village schools

**3.4.2.** But that on its own would not be enough. We are determined to ensure that rural schools not only survive but are able to continue to produce high quality education. We are therefore taking action to ensure their long term viability. This includes:

- From September 2000 **we have introduced further safeguards against the closure of a site of a multi-sited school.** Where sites are a mile or more apart they will be afforded the same level of protection as a single sited school. Where necessary this should give very small schools the confidence to be able to co-operate in order to increase their effectiveness and long term viability;

- **£80m is being made available between 1999-2001 under the Administrative Support Fund for Small Schools** to reduce the burden of basic administration placed on teachers, deputies and heads in those schools;

- **Additional funding of £20m** is available over 2000-2001 to encourage small schools to pilot innovative ways of working collaboratively with others to overcome difficulties due to small size; more money will be available under a new merged fund from April 2001;

- The extra money for schools announced in the last Budget will give **an extra grant of £3,000 for every primary school with less than 100 pupils** this year and £6,000 from April 2001;

- And we need to create **a fairer financial regime for schools.** The Green Paper 'Modernising Local Government Finance' included proposals for reforming education funding.

**Ebrington and St James' Schools**
Credit: St James' and Ebrington C of E Primary Schools (Federated)

**3.4.3. Information and communications** technology has a vital role in extending access to learning and teaching opportunities, opens up a whole range of possibilities, including: access to study support and discussion groups for teachers and pupils who, for reasons of distance, cannot otherwise link into training or after school hours activities; availability of school ICT facilities for use by the community; and opportunities for fully interactive distance learning, which the roll out of broadband technologies to rural schools will bring.

- We will connect all schools to the National Grid for Learning by 2002.

## Shared and community use of school facilities

**3.4.4.** This can enlarge opportunity for the whole community through providing facilities not otherwise available including: sports facilities, after school clubs, neighbourhood learning centres, libraries, play schools and nurseries and lunch clubs for pensioners. Schemes of this kind can make a big contribution in many locations and help people from all backgrounds. They may be particularly helpful to children from poorer backgrounds who are disproportionately affected by travel problems in rural areas. They are more likely to be dependent on the school bus for travel to and from school, and therefore find it difficult to participate in both formal and informal after-school activities. Those who are most likely to benefit from homework clubs, access to computers and leisure activities are least likely to be able to take part unless the service is provided close to their homes.

*"And what I found when I was at school at Sherborne was the schools were excellent, but so much of it required you to stay after school, and I couldn't get home because there was no bus back, and so I could never participate in any of those things."*

- To encourage more LEAs and schools to become involved in **community use of schools**, we have published guidance *Raising Standards, Opening Doors*. This sets out the many advantages in opening up schools for wider use, and also shows how some of the potential practical difficulties can be overcome. We have provided funding of £20m over four years for innovative community based projects from the Adult and Community Learning Fund.

### Case study – Community use of schools

Examples include:
**South Northamptonshire Adult Education** – provides basic and study support skills training for disadvantaged parents through five village schools.
**Barrow Primary School in** Lancashire provides activities for pupils until 5.30pm and then from 6 to 9pm, any pupil or ex-pupil (up to age 18) can come to the school and use the computer or library to do homework or play games. Some parents also attend.

## 3.5. Better access to childcare and early education

**3.5.1.** Access to convenient childcare is essential for families with young children. Not only does this offer children the opportunity to interact with others and prepares them for school, but it also gives those looking after children, usually women, the opportunity to take up employment, training or educational activities which can be of long term benefit to the whole family, and indeed to the community as a whole.

Somerset Rural Youth – after school homework in mobile unit
Credit: The Countryside Agency – Nick Smith

### The National Childcare Strategy

**3.5.2.** *The National Childcare Strategy* aims to provide good quality affordable accessible childcare in every community across the country. £470m, including £170m raised from the National Lottery and distributed through the New Opportunities Fund, was allocated to support childcare provision in 1999–03. On 9 October 2000, we announced a threefold increase in the annual investment in childcare from £66m in 2000–01 to over £200m by 2003–04. In 1999–00 Early Years Development and Childcare Partnerships reported the creation of 140,000 new childcare places.[1] These included 1,246 new places created in Cornwall, 1,276 in Durham, 992 in Lincolnshire and 2,271 in Devon.

- **The target for 2000-01 is 128,000 new childcare places.** To help overcome difficulties in rural areas, the Countryside Agency and DfEE have launched the **Rural Children and Young People's Forum** which will help shape policy and practice on childcare to meet rural circumstances.

### Early education

**3.5.3.** Rural areas will benefit from our commitment to provide all four year olds with an early education place if their parent wishes, while provision for three year olds is being expanded with co-ordination between maintained, private and voluntary sectors through Early Years Development and Childcare Partnerships, aiming for an option of a place for all by 2004. The pilot Early Excellence Centres are providing models of good practice in integrated approaches to high quality early education, childcare, and family support. They include schemes in rural areas.

The ACE Centre in Chipping Norton
Credit: The Countryside Agency

*"Yetminster's a very sought after village because it's a hub village for the others around it. We've got the school, we've got the surgery, there's the stores, the hairdresser, the butcher, grocer. We've got the stop-me rail – you literally put your hand out and the train stops for you."*

---

1    These have provided childcare for more than 244,000 children and, taking into account turnover, have added more than 74,000 to the stock of childcare places across England.

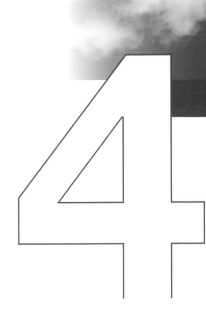

# modern rural
## services

## The issues

- Quality of life for people in rural areas is generally good, but deprivation exists for people at all stages of life. Isolation poses special challenges for delivering rural services, especially to older people and those without cars, and can make it difficult to access employment.
- As services have become more specialist and diverse they have relocated away from rural communities, making access more difficult. On the other hand, new technology is making it easier to transmit information, bringing new solutions to bear on the problems of isolation. But people also need to be helped to adjust to these changes.
- There is increasing concern about levels of property crime and related issues, including drugs and youth offending. Crime and the fear of crime, especially for the elderly and those living in isolated places, damage quality of life.

## The future – what we want to see

- Clear helpful information from service providers on access levels for all services in rural areas.
- A new deal on services which ensures that rural communities benefit from increased investment in public services and which tackles deprivation and social exclusion for all groups, including the jobless.
- Service delivery tailored to suit the needs of rural communities, exploiting ICT and new technology in areas such as health and education. A bigger role for service users and communities in designing solutions.
- Public facilities located to take account of their impact on user travel costs and on access for rural users. Service providers increasingly joining together to deliver a range of services from a single building.

### Summary of measures

- Modernised family doctor facilities will improve access to services for most people in rural areas, with over 100 new primary care one-stop shops or mobile service delivery units by 2004;
- More help for elderly people in rural areas to stay at home;
- More resources to give more rapid rural ambulance response;
- Extension of education maintenance allowances for 16-18 year olds;
- More resources for the most deprived rural areas to improve service delivery to poorer people;
- More resources for rural policing – an extra £15m in 2000–01 and £30m in 2001–02.

# 4

## Contents

## 4.1. Introduction

**4.1.1.** The problems of rural communities – isolation, lack of information, high travel costs – and of service providers in rural areas – sparsity, extra costs, scattered clients – are two sides of the same coin. Our new approach to delivering rural services will:

- **Tailor services to rural needs** and conditions, using new technology where it can help;
- **Work flexibly**, across organisations and making use of shared facilities;
- **Understand the needs of users** and plan services to their convenience;

**4.1.2.** Better services are key to tackling rural deprivation and exclusion, often linked to a severe lack of access to the most basic services or social and economic opportunity. The measures we are taking on health, education and social care will help address this. We aim to ensure that people no longer fall between the cracks: unable to access work or training because of poor public transport; feeling that they are outside the geographical reach of the social services; without a dentist, library or advice centre within easy reach. We want to be sure that the needs of people living in the countryside are consistently and equitably taken into account in the planning of services – whether provided by central Government, national agencies, local government, regionally based bodies or the private sector. The very fact that there will be a published set of targets and standards covering rural access to services (as set out in chapter 2), will focus attention on rural needs.

**4.1.3.** Not all services will be available in all towns and all villages (although the new initiatives set out in chapter 3 will help). But the ease of access to services is a crucial dimension for planning services in rural areas. It may be helpful to see how we envisage new rural services will be delivered. Services may be delivered to the home, eg by phone/internet, to the village service point (eg the post office) or to the nearby market town (see table below).

**Table 4.1: improving rural services – home, village and market town**

| In the home | In the village | In the market town |
|---|---|---|
| • Health advice by phone – 'NHS Direct' (4.2.4) | • A new range of services at the ICT linked Post Office including<br>– business services<br>– banking<br>– pensions and travel passes<br>– health and education applications<br>(3.3.2 – 3) | • Improved primary healthcare using telelinks and ICT to specialist centres (4.2.6) |
| • Social Services – 'Care Direct' (4.2.9) | • Re-establishing shops and other community services (3.2.2 – 5) | • ICT learning centres (4.4.10) |
| • Education and employment services online and by telephone (ch.2 and 4.3 – 4) | • Community use of school facilities (3.4.4) | • Better transport links – bus and rail (Chapter 6) |
| • Car share and community transport schemes run by parish councils (6.3.5) | • More childcare places (3.5.1 – 2) | • Improved ICT and business support (7.5 and 7.6) |
| | • Better bus links to market towns and more flexible local transport (6.3 – 6.4) | • Strengthened role as retail and business centre (7.2 and 7.3) |

**4.1.4** In reaching decisions on locations of service outlets, it is important that service providers take account not only of the consequences for their own costs, but also of the consequences for their users and other providers – for example additional transport journeys to reach a more distant centre.

- **We will ensure that rural needs are taken into account when policies are developed** (see chapter 13) and improve the guidance on how to do this. DETR has commissioned research on how external costs such as those relating to rural access can be taken into account in assessing policy options. As a result of this work, a best practice guide will be published next year and made widely available.

## 4.2. Health and social services

**4.2.1. The challenge for health services in rural areas** is to provide good quality accessible care to an often scattered population, and to ensure that people living in the country with particular needs have the same opportunities to benefit from targeted help as those living in towns. We are committed to the provision of comprehensive, high quality health care for all those who need it, regardless of ability to pay or where they live, and to ensuring greater consistency of access across the country.

**4.2.2.** The aim of the *NHS Plan* is to transform the health system so that it produces faster, fairer services that deliver better health and tackles health inequalities. Expenditure on the NHS will grow by one third in real terms in just five years. New investment – and new solutions tackling the problems of isolation – will deliver real improvements for people in rural areas through:

- Care and advice to people at home, and close by in modernised GP surgeries, primary care centres or through mobile service units;

- New primary care centres and new intermediate care facilities to bring care closer to the patient;

- Round the clock medical care for minor ailments and accidents will be available for all within convenient travelling distance;

- More accessible high quality specialist care in modern hospital settings;

- A more responsive pharmacy service.

**4.2.3.** The NHS Plan sets out the main national priorities. Patients should have fair access and high standards of care **wherever they live**. At national level the Department of Health will set national standards in the priority areas. *National Service Frameworks (NSF)* which set national standards for key conditions and diseases have already been produced covering mental health and coronary heart disease. *A National Cancer Plan* was published in September 2000, the NSF for older people will be published in autumn 2000 and the NSF for diabetes in 2001. Further NSFs will be developed on a rolling basis over the period of the *NHS Plan*.

### Better access to health services in rural areas

*"I had to go down and see a specialist and had to go to Poole and we had to leave here at 7.30 in the morning for the appointment, and when I got there it was only 3 minutes but even so it seemed such a... – when you could go just 5 miles to Yeovil."*

**4.2.4.** We are committed to improving services for rural areas through access to quick, authoritative health advice. A single phone call to **NHS Direct** provides a one-stop gateway to healthcare, to give patients more choice, advice on care at home, getting further treatment, or dealing with an emergency.

- **The 24-hour NHS Direct telephone advice service now covers the whole of England.** In time NHS Direct will also be able to offer the option of ordering prescriptions and arrange for delivery to the patient's door with a single phone call, even in remote areas.

**4.2.5.** We published a programme for modernising pharmacy in the NHS in September *Pharmacy in the Future: Implementing the NHS Plan*. Measures that will improve access for those in rural areas include electronic prescribing by 'e-pharmacies': by 2004 your doctor will be able to send your prescription over the NHS net to a pharmacy of your choice – for example, one which will deliver medicines to your door.

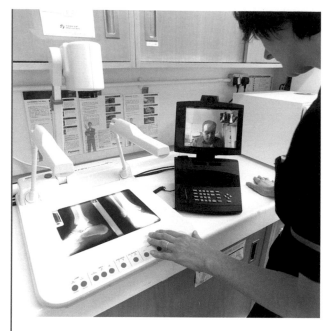

Falmouth Minor Injury Unit consults the A & E Department of the Royal Cornwall Hospital via the telemedicine system
Credit: Roger Dovey

**4.2.6.** Primary care services are being redesigned to offer faster, more convenient access to a wider range of services. These changes will bring many treatments closer to the patient and improve access to primary care services outside normal working hours and provide quicker and easier access in rural areas. Many more GPs will be working from modern multi-purpose premises alongside nurses, pharmacists, dentists, therapists, opticians, midwives and social care staff. These will include provision for video and telelinks to hospital specialists to help in diagnosis and test results, and direct local booking of operations and outpatients' appointments. An increasing number of consultants will take outpatient sessions in these centres, working alongside GP specialists.

- Capital investment of up to £100m under the NHS Plan in rural areas to provide over 100 one-stop primary care centres or mobile service units will provide **better access to services for the majority of rural people.**

**4.2.7.** Many of the new resources for dentistry are going to health authorities with a rural population, including over half of the new Dental Access Centres and about three quarters of this year's £4m Dental Care Development Fund (see *Modernising NHS Dentistry – Implementing the NHS Plan*).

- NHS dentistry will be made available to everyone who needs it, no matter where they live, by September 2001.

**4.2.8.** Many rural areas have a higher than average proportion of **older people**. The NHS Plan sets out a major package of investment to improve standards of care for older people. By 2004 the Government will be making available annually an additional £1.4bn for older people's health and social care services, of which £900m will be invested in **intermediate care**. This will promote independence and improve quality of care for older people, for example through specially designated hospital wards run by nurse consultants, and step down facilities in the community, including a new role for cottage hospitals. It will also include improved care services in the home.

- The NHS Plan will mean more patients recovering from operations in a smaller hospital setting close to home, such as in a community or cottage hospital.

Coquetdale Cottage Hospital, Northumberland
Credit: The Countryside Agency, Liane Bradbrook

- Rural areas will benefit from the Government's **hospital building and modernisation** programme creating 7,000 extra beds in hospitals and intermediate care facilities and over 100 new hospitals by 2010.
- Booked appointments will allow people to go for treatment at a time when it is more easy and convenient for them to do so, enabling them to plan travel arrangements in good time if they have to travel far.

- New **ambulance response time targets** will apply from March 2001 (see table in Chapter 3) reducing risks to people in rural areas. The target of 8 minutes for life threatening (category A) calls is supported by additional funding for emergency ambulance services in areas where population density is low. And increasingly ambulance services are working with the fire and police services and with community volunteer schemes to deliver basic life support in an emergency, such as a fire or a road accident. For example in Essex, there are now increasing numbers of schemes using volunteers trained in basic life support and defibrillation to improve emergency health care in rural areas.

**Health Improvement Programmes** (HImPs) are the local strategies for improving health and healthcare in each Health Authority through the NHS and its partner agencies. They combine a range of nationally and locally oct targets, including distinctively rural health needs – for example of elderly people living remotely who have difficulty accessing GP and hospital services. In Northumberland, one of the challenges identified in the Health Improvement Programme is that of getting services to people living in isolated and dispersed communities within rural areas. Young People's Drop In Centres have been developed in schools serving large rural catchment areas to address health, education and other social exclusion issues. Schools have been selected because they are at the centre of existing transport networks.

## Social services

**4.2.9.** Social services provided by local authorities in rural areas have a vital role in helping vulnerable people such as the elderly and disabled in their own homes and communities as was shown in the first comprehensive inspection of community care in rural areas *Care in the Country* published in 1999. They provide access to day care centres and home support such as home helps. We are working to improve access to a consistent standard up and down the country. There will be clearer responsibilities for local government to show how well they are serving local people, and a clearer role for central government to take action where standards are not being met.

**Health Action Zones (HAZs)** are multi-agency programmes in 26 deprived areas involving NHS, local government, the voluntary and private sectors and community groups, to tackle major health problems such as coronary heart disease, cancer and mental health. They also represent a new approach to public health, linking regeneration, employment, education, housing and anti-poverty initiatives. Rural or part rural HAZs include North Cumbria, Hull and East Riding, Northumberland and Cornwall and the Scilly Isles. North Cumbria's Health Improvement Programme and Health Action Zone focuses on poverty, deprivation, rural issues and isolation as key determinants of health inequalities. £160,000 was allocated in 1999 – 2000 for innovative services for people living in rural areas in the county such as training a network of volunteers to develop new rural transport services, supplementing the services already available.

**New initiatives for addressing stress and mental illness,** which are as prevalent in rural areas as elsewhere, and where the suicide rate is higher, partly reflecting the higher suicide rate among farmers. The Department of Health is funding the mental health charity MIND to carry out a project called RURAL MINDS to develop training and education for those providing emotional support in isolated rural communities and to help people living in the country to feel that support and understanding of their problems are close at hand and a national network of support for people in rural communities who are suffering from stress and need help.

As part of the Action Plan for Farming, MAFF is giving £500,000 towards a rural stress action plan agreed and implemented by the voluntary sector, including the Rural Stress Information Network (Telephone: 024 7641 2916, e-mail: rusin@btinternet.com). Several organisations are working in partnership to deliver support to make a difference to those in distress; details of the plan were announced in October 2000 (MAFF News Release 351).

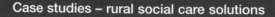

**4**

## Case studies – rural social care solutions

**Dorset, Bedfordshire and Lincolnshire** have negotiated with housing agencies to provide day care in the communal lounges of sheltered housing units in villages, which are nearer to rural service users than day care services in towns.

**In Wiltshire**, arrangements with cafes and public houses allow for the delivery of meals to recipients' homes or to be taken on the premises.

**Careline, a service in Derbyshire**, provides a network of volunteers to make a daily telephone call to elderly or disabled people living alone and at risk.

- We will pilot a **24 hour 'Care Direct' phone line** to provide general advice on care and support services and benefits in rural as well as urban areas. When necessary, callers will be referred to advisers to answer detailed queries and help them obtain the services they need.

- We will ask the Social Services Inspectorate to report on the degree to which the national agenda for modernising social services is being delivered in rural areas.

- We will be making sure that our national frameworks for health and social services require providers to assess rural needs, and give clear information about what is available.

## 4.3. Education and learning

**4.3.1.** Improving education and learning opportunities for people throughout their lives is fundamental to our objectives for a globally competitive economy, a highly skilled and productive workforce, equality of opportunity, the elimination of child poverty within one generation, and a better quality of life for all. This applies in rural as much as urban areas. We intend to make sure that people of all ages living in rural areas have full access to the range of opportunities available and that obstacles to access are addressed.

**4.3.2.** Rural transport problems and the location of training can be barriers which deter young people from engaging in further education and training after finishing compulsory education at 16. The New Start and Learning Gateway initiatives involve personal advisers dealing directly with young people to help them overcome these difficulties – as, for example, in Norfolk, where public service providers are working together to find solutions. Across the country, local education bodies are helping to fit budgets for supporting students with ways for students to travel to classes.

**Alford IT project, Lincolnshire**
Credit: The Countryside Agency

- The new **Connexions service** will build on this by providing young people with access to a personal adviser who will provide help, support and guidance through their teenage years. The Connexions service will be phased in from 2001 with pilots currently testing aspects of the service in 13 areas around the country. Pilots in Cornwall, Devon and Lincolnshire are focusing on rural issues as part of their activities. As part of the Connexions Strategy the Connexions Card aims to increase participation and attainment in learning by reducing some of the financial barriers, such as transport costs, preventing young people remaining in education.

**4.3.3.** From September 2000 we will pilot the use of **Educational Maintenance Allowances for 16–18 year olds** to pay for education-related transport costs so as to help widen participation among 16–18 year olds from low-income families. The scheme will be piloted for three years in five areas, including Suffolk, Worcestershire and East Lancashire, and will include two approaches: one which pays the entire cost of the transport, the other which combines a weekly allowance with subsidised transport.

- We will consider **extending to the rest of the country education maintenance allowances for 16-18 year olds** in the light of the most successful approaches from these pilots.

**4.3.4. Higher education (HE)** establishments are mainly located in larger urban centres and so less accessible to people in rural areas. One response is to take advantage of the increasing availability of distance learning. Degree courses and other HE qualifications available online – including full tutorial and other support services – are being developed by the Higher Education Funding Council for England in the 'e-Universities' project. For those in rural areas travelling to more traditional campuses a **Hardship Fund** of £57m (which covers both urban and rural areas) and bursaries are available to institutions offering higher education courses for 2000–01 for students who have difficulty in meeting their living and course costs, including travel to and from their place of study.

## 4.4. Tackling social exclusion

**4.4.1.** Social exclusion and deprivation in rural areas are significant and persistent problems. Although poverty is less prevalent than in urban areas, distance, isolation and poor access to jobs and services compound the problems of poorer people in rural areas.

### Neighbourhood deprivation

**4.4.2** In some cases deprivation will be evident across an area. A number of rural areas will benefit from a series of national targets set out in the cross-cutting spending review on *Government Intervention in Deprived Areas (GIDA)*. These are designed to secure major improvements in rates of employment, educational attainment, health improvement, and crime reduction in areas where outcomes fall below the minimum standard we expect. Local communities have a vital part to play in identifying priorities for tackling deprivation and improving services in their areas, and in creating a strategy to tackle these priorities. We are currently consulting widely on our proposals for Local Strategic Partnerships (LSPs) (see para 12.4.5). These will be an important element in the fight against rural social exclusion.

**4.4.3.** We are allocating £800m over the next 3 years to the new Neighbourhood Renewal Fund (NRF) to help local authorities in the most deprived areas improve services for poorer people and deliver the targets. A number of rural areas will benefit – for example £3.1 million will be available for Kerrier and £1.7m for Allerdale over the next three years. A commitment to work towards the establishment of a Local Strategic Partnership (LSP), or alternative acceptable partnership working arrangement, is one of the conditions for those local authorities receiving NRF resources.

**4.4.4.** We are allocating an extra £210m over the next 3 years for the New Deal for Communities to help implement the Action Plan for Neighbourhood Renewal to be published by the Social Exclusion Unit in the near future. Funds will be used to establish:

- The **Centre for Neighbourhood Renewal**. It will promote best practice and improve the skills and expertise of those involved. This will include what is likely to work in deprived rural areas.

- **Community capacity building projects** and pilot projects for **neighbourhood management** in deprived (mainly urban) areas, will benefit a number of rural places.

---

### The Indices of Deprivation 2000

These are a major step forward in assessing deprivation in both rural and urban areas. They provide new fine-grain information on six key elements or 'domains', so that – for the first time – small areas experiencing deprivation can be properly identified. The six aspects are:

- Low income
- Employment deprivation
- Education, skills and training deprivation
- Poor health and disability
- Poor housing
- Poor geographical access to services for benefits claimants

All 8,414 wards in England are ranked, showing how deprived individual wards are under each domain, as well as in an overall index of multiple deprivation. Information is also available at the local authority district level.

The *Indices of Deprivation 2000* will raise understanding of the complex nature of deprivation, including rural aspects like access to services. They will also be used across Government to target policies and allocate resources to the most deprived areas.

---

### Social exclusion in the wider rural community

**4.4.5.** Where deprivation is more isolated and less concentrated, we will tackle it through improving the targeting and delivery of main programmes, improving information and ensuring that **new initiatives are piloted in rural areas** (as with Health, Employment and Education Action Zones) so that in developing policies and disseminating best practice, rural impacts are fully taken into account and rural communities can fully benefit.

## Employment and income

**4.4.6.** Providing employment opportunities for all is the single most effective means of tackling poverty and social exclusion. Employment enables individuals to improve their living standards; it also makes constructive use of human resources.

Casual labour – Strawberry picking
Credit: MAFF

**4.4.7.** We are is delivering macroeconomic stability so there can be increasing employment opportunities for all; and employment in the UK is at a record level – up by over 1 million since the last general election. The employment rate of 74.7% is the second highest in the EU. We are making work pay through various tax and benefit reforms; raising standards of education to equip young people with the skills and knowledge they need to be able to take up jobs; and developing a culture of lifelong learning so we have a skilled, flexible and adaptable workforce.

**4.4.8.** We are also **assisting unemployed people** to acquire employability skills and find work through: the New Deals for unemployed claimants; helping those on sickness and disability benefits get back into the labour market and from there into employment through other welfare to work programmes such as the New Deal for Lone Parents; and taking a wide range of local initiatives designed to improve the functioning of regional and local product and labour markets. To help people further to make the transition from welfare into work, we announced in Budget 2000 a £100 job grant to help people make the transition from welfare into work; extended payments of Income Support for mortgage interest when moving into work, to match the housing benefit run-on already available; simplified rules for applying for these payments to increase take up; and a new childcare tax credit.

**4.4.9.** In rural areas employment among those of working age is generally higher (78% in rural districts compared to 73% for urban in 1999) and unemployment is generally lower than in urban areas (4.3% for rural compared with 7% for urban districts in England in 1998). But changing employment patterns, relatively high levels of casual and seasonal work, and problems with access to transport are all particular challenges in rural areas. There is also higher self-employment, with many on low incomes. Low wages are common.

*"We've got one local supermarket at the moment. So that's retail, pack house work or farm – and that's it."*

**4.4.10.** Although jobs come up all the time even in areas where employment is low, joblessness tends to be concentrated amongst certain groups and in certain localities in both urban and rural areas. A key element of our policy is about addressing this inequality. It is vital that people living in rural areas have good and flexible access to the employment services which will help them find suitable jobs; and that the services provided, such as the new Action Teams for Jobs in some rural areas, address the particular mobility and childcare problems people living in the country may have (see paragraph 6.3.3). New developments such as the telephone advice service Employment Service Direct are already making a big difference as people no longer have to go to job centres.

- From this Autumn 2000 vacancy information will be available on the internet and via computerised information kiosks at conveniently located public places. ICT Learning Centres will give access to **Employment Service Direct and the Employment Service Learning and Workbank.** This will increase the availability of access to jobsearch facilities and help for those people in isolated rural areas.

**4.4.11.** Our **welfare to work** policies aim to assist people not in employment, particularly those on welfare, into work. The New Deal programmes (for 18–24 year olds, the long term unemployed, the over 50s, lone parents, partners of unemployed people and disabled people) concentrate support on those who find it most difficult to obtain work and improve their prospects of remaining in sustained employment. Personal advisers consider with participants how to break down barriers to employment through programmes such as improving basic skills and understanding of the qualities employers are looking for, training opportunities, in-work benefits and information on local childcare provision.

**4.4.12.** For Job Seeker Allowance claimants and participants in the New Deal and New Deal for Lone Parents schemes, individually tailored help is available for people living in rural areas, including help with transport and childcare (see chapter 2). The **National Minimum Wage** will particularly benefit rural workers because a higher proportion of rural workers are on low wages.

## Case study – Working Family Tax Credit: North Cumbria

The Working Families Tax Credit (WFTC) provides support for low and middle income working families. The WFTC, together with the National Minimum Wage, provide a guaranteed minimum income of £208 a week for a family with someone working at least 35 hours a week. In Northern Cumbria a partnership approach led by the county council, and involving other local authorities, the voluntary sector, NHS, and parish councils, has successfully increased the uptake of this scheme. Some 5,400 local families with children are benefiting from the WFTC. The increase in the take up of the benefit was particularly noticeable in rural areas of the country, where many people are on low incomes.

## Case study – Sure Start South Fenland

The Government's Sure Start initiative brings together early education, health services, family support and advice on nurturing to disadvantaged families. One rural area selected as a Trailblazer for the approach is South Fenland in Cambridgeshire. The area has considerable problems including: low population density and isolation making it difficult to sustain community facilities and services and to access them; low wages and high unemployment; the highest crime rate in Cambridgeshire, including youth offending and drug misuse.

Central government funding of nearly £2.9m over three years will enable a programme to go ahead to include: a mobile play and learning centre; a Sure Start shop; improvements to buildings and upgrading of outdoor play areas; a bookstart scheme; a network of trained childminders; information and advice for families, including early support for families who may be facing difficulties; specialist teaching and support for children with special needs; and a community transport scheme to improve access.

The aim is to achieve social cohesion within communities in the area, with equal opportunities for quality, confident and independent lifestyles for tomorrow's children and their families.

Sure Start South Fenland will be one of 500 programmes aimed at deprived communities in urban and rural areas. £1.4bn has been allocated to this initiative over the financial years 1999–00 to 2003–04.

**4.4.13.** Successful action to tackle **social exclusion** in rural areas requires partnership action involving both local and specialist agencies. The Countryside Agency has a key part to play in developing expertise and knowledge, and we have already allocated an additional £3m over three years to the Agency to develop its programme of research, pilot projects and dissemination of information and good practice.

- The Countryside Agency is launching a **Rural Social Exclusion Advisory Group** to guide its work and provide links with other key social exclusion initiatives including the Social Exclusion Unit (SEU) who will be taking account of the rural dimension in their future work programme.

**4.4.14.** Over 50 rural **local authorities** are actively working with anti-poverty and social exclusion strategies. The Improvement and Development Agency (IDeA) is working to encourage networking and good practice sharing, including between urban and rural authorities. Improved access to fine grained local benefits data has recently helped authorities to identify very small pockets of need in their areas. **Local community action**, through rural community councils, parish councils and voluntary organisations, is important in helping to assess and present needs, develop solutions and deliver services. Much hidden need has been identified and valuable innovative practice put in place as a result of community level action (for instance through the formation of village companies in coalfield areas with support from the Coalfields Regeneration Trust).

- We will be strengthening this work by an extra £4.5m over the next three years for the Countryside Agency to fund additional community development work in every county to help communities set up new projects to tackle problems of social exclusion.

Raindrops community project on the Royce Road estate in Spalding. A multi-agency community development project, in Spalding which brings service providers and the community together to help solve social problems. The photo shows a mother and toddler group which has helped residents' confidence grow through their involvement.
Credit: City Graphics Partnership

## Cultural and leisure services

**4.4.15.**   Access to cultural and sporting activity helps to provide an increased quality of life for rural communities. We are encouraging all local authorities to develop local cultural strategies which are based on a partnership approach. These encompass sport, countryside, parks and tourism as well as arts, cultural heritage and libraries.

**4.4.16.**   **Libraries** play an important role in providing local facilities in rural areas through their branches and mobile units. They can draw on new technology to improve services and provide easy access to information about the locality and its services. Our aim to ensure a high quality library service will lead, in April 2001, to the introduction of the first library standards. These will cover location and opening hours to mobile as well as branch libraries.

Mobile Library, St Buryan, Cornwall
Credit: The Countryside Agency, Liane Bradbrook

**4.4.17.**   The Government and three Lottery distributors have recently announced the **Spaces for Sports and the Arts scheme** providing £130m aimed at improving facilities in primary schools for dual school and community sports, drama, dance and other activities. It is targeted at areas of greatest need, including 14 largely rural counties such as Cornwall, Cumbria, Derbyshire, East Sussex, Kent, Norfolk, Northumberland and Somerset. This is part of our strategy for sport, *A Sporting Future for All,* the twofold purpose of which is for more people of all ages and social groups to take part in sport, and more success for our top competitors and teams in international competitions. This support is in addition to the commitment given by Sport England to fund 500 different facilities projects in rural areas as part of its current 10-year Lottery strategy.

## Access to legal and advice services

**4.4.18.**   Advice services, which help people resolve disputes and enforce their rights effectively, have a vital role in tackling poverty and achieving social inclusion. People in rural communities have traditionally had poor access to advice and many do not claim all the benefits due to them. We launched the Community Legal Service (CLS) in April 2000 to improve access to good quality legal advice. The CLS will focus particularly on access to advice on benefits, housing, debt, immigration and employment problems, based on an assessment of local needs. Local networks of legal advice services, consisting of solicitors, Citizens Advice Bureaux, independent advice agencies and local authority services, will be created and supported by local CLS partnerships – local authority, Legal Services Commission and other local bodies involved in advisory services. Their job is to find the best means of meeting local needs. In rural areas, this will mean overcoming problems of reaching remote and disperse rural communities.

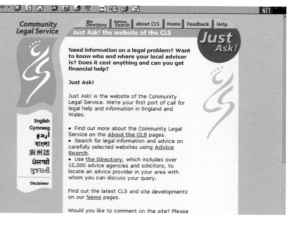

Just Ask! Website of the Community Legal Service
Credit: Community Legal Service

## 4.5. Safer communities

**4.5.1.** Evidence from the British Crime Survey shows that the levels of general crime, and fear of crime, are significantly lower in rural than in urban areas. Burglary, violent and vehicle crime in rural areas declined from 1995 to 1997 and again from 1997 to 1999; violent and vehicle crime declined more in rural than in non-rural areas. But the threat of crime felt by rural communities is still very real. Greater isolation, personal experience and publicised cases can all add to this. Some crimes are specific to rural areas – thefts of livestock and farm equipment, wildlife crime and mass trespass. In some areas and for some individuals, these can pose particular and serious problems.

### Our approach

**4.5.2.** There is no 'acceptable' level of crime, and we are fully determined to tackle crime, and the fear of crime, wherever it exists. We have already launched a range of rural initiatives and are now building on these by

- promoting partnership working in ways that meet rural needs;
- providing extra resources to tackle the extra costs of policing rural areas;
- introducing new ideas and ways of working.

**4.5.3.** Local communities can identify problem areas, contribute to joint solutions with the police and provide vital intelligence through initiatives such as neighbourhood watch. This is additional to, not a substitute for, the growing resources committed by the police themselves and gives the community access to sophisticated crime fighting techniques.

**4.5.4. Local crime reduction partnerships and strategies** (set up under the Crime and Disorder Act 1998) bring together local authorities and local people, including parish councils. They are developing solutions such as **'Watch' schemes** covering farms, vehicles, horses, and increased provision for young people (such as dial-a-ride, schools-based community activities and young people's projects) to help prevent young people drifting into anti-social and criminal behaviour. Police and the farming community have together established 500 farm watch schemes across England and Wales. New regional crime directors will help local partnerships to deliver their goals.

**Neighbourhood Watch** (Rural Watch in the countryside) is based on the idea that getting together with your neighbours can not only cut local crime but can help to create communities which care. The aims of Rural Watch are to improve two-way communications between rural communities and the police, to reduce opportunities for crime, and to strengthen community spirit.

It has given rise to a number of specialized "watches", including Horse Watch and Farm Watch. **Horse Watch** has resulted in many animals being freeze-branded and some having their owners' postcodes etched into their hooves. Tack is postcoded and postcodes are painted onto the roofs of horseboxes. **Farm Watch** schemes have arranged such measures as postcoding property, wheel-clamping mobile equipment, and painting postcodes on the roofs of vehicles.

**Gloucestershire Rural Watch**
Credit: Gloucestershire Constabulary

**Hexham, Northumberland – Policeman and CCTV camera**
Credit: The Countryside Agency, Liane Bradbrook

**4.5.5. Closed circuit** TV (CCTV) is increasingly being introduced by local partnerships as a proven way of tackling local crime problems, such as rowdy behaviour in small towns. A CCTV fund of £153m was announced in July 1998. Only 16 of 350 first round bids had a clear rural element, but rural bids have been specifically encouraged in the second round. Local communities can apply for Home Office funding through their local crime and disorder reduction partnership, perhaps contacting their local crime prevention officer or community safety officer in the first instance.

**4.5.6.** The use of **neighbourhood wardens** by rural communities to provide a uniformed, semi-official presence is another potential option for tackling crime at local level. Wardens can promote community safety, assist with environmental improvements and housing management and also contribute to community development.

## Case study – Neighbourhood Wardens

The village of **Mullion in Cornwall** is setting up a neighbourhood wardens' scheme with assistance from the Home Office/DETR Neighbourhood Wardens' Grant Programme. Mullion is in an isolated location and has high levels of unemployment and deprivation. The wardens' scheme aims to reduce crime and fear of crime, and reduce anti-social behaviour by involving the community in finding solutions to these problems. Two part-time neighbourhood wardens will provide an interface between the police, local authorities, older residents and the youth of the village, in an attempt to improve community relations. The wardens will take a proactive approach to tackling vandalism and will encourage the repair of existing community facilities. The wardens will work very closely with Cornwall's Youth Service.

**4.5.7.** A rural family suffering **domestic violence** will feel extremely isolated when there is often literally no-one nearby to turn to. Four of the 34 projects being funded under the £7m Violence Against Women initiative of the Government's Crime Reduction Programme specifically address issues of rurality in connection with domestic violence

## Case study – domestic violence support

Victim Support in the Cotswolds have recently produced a publication entitled 'Raising awareness of domestic violence in rural areas'. This covers an enormous number of initiatives they have been organising such as information stickers with contact numbers for Victim Support which are placed in public toilets. Another initiative involved Victim Support Cotswold working with British Telecom to place information sheets in all telephone kiosks throughout the Cotswolds – approximately 500 in total – to raise awareness of the services Victim Support offer and to enable victims to make untraceable calls for help. They advise that in many isolated communities there may be no Church or Village Hall, but there is always a phone box.

### More resources, and more police on the ground

## Case study – Community Safety Partnership

The **Boston Community Safety Partnership** scheme involves extending a current town centre CCTV system to cover a housing estate and to provide a mobile system for rural areas. The rural system will be targeted at crime hot spots but will also address the high level of fear of crime that exists in the rural area.

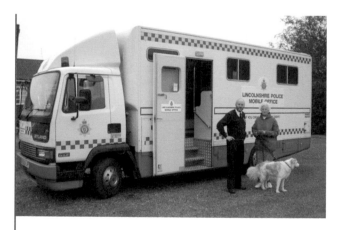

Lincolnshire Mobile Police Van
Credit: Lincolnshire Constabulary

**4.5.8. Funding for rural policing** has increased steadily since 1997. £15m from the Police Modernisation Fund has been earmarked for rural policing for this year and £30m next year. It has been allocated to police authorities on the basis that they must demonstrate real improvements in the policing of rural areas, responding to the needs of rural communities, including the farming community, for whom crime and fear of crime are a real concern. Police authorities will be required to set out clearly in each year's Best Value performance plans how that money has been used to improve services and how it will be used in the coming year. They will be required to demonstrate improvements that can be measured by *Best Value Performance Indicators*, focusing specifically on rural force areas. Her Majesty's Inspectorate of Constabulary will inspect on the basis of this.

---

### Case study – response times

Each police force sets and monitors key performance targets, including speed of reaching incidents requiring immediate attention:

**Lancashire Police Authority** covers both major towns and extensive rural areas such as the Ribble and Lune Valleys. The target is for officers to arrive at an incident requiring an emergency response within 15 minutes, in both urban and rural areas. The force has consistently achieved a high success rate over the past four years. In 1999/2000, officers attended 83,063 emergency incidents, arriving at 95% within the target 15 minutes. Response times are inevitably quicker in urban areas (average 5.5 minutes over a three-month period) than rural areas. But a well-developed road infra-structure assists in providing rapid access to rural communities when needed. For example, in one rural area the average response time to emergency incidents was 11.5 minutes (over three months). Both the Police Authority and the force place a high priority on officers arriving at an emergency both as quickly and, very importantly, as safely as possible.

- **We will be looking for positive improvement in this aspect of police performance in rural areas.**

---

**4.5.9.** Rural police forces have also benefited from the ring-fenced **Crime Fighting Fund (CFF)** money, which will allow forces in England and Wales to recruit 9,000 officers over and above their previous plans over the three years to March 2003. The Government and the public will expect to see results from the CFF recruitment – reduction in crime, with more offenders being brought to justice.

**4.5.10.** In the past 10 years, the pressures of modern policing have led to a reduction in the number of local police stations and of a permanent policing presence in many rural areas. An efficient police service does have to reappraise its estate. But we recognise the concern of many in rural areas at the loss of a visible police presence. **We will encourage more active public consultation by police authorities and forces before any police station is closed.**

**4.5.11.** We are also working to increase the number of **special constables** in rural areas. Not only will this provide an additional visible presence in rural areas, but local recruits will bring local knowledge and expertise to the job of reducing crime and offending.

**4.5.12.** **Illegal drugs** are not just a problem of the inner city, but have spread deep into the countryside. We are ensuring that treatment services will follow by investing an extra £33m in drugs treatment services over the next three years.

- Every major rural police station will have a drugs worker to help to break the link between crime and drugs. The National Treatment Agency will ensure that national standards apply to drug treatment services and that access to services is fair.

### Racism in rural areas

**4.5.13.** Research suggests that, relative to the number of ethnic minority people in an area, racist incidents and crime may be more common in the countryside than in urban areas. We are determined to tackle racism everywhere.

---

#### Challenging Racism in the Rural Idyll
This rural racism project reported in July 1999 and contains important information. Isolated families and members of ethnic minorities lack the support of a larger community and can feel, and be, more threatened. There is little official infrastructure to support ethnic minorities, by comparison, for example, with the activities of Race Equality Councils in more urban areas. "**No problem here**" is a common approach on the part of statutory agencies.

---

**4.5.14.** Local crime reduction strategies should ensure that racist crime, and racist overtones to crime, are properly tackled. Low level vandalism and other nuisance directed at people from ethnic minorities may be especially significant. The Racist Incidents Standing Committee produced guidance in 1998 on multi-agency working, including in rural areas. Local crime reduction partnerships in rural areas should use positive recruitment campaigns to attract members of ethnic minority communities

- The Home Office will be launching a new Race Equality Grant to provide funding of £5m per year. Some of it has been used to fund a number of projects in rural areas to help combat the problems found in the research.

## New ways of working

**4.5.15.** We are enabling police officers to be more visible and effective on the ground, by reducing bureaucracy and by investing in new police technology so that police officers do not have to return to the police station to complete paperwork, but can process arrests and send the information back to the station on the move.

This year's budget provided a total of £285m to be spent on this area. Measures of particular benefit to rural communities include:

- A **new police radio system** for which £500m will be provided over the next three years.

- Introduction of **Geographical Information Systems** to improve the speedy location of incidents and police response times;

- **The Public Safety Radio Communication Project** (Airwave) which will provide every officer with secure and reliable communications, giving direct access to the information needed to resolve incidents;

- A new **Command and Control computer system** now under development will speed up the reaction to calls and dispatch of resources;

- £4m for **police aviation**;

- The development of a **rural crime toolkit**, drawing on research and existing examples of good practice, will offer a new resource to help the police achieve this in rural areas. The rural crime toolkit, with others, will be available on the Government's crime reduction website at www.crimereduction.gov.uk

- The **Targeted Policing Initiative** which is helping police forces develop improved ways of tackling local concentrations of crime, such as in Norfolk, Cambridge and Lincolnshire where improved cross-border co-operation and other enhancements are being made with £600,000 extra funding.

## Greater visibility

**4.5.16** One of the main concerns which rural people have on policing is to see and know more about how their area is being policed – how many officers patrol their area and what is being done to fight crime. Several police forces have developed good practice in this area, for example through measures to provide a regular police presence in village facilities such as the Post Office or community centre or a mobile police station, and to inform local communities how policing in the area is being delivered.

- Home Office Ministers have announced that they wish to discuss, with the Association of Chief Police Officers, and the Association of Police Authorities, how each police authority might better inform the public about the steps it is taking to maintain and improve police visibility and effectiveness in all parts of England and Wales.

# an affordable
## home

## The issues

- There is a shortage of affordable housing in many rural towns and villages which are frequently popular and attractive places to live. Demand for housing is high, both from local people and from new residents – commuters, the retired and second home owners. This can create unbalanced communities and deny local people the chance to acquire a home.
- The Right to Buy scheme has helped tenants to realise their aspiration to own their own homes and in many cases it has helped to create stable, mixed-income communities. But it has been a costly scheme and in the absence, under the previous government, of sufficient investment to replace housing being sold, has led to the removal of more desirable homes from the social rented sector. This has left local authorities with a smaller stock of poorer quality properties in which to house people who need affordable housing to rent, particularly in small rural communities with only a few homes for rent.
- There is less obvious homelessness in the countryside, but homelessness cases accepted by rural authorities have increased as a proportion of the total in the last decade.
- There is often resistance to new housing in small villages because of the fear that it will not fit in.

## The future – what we want to see

- A high proportion of affordable and decent housing, both for rent and sale, in market towns and villages to support a living, working countryside with inclusive rural communities which help young people to remain in the area where they grew up.
- New housing development built sustainably in market towns where it is accessible to jobs and services and will reduce car dependence. By making use of previously developed sites we can reduce the amount of new development in the open countryside; an urban

renaissance so that our larger towns and cities will become more attractive places to live.
- Sensitively designed new housing in towns and villages using materials which blend with nearby buildings and that is carefully sited so that it fits into the surroundings.

---

### Summary of measures
- Doubling funding for the Housing Corporation between 2000 and 2003 to benefit both rural and urban areas;

- Doubling the size of the Housing Corporation's programme in small rural settlements from 800 to 1,600 homes a year;

- Local authorities able to charge the full council tax on second homes and retain extra revenue (subject to consultation);

- Better use of the planning system to secure more affordable homes as part of mixed developments in market towns and rural areas. There is no reason why, in small villages if there is evidence of need and subject to financial viability, every new market house should not be matched with an affordable home;

- Better designed homes to fit in with rural surroundings;

- Package of VAT reforms to encourage additional conversions of properties for residential use.

# 5

## Contents

*"So what happens to the young people when they get to the age when they want to make a household?"*
*"They leave, or they stay at home with mum and dad, or they go off to somewhere like Chesterfield where house prices are more reasonable."*

*"So you really wouldn't be able to afford anything in your own village?"*
*"Not in my village, no"*
*"Does that bother you, or not?"*
*"It does really, yeah, 'cos I do like where I live, but there's just nothing – I would stay there if I could afford to."*

## 5.1. Introduction

**5.1.1.** We are putting in place a framework to ensure the housing needs of rural areas are better met. Our strategy is to ensure that rural affordable housing needs are properly identified; that a higher proportion of housing provided in rural areas is affordable; and that new housing is designed to enhance the countryside. We will deliver this strategy through a substantial increase in resources for affordable housing and by making better use of the planning system to provide a higher proportion of affordable housing.

Estate agents in Liskeard, Cornwall
Credit: Philip Wolmuth

**5.1.2.** In the Spending Review 2000, we announced an additional £1.8bn investment in housing over the next three years. This is in addition to the extra £5bn announced for housing as a result of our Capital Receipts Initiative and the 1998 Comprehensive Spending Review. This means that around £13bn will be available over the next three years for more and better housing.

**5.1.3.** However our aim is not just to increase the amount available for housing overall, but also to ensure that an adequate share goes towards those rural areas where additional resources are most needed.

## 5.2. Identifying the need for affordable housing

**5.2.1.** We know that the housing needs of rural areas are not always properly assessed at the local level. Responsibility for assessing housing needs rests primarily with local authorities. A robust needs assessment is an essential input to the housing strategies authorities are required to produce. Making such an assessment is not easy because of the scattered nature of rural communities. But it is essential that it should be done, and done in consultation with the local communities themselves.

- We are therefore asking all authorities with rural areas to make **a specific assessment of the rural housing needs in their area,** and to include in their strategies a plan for meeting these needs. We have recently issued guidance **on how to ensure the needs of everyone in their area are taken into account**, including the particular circumstances of sub-areas, including rural areas. This stresses the importance of local authorities consulting local communities including parish councils; and we have endorsed the recently published guide to local authorities *Developing Housing Strategies in Rural Areas* which has been developed by the Chartered Institute of Housing, along with the Housing Corporation and the Countryside Agency;

- In making recommendations on **funding allocations** for housing, the Government Offices in the regions will take into account how effective local authorities have been in identifying rural need. To this end the Government Offices will monitor local authorities' rural needs assessments;

- **The Housing Corporation** is now adopting an increasingly strategic approach to the allocation of resources under its Approved Development Programme. This ensures that investment decisions are based on regional and local priorities. The Corporation will continue to include allowance for the higher costs which can be incurred in developing small schemes in villages in its scheme cost criteria. It will also include issues relating to development in rural areas in its forthcoming review of total cost indicators and social housing grant rates.

## 5.3. Providing the resources for affordable homes

**5.3.1.** It is clear that there is a need for more affordable houses in many rural areas. We are providing an additional £50 million this year, followed by an extra £872 million between 2001–02 and 2003–04 for building new social housing in both rural and urban areas. This will mean that by 2003–04 we will have doubled annual funding for the Housing Corporation's Approved Development Programme (ADP).

### Case study – rural housing development with local authority support

A council-owned in-fill development site in Chapel Lane, Weston Sub Edge, Gloucestershire was released from adjoining secure tenancies and originally granted planning consent for a single detached house. The Parish Council and Ward Member were concerned about the lack of affordable housing for local young people. Two one-bedroom homes were built instead.

The development was possible through the benefit of the partnering contract which batched a number of small rural schemes with a significant 20 unit scheme at Willersey. The scheme was completed in February 2000. The units were joint funded with Social Housing Grant by the Housing Corporation and Cotswold District Council.

Construction of 2 one-bedroom houses for rent with local authority social housing grant. In-fill development site in Gloucestershire
Credit: Cotswold District Council

### Funding for social housing
The main mechanisms for financing provision of additional social housing (rented housing at below marked rates) are:

- Funding by the Housing Corporation through its Approved Development Programme (ADP) to Registered Social Landlords (RSLs) which provide lower than market cost housing;
- Funding for new or replacement social housing by means of Local Authority Social Housing Grant (LASHG) through local authorities' housing capital programmes. This is financed partly from allocations from central government and partly from authorities' own resources.

## Affordable homes in small rural settlements

**5.3.2.** There is a particular problem in small rural settlements, where often all the new housing has recently been executive homes that local people cannot afford to buy. To make sure that a fair share of the additional funding goes to small rural settlements where there is a need for affordable housing:

- **We will double the number of dwellings which the Housing Corporation's rural programme will deliver in settlements of less than 3,000 people over the next three years.** By 2003–04 we expect 1,600 dwellings a year (provided by Registered Social Landlords) to be approved in those settlements compared with about 800 dwellings in the current year. This means that the proportion of the dwellings in small settlements approved by the Corporation will rise from the current target of 3.4% to a new target of 6.4%;

- **We will encourage local authorities to provide more new affordable housing in small rural settlements where there is high demand through use of local authority Social Housing Grant.** This, together with the judicious use of planning powers (see para 5.4 below) should bring 1500 or so affordable social homes annually to small rural settlements – ie together with the Housing Corporation rural programme a total of over 3,000 by 2003–04.

Challock, Ashford, one of 20 small village schemes built on exceptions sites in Ashford District.
Credit: Rural Housing Trust, Mary Allwood

## Affordable homes in market towns

**5.3.3.** While it is important to provide new affordable homes in villages where there is a need, about half of rural people live in market towns, and that is where we expect most new affordable housing to be provided.

- **Some 3,800 affordable homes (16% of the total Housing Corporation programme) were approved in 1999-2000 in local authority districts with rural areas, including market towns.** (This was in addition to the housing provided in settlements of under 3,000 people

under the rural programme.) We expect this to grow, alongside urban approvals, as they benefit from the extra resources which the Government is providing for the Approved Development Programme over the next 3 years.

- **Local authorities** also finance new affordable homes. On average we estimate that some 8,000 social housing dwellings are provided by this means annually in England, of which the majority are in the south east and south west. In 1999–00 around 2,500 dwellings were approved in rural districts. We expect rural local authorities to use this route to provide homes in market towns and small villages which help people to live and work in the countryside. They will be assisted by the massive boost in the overall resources provided to local authorities for housing investment. **The resources allocated for 2000–01 are around twice the amount allocated for 1997–98 and will increase by a further 40% over the next 3 years.**

- **The Housing Corporation will be reviewing its rural strategy following the White Paper** to ensure that it responds effectively to the housing needs of rural communities. The Corporation wants to fit its rural policy within their broader investment strategies and acknowledge the key role of market towns alongside the village programme.

## Cheaper homes to buy

*"It's a very difficult problem, it's not just young people, it's people like, for example, young teachers. When the schools advertise here for teachers they don't get many applicants, frankly, because they just can't afford to come and live here – very, very difficult for them."*

**5.3.4.** In addition to the need for more social housing, there is a demand for cheaper housing for purchase in rural areas, for example to help young couples get their feet on the housing ladder.

- **We will therefore increase the level of support to help those on modest incomes acquire their own homes.** There are several existing schemes which help people into home ownership. Options include part buying and part renting homes from Registered Social Landlords (RSLs) or using an interest free equity loan from an RSL toward the cost of a property eg Homebuy.

- In addition our Housing Green Paper *Quality and Choice – a Decent Home for All* announced the new **Starter Home Initiative** which will assist key workers with home ownership in areas of high prices and high demand. The Spending Review has provided £250m to support this important initiative and we will make sure that these funds will be available to benefit rural high demand hotspots, among other areas.

**5.3.5.** Through these measures we can substantially increase the supply of affordable homes in rural areas. **We expect to deliver around 9,000 affordable homes annually in rural districts by 2003–04 (including 3,000 in small settlements).** However, the precise amount will depend on local authorities' investment decisions and additional housing provided through the planning system.

---

### Case study – shared ownership housing

Uttlesford District Council gave planning permission in 1988 for ten houses on its first exception site (see paragraph 5.4.4) in Ashdon, near Saffron Walden. Because of the negligible land cost, English Villages Housing Association was able to provide shared ownership houses (at 50% of value) on this site without any public subsidy.

The scheme is now eleven years old and some of the houses have changed hands – always to people from the village of Ashdon. Building Societies remain willing to provide mortgages on the properties. Further non-subsidised shared ownership houses have been built by English Villages Housing Association in a further 6 villages in the District. Altogether, the association has built 397 non-subsidised shared ownership houses in 89 villages in England.

---

## 5.4. Planning for affordable housing

*"To the best of my knowledge all the recent planning has been for medium-to-upper group housing."*

**5.4.1** The planning system has a vital role to play in the provision of both affordable housing for rent and for purchase. Our new planning guidance on housing *(PPG3)* emphasises the importance of an affordable housing policy based on an assessment of local need.

**5.4.2.** When developers apply for planning permission to build new houses, the local authority can seek a contribution to affordable housing, usually by asking for a proportion of the units to be built on site as social housing. Local authorities outside London can do this if the development covers a site of at least one hectare or involves at least 25 dwellings or more. But where acute pressures can be shown to exist and smaller schemes would be viable, authorities can adopt policies in their plans to use lower thresholds down to developments on sites of only half a hectare or with as few as 15 dwellings. This offers particular flexibility for small housing development in market towns.

**5.4.3.** Furthermore, **in settlements of 3,000 or less, no thresholds apply.** So in villages where there is a clear need for affordable housing, the local authority can seek a proportion of affordable housing even on the smallest site. This provision, which is of particular benefit to rural areas, is not always used to full effect, and **we believe that its wider adoption could generate significant numbers of affordable houses in rural villages.**

Ashdon, Essex: the first exceptions site, where 10 fixed equity, shared ownership homes were completed in 1989
Credit: Rural Housing Trust, Mary Allwood

### Exception policy

**5.4.4.** We also want to encourage the use of the **rural exception policy.** This is a special provision which applies only in rural settlements (but regardless of size) where permission would not otherwise be given for new housing development. It can provide a significant number of affordable homes for local people in rural areas – around 1,500 in 1998 – which is in addition to those delivered as a result of an authority's general affordable housing policy. The exception applies to additional affordable housing made available only for local people in perpetuity. Local authorities who include an exception policy in their local plan can grant planning permission for small sites within or adjoining villages which would not otherwise be released for housing. Again we would like local authorities to make more use of the exception policy.

*"Yeah, but we sold some land for eight bungalows, and if it wasn't for those bungalows our church would fold – mother and I used to be about the only ones that went to church, and now we get about 16 – and they have really brought life."*

**5**

### Case study – Sussex Rural Community Council helps deliver affordable housing

In Sussex, seven district councils work together along with the Sussex Rural Community Council to address affordable housing issues in a consistent and constructive way. In 1998–99 they secured over 450 houses, three quarters of which were in small villages. A Housing Enabler has recently produced *Guide to Good Practice, Affordable Housing for Rural Communities*. The Guide provides step by step advice to parish councils on ways they can participate in providing affordable housing in their village – assessment of local need and the use of local surveys, identifying a potential site, consulting with the community, choosing a developer (typically an RSL) and obtaining planning permission. It sets out the role parish councils can play in advising local people on the process of nomination to one of the new homes in their village.

### Case study – exception sites

**Hartpury and Staunton, Forest of Dean District Council, Gloucestershire**

These two recent newbuild developments are mixed tenure schemes to meet local housing needs on a rural exception sites using Housing Corporation Social Housing Grant. It is the outcome of a local housing needs surveys in both villages. Both settlements are in higher house price areas causing a significant 'affordability gap' for local people to access housing. Each seheme is on a site bordering the village Planning envelope consisting of 8 two- and three-bedroom houses for rent and shared ownership. Rents are between £50 and £62 per week with shared ownership starting from £22,500 for a 50% share. Both schemes were oversubscribed and households housed all had strong local connections:

    5 locally resident households
    8 previous lengthy residence
    10 with close relatives in the village
    4 with employment in the village.

### Putting affordable housing policies into practice

**5.4.5.** Local authorities' success in using these planning policy tools is variable and some have not exploited them fully. We think authorities could and should make greater use of these policies.

- **Local authorities should negotiate an appropriate element of affordable housing and there is no reason why, in small villages if there is evidence of need and subject to financial viability, they should not seek to match every new market house with an affordable home.**

**5.4.6.** Closer working between housing and planning authorities, the Housing Corporation and Registered Social Landlords (eg Housing Association) is critical and this is something we are trying to encourage. We have already commissioned wide-ranging research on the use of current planning policy to provide for affordable housing and will advise on good practice guidance for local authorities and others on delivering affordable housing through planning policy.

**We will issue best practice guidance which will:**

- Provide practical examples of where rural authorities are planning successfully for affordable housing;

- Encourage local authorities to consider whether Local Authority Social Housing Grant, could be used to ensure that the potential of exceptions sites is used to the full;

- The Countryside Agency will continue to fund its successful Rural Housing Enabler programme and explore extending it to more rural areas.

**Further help from the Countryside Agency**
**The Countryside Agency** is already helping local authorities and rural communities to secure affordable homes in villages – eg through its Rural Housing Enablers programme. It is exploring further ways to help including using a community trust to purchase the land and through a combination of private funding and mortgaging the land, raising finance for social housing. This could be combined with mechanisms to retain the low cost sale element in the affordable housing sector in perpetuity.

The Rural Housing Enabler (RHE) in Northumberland, based with the Rural Community Council, operates over the four district councils covering the rural parts of the county. Through joint working, now formalised in the **Northumberland Rural Housing Forum** the RHE has helped 45 communities identify needs and supported the development of 59 new affordable homes in 10 villages. With her support the community on Holy Island established a Community Trust. This has funded five rented homes for local people which are owned by the Trust. It has bought a vacant hotel and converted it to a community centre and hopes to do a further conversion to create two additional flats.

1 to 5 Kyle Gardens, Holy Island, a courtyard of two and three bedroomed houses for local people. Developed by a Community Trust supported by a Rural Housing Enabler
Credit: The Countryside Agency, Lianne Bradbrook

## 5.5. Making better use of existing housing stock

Housing tenure in rural areas compared with England as a whole

**Rural areas**

11%
4%
9%
76%

**All England**

10%
5%
16%
69%

■ Owner occupied  ■ RSL tenant
■ Council tenant  ■ Private tenant

*Source: DETR Survey of Housing 1998/99*

**5.5.1.** One of our main priorities is to ensure that all social housing is brought up to a decent standard within ten years. Our strategy for improving the quality of housing and service delivery was set out in the Housing Green Paper *Quality and Choice: A decent home for all*.

**5.5.2.** We also want to make sure that more of the existing housing in rural areas is available to local people. In some rural areas, a high proportion of houses are used as second homes, empty for much of the year, thus increasing the pressure on the existing housing stock. Another concern is that dwellings originally provided as social housing can be bought by the tenant and then sold on, reducing the low cost housing stock available for local people and those who need to work in the area. That is why we need the possibility of imposing some restrictions on resale.

### Restrictions on resale of right to buy homes

**5.5.3.** Secure tenants – most council tenants and some tenants of Registered Social Landlords – have the right to buy their home at discounts of up to 70%. Tenants in rural areas have the same right to buy as tenants in other areas. But right-to-buy landlords in certain rural areas can impose conditions on the resale of such homes, in order to maintain a supply of affordable homes for local people. In a National Park, an Area of Outstanding Natural Beauty, or any area designated by the Secretary of State as rural they can impose one of two restrictions:

- They can require the tenant, if reselling within 10 years, to offer them the first chance to buy the home. This enables them to bring the property back into their stock of affordable homes for rent; or

- They can require him to resell only to someone who has lived or worked locally for at least 3 years. This requirement binds all subsequent buyers of the property. Such a restriction tends to reduce the value of the property, and so makes it more affordable as well as available to local people. As this limitation will have applied when the tenant first bought the property it will have been reflected in the purchase price, so the tenant will not lose out. This policy gives rural tenants the same rights as others while at the same time helping to promote the supply of affordable homes in rural areas and assist smaller communities to thrive.

**5.5.4.** Twenty four areas of England – mainly districts or parts of districts – have been designated as rural for resale restrictions since 1980. Applications for other areas to be designated can be made to DETR. These should be made or supported by the local housing authority. In reaching decisions the Secretary of State uses a number of criteria including size of settlement, population density and the incidence of second homes in the areas.

- We will remind authorities in rural areas where there is a significant demand for affordable housing to consider the possibility of applying for designation.

**5.5.5.** Our housing Green Paper *Quality and Choice – a Decent Home for All* made clear that we have no plans for further significant changes to the right to buy scheme.

## Making housing available for local people

**5.5.6.** We are taking other measures to make sure that more existing dwellings in the countryside are available to local people on lower incomes:

- **We propose (subject to consultation) to give local authorities discretion to charge the full council tax on second homes**, rather than the 50% discount that they are required to apply at the moment. We propose that this should be discretionary, as pressure on housing varies from one area to another and some authorities may wish to encourage second home owners who can bring a useful input to the local economy. We propose that the extra revenue raised should be retained by the local authorities concerned and we will consult on whether the funds should be earmarked to provide affordable homes in the areas affected;

- Last year we introduced **fairer right to buy discounts**, replacing the cash limit of £50,000 by new regional cash limits ranging from £22,000 to £38,000. These better reflect house prices in each region and offer the taxpayer better value for money. The new limits mean that the most expensive properties in attractive high demand rural areas will be sold only at a fair price;

- **We will promote more flexible lettings policies by local authorities, so as to take more account of specific rural needs in their area.** We propose changes to social housing lettings to promote a more customer-focused approach giving applicants more say and greater choice in where they live. There would be increased opportunities for people to move more easily between different landlords and different areas; although landlords could choose to give local people priority over incomers so as to reduce the pressure of demand on limited stock. Over the next three years, we will be providing £11m to support pilot schemes involving local authorities and registered social landlords which test choice-based lettings policies. We intend to invite pilots from rural areas;

- **We are funding the Empty Homes Agency to work with local authorities to bring more empty rural property back into use.** As a follow up to its challenge document *Wasted Rural Homes – a Blueprint for Action*, published last year, the Agency will shortly publish a good practice guide entitled Wasted Rural Homes, Putting the Blueprint into Action. The guide highlights good practice from the best rural local authorities and includes imaginative strategies that tackle empty properties. The Agency, with the full backing of Government, will continue to press authorities which have done little to tackle their wasted homes;

- We will ask the Regional Development Agencies and the Countryside Agency to address the issue of **empty properties** and promote the actions required to bring more of them back into productive use as part of the economic regeneration of rural areas. This measure was recommended by the Empty Property Advisory Group which was established at the end of last year. Following other recommendations of the Group, the Government is working with the Empty Homes Agency, the professional bodies and others in the property field to raise awareness and spread best practice among property owners, professionals, local authorities and others;

- As announced in the November 2000 Pre-Budget Report, we plan to encourage additional conversion of properties for residential use by **cutting the VAT rate to 5%** for residential conversions and removing the VAT burden on the sale of renovated houses that have been empty for ten years or more. These measures will help encourage the redevelopment and better use of buildings and improve the environment for local residents.

Vandalised empty homes in the former mining village of Grimethorpe, South Yorkshire
Credit: Philip Wolmuth

## 5.6. Rural homelessness

Summary of Homeless Acceptances in England by population

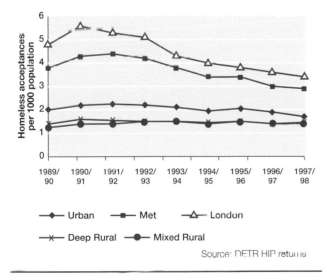

Source: DETR HIP returns

**5.6.1.** Rural homelessness is not as obvious a problem as urban homelessness. It is less visible than the street homelessness seen in many cities and towns. But the misery felt by individual households who find themselves without a home of their own is just as acute whether they live in the countryside or in a major city.

**5.6.2.** Our Homeless Action Programme provides resources to develop practical measures to help those who are particularly vulnerable to homelessness. Services provided under this fund include **housing advice and resettlement services for those in rural areas**.

**5.6.3.** Tackling homelessness in rural areas helps to prevent rough sleeping in larger towns and cities. Our Special Innovation Fund to prevent rough sleeping supports local initiatives such as the Benjamin Foundation in North Norfolk, which helps young homeless people through specialist advice and counselling and a direct access hostel, to expand the services that it provides. This will help prevent rough sleeping by tackling the root causes of social exclusion of young people in rural areas. The Foundation will now be able to set up a rent deposit and housing support service for young people who are vulnerable to homelessness. This will provide practical help to enable young homeless people to find and secure accommodation locally, close to their natural support networks. We will also be producing good practice guidance for councils which will address the particular difficulty in ensuring access to housing advice and homelessness services in rural areas.

### Case study – Newark and Sherwood Foyer tackling homelessness and unemployment among young people

Research identified that the greatest unmet housing need was among young unemployed people whose lack of job or skills often meant they were homeless. In response a 'dispersed foyer' has been established to offer both houses and training. It provides 18 places for young people aged 16–25 years old for up to two years.

Temporary furnished housing is provided through housing association and local authority vacant stock in villages throughout the district. This cuts costs and means the young people can stay in or near their family and friends. At the end of their placement some move on to permanent accommodation provided as part of the scheme. Others become permanent tenants of the homes they occupied when with the foyer.

The training, tailored to individual need, is provided through the local colleges and training agencies. An outreach service provides life skills support for the young people in their foyer accommodation. This support remains available for the young people for six months after they leave the foyer.

Between January and March 2000 the foyer had received requests for help from 133 young people. The project has been developed through a partnership of the local district council, three housing associations, Social Services, a local hostel, NACRO, other key agencies and the RCC.

Official launch of the Newark and Sherwood Foyer 3rd April 2000
Credit: Nottingham Community Housing Association

## 5.7. Improving housing quality and design

**5.7.1.** New housing is not always well designed and attractive. Poor housing can change the character of a settlement, particularly in a village setting. New housing needs to be sympathetically sited and built in a style and use materials which blend with the rest of the village – for example using local materials. This does not mean that housing should always be based on traditional architectural patterns – sometimes modern architecture can make a real contribution to a locality.

Abbots Cottages, Corfe Castle – This infill housing development of 6 cottages arranged in a courtyard plan won a Civic Trust Rural Housing Award.
Credit: Civic Trust

*"I would say in our village the development's quite tasteful, blends in well"*
*"They look as if they've been there all the time, don't they?"*
*"Beautifully done"*

**5.7.2.** Creating better-designed places is a central message of our new planning guidance for housing (PPG3). We have made it clear that planning authorities should promote developments that bring together environmental, transport, planning and architectural best practice to create places with their own distinct identity and in harmony with the local environment. Authorities can include planning policies in local development plans covering new buildings in the countryside which refer to local character, building styles and materials. They can also develop design guides, which may be approved as supplementary planning guidance.

**5.7.3.** We are strongly committed to promoting earlier, greater and better-informed attention to design wherever new development takes place. This was underlined when we published a 'good practice' guide earlier this year. We believe that better attention to design considerations from the outset will help to achieve high quality places in which people live, work or relax, not just in towns and cities but in villages and other rural areas as well. To promote better design we will encourage the preparation of village design statements as part of the Town and Village Plans described in chapter 12. These can be a particularly helpful design tool when considering new development in villages, or other rural settlements.

### Case study – The Piggeries housing scheme, Frome

The Piggeries is the product of dedicated efforts by Mendip District Council to turn round a derelict part of Frome blighted by road proposals. Through land assembly and a clear design philosophy the Council has fostered a re-development that provides an attractive living environment sensitive to its surroundings. The establishment of a multi-disciplinary project group early on in the process was crucial to the scheme's success, as was the involvement of the local community.

# flexible local
## transport

## The issues

- Distances between people and between settlements mean that difficulty with transport is often a dominant consideration for those who live in the country. With public transport services often sparse, communities are typically highly dependent on the private car. 84% of households in rural areas own a car, compared with only 69% in towns and cities; and the poorest 10% of households are twice as likely to own a car if they live in a rural area compared to a metropolitan area.
- There are particular problems of access to services for the one sixth of rural households who do not have the use of a car. These include many older people (and those who are frail or disabled), and young people, for whom it is often difficult to get access to training and job opportunities – or even to enjoy a night out with friends. Even when a family has a car, some members may not have access to it during the day and women in particular are often more dependent on public transport.
- Whether car users or not, all rural residents are affected by traffic levels, rising fastest on rural roads, and by concerns about road safety, with casualty rates falling more slowly on rural than on urban roads.

## The future – what we want to see

- More locally provided services (shops, banking, health services) which people can reach without the need to travel long distances.
- Recognition of the important role of the car.
- Good quality public transport, responsive to people's real needs; flexible, well marketed, well integrated, stable and reliable.
- Better co-ordination of services to make best use of what is available, with an expanded community and voluntary transport sector, working with bus and rail service providers and filling the gaps in those areas which are not adequately served by scheduled services.

- A stronger role for local communities in identifying local needs and in deciding how those needs can be met, and more funds for small local projects.
- Improved rural road safety; with measures to minimise the impact of traffic in rural areas and to facilitate cycling and walking.

### Summary of measures

- Additional rural bus services through increased funding: £132m over three years for Rural Bus Subsidy Grant and £60m over the same period for Rural Bus Challenge;
- A doubling of Rural Transport Partnership funds from £6m to £12m to deliver to up to 500 new Rural Partnership schemes over the next three years and at least one partnership in every county by April 2001;
- A new Parish fund of £15m over three years to support small-scale, locally generated transport solutions;
- Early consultation on measures designed to relax restrictions on rural transport services so as to allow for more responsive and flexible provision in areas not well served by scheduled services;
- New pilot schemes and funding for car sharing schemes and car clubs in rural communities;
- Better and more integrated travel information, including developing a comprehensive internet information and retailing service 'Transport Direct';
- Additional funding for Community Rail Partnerships – local authorities and businesses working together to promote local rail services;
- Rail franchises which protect rural rail services;
- Actions to make towns, villages and rural roads safer – through reduced speed limits, more investment in traffic calming, and some 50 rural bypasses.

# 6

## Contents

*"With work as well I can do 100 mile a day quite easy without even realising it. It's just nipping backwards and forwards, it just builds up very quickly."*

## 6.1. Introduction

**6.1.1.** We want to build on the new policies and substantially increased funding set out in the *Integrated Transport White Paper* and its supporting documents, and in the *10-Year Plan*.

### The Integrated Transport White Paper

This set an extensive policy agenda to improve the framework within which transport is planned, provided and funded including:
- Support for regeneration and sustainable growth of rural communities;
- Improved access to services (including through reducing the need to travel);
- Combating social exclusion (including through improved mobility).

**The 10 Year Transport Plan:**
- Increased financial support for rural public transport;
- Set out proposals for relaxing rules to achieve greater flexibility in meeting rural needs;
- Made provision for some 50 new rural bypasses to take traffic out of towns and villages; and for investment to provide safer roads with less impact on the environment.
- Increased investment in total road maintenance in England to £31 billion over the next 10 years.

Accessible transport for all
Credit: Interconnect Project-Stephen Pauling

**6.1.2.** We have already transformed funding for rural transport.

| Rural Public Transport Funding | 1995/96– 1997/98 | 1998/99– 2000/01 | 2001/02– 2003/04 |
|---|---|---|---|
| Rural Bus Subsidy Grant | | 90m | 132m |
| Rural Bus Challenge | | 48m | 60m |
| Countryside Agency | 4.8m | 17m | 47m |
| **Total** | **4.8m** | **155m** | **239m** |

**6.1.3.** Our aim across the country is to promote public transport, both as an alternative to the car to reduce the impact of rising traffic levels, and to meet the needs of non-car users. But we recognise that, in rural areas, there will continue to be an essential role for the car. Our rural transport strategy takes account of this fact; but will make a real difference to the choices and opportunities of all people living in the country.

---

**Commission for Integrated Transport**

Our approach to the delivery of integrated transport draws on advice from the Commission for Integrated Transport (CfIT), the independent body which brings together a wide range of transport interests. For rural areas CfIT believes that transport policies should seek to **reduce reliance on the car** and the need to travel in total by:

- Ensuring effective integration, both between different types of transport and between transport and land use planning;
- Improving the availability of travel choice, including safer conditions for walking and cycling;
- Enhancing the opportunities for local access to shops and services.

To support its further advice to Government on the further development of rural transport policy, CfIT is carrying out research on the relationship between car dependence and declining service provision; the reality of car dependence; expenditure on rural travel; the availability of transport choice and rising traffic levels.

CfIT is also preparing advice for Government on how to obtain **best value from subsidy to the bus industry**. It has already recommended that buses without a fixed route (including Dial a Ride services) should be eligible for Fuel Duty Rebate in the same way as registered bus services and this should encourage new services in rural areas.

It is also considering: whether and how the money currently paid as fuel duty rebate could be applied more effectively so as to maximise the role of the bus, in tackling social exclusion, attracting traffic from the car and in meeting environmental objectives; and how to determine circumstances where other appoaches – car clubs, community mini buses or taxis – would provide more effectively for people's travel needs.

---

*"It's not just that the fuel is more expensive and the mileage you do is more, it is the fact that you have to have a car here – I mean I don't like having a car, if I lived in a town there's no way I would have a car."*

Long Melford bypass
Credit: Suffolk County Council

## 6.2. Bringing services closer to people

**6.2.1.** Addressing rural transport issues is not simply about how to improve people's personal mobility. A major part of our strategy is to make access to important services less dependent on travelling, whether by car or other means. We will be issuing planning policy guidance *(PPG13)* emphasising the need to site new development where it is accessible by public transport or where, in the case of housing, people can access other services. Chapter 3 of this Paper describes how new technology will be used to provide more services direct to people's homes (eg NHS Direct) and locally – in the Post Office, or community centre. This offers important benefits for users of services and for the environment if journeys are reduced. It can help to strengthen and sustain smaller rural communities by reducing the need to look further afield for the services on which people rely.

**6.2.2.** However, people in rural areas also want and should be offered the level of consumer choice which comes with being able to travel to local or regional centres. Measures to improve transport and mobility will therefore continue to be an important element in ensuring fair and equitable access to services in rural areas.

## 6.3. Improving personal mobility

### Recognising the role of the car

**6.3.1.** For many people who live and work in rural communities, using a car is the only practicable means of undertaking many journeys. They are 50% more likely to use a car for their journey than are urban residents. Where a car is needed, but not available, there can be real hardship. The vicious circle of "no job no car; no car no job" is all too familiar to some people living in the country. We aim to offer more help to individuals who need the use of a car.

In the **Pre-Budget Report** of November 2000 the Government announced that it is consulting on a package of measures to reduce taxation for motorists which will be helpful to people in rural areas, given their high level of dependence on the private car, and the fact that rural households are twice as likely to have more than one car.

- The 83% of rural households who own cars will benefit from the freeze on fuel duty in cash terms in the 2001 Budget and the proposed reduction in duty on low sulphur petrol and diesel. Those with older cars will benefit from the proposal to **remove the duty premium on lead replacement petrol** (subject to an assessment of the environmental implications). This will help people on lower incomes who are more likely to own a car which is over 10 years old.

- The Goverment's proposals to extend a **reduced rate of vehicle excise duty** to cars of up to 1500cc will reduce the tax payable on a quarter of the cars in rural areas.

Our proposals to help **rural garages** by extending mandatory rate relief – subject to consultation – are set out in paragraph 3.2.3). These should help protect a valuable local service by improving the financial viability of rural petrol stations.

**6.3.2. Car clubs** are well established in some European countries. They have yet to catch on in this country, although there are one or two pilot projects in urban areas and paying for a lift either in a social car scheme or independently is becoming increasingly common. We believe that car clubs and informal car-sharing arrangements could be a practical solution in at least some cases. Typically, car clubs involve common ownership of a mix of vehicles which members can book for specific trips for which the car is the best option. They have the potential to provide access to a car for the many people who do not need a car every day, but who depend on one for particular journeys. To make it easier to set up such schemes:

- **The Countryside Agency, through the Rural Transport Partnerships scheme will encourage a wide variety of car-based schemes in rural areas.** Rural Transport Partnerships, are designed to bring together local community interests to develop new ideas for transport in co-operation with local authorities. The Agency will specifically invite bids to support pilot car-clubs;

- We are also discussing with the Motorists' Forum[1] what else can be done to make car clubs and other forms of car-sharing easier in rural areas (including through better use of ICT); with a view to developing practical advice and disseminating good practice.

**6.3.3.** The lack of a car is particularly serious for jobseekers and young people seeking training. The Employment Service (ES), as part of its local labour market mobility strategy, is working with local authorities, rural development agencies and transport providers to overcome transport problems for jobseekers. Action Teams for Jobs (ATs) offer flexible funding for jobless people living in areas, both urban and rural, where employment rates are low and for people who find it difficult to get work because of their background or where they live.

### Case studies – Cornwall and Thanet

The **Cornwall ATs** plans include access to 'Wheels to Work' – a scheme which provides the loan of a moped for the first three months of employment, including CBT tests, insurance, helmet, top box and support services. To help people back into employment **Thanet AT** has provided funding for obtaining the new 'clean' driving licences to which they are entitled following expiry of penalty points.

**6.3.4.** The Rural Transport Partnership Scheme can also be used to support schemes to help people in rural areas travel to work, for example through the provision of mopeds or bicycles, help with car purchase or repair or public transport subsidy.

- **We shall double the resources currently available for Rural Transport Partnerships from £6m to £12m over the next three years.** By April 2001, we expect to see at least one Rural Transport Partnership per county, and up to 500 new Partnership sponsored projects over the next three years;

- The Countryside Agency will also encourage a more systematic approach by evaluating existing 'Wheels to Work' schemes and developing good practice advice based on those projects which have been particularly successful.

---

1     The Motorists' Forum has been set up under the Commission for Integrated Transport (CfIT) to give motorists a voice in the development of Government policy.

### A new Parish Fund

**6.3.5.** We also want to encourage rural communities at the local level – particularly in areas least well served by public transport – to identify and express their own local transport needs and to be able to take steps to meet them. We want to provide the means for parishes to develop and run their own projects, as they are well placed to know what will help at the most local level. We want parishes to think innovatively about what would best solve their problems

> - **We are therefore creating a new fund of £15m over three years to support small scale transport projects identified by parishes. Parish Councils will be able to apply to the Countryside Agency for grants of up to £10,000 to fund schemes which meet local transport needs.**

**6.3.6.** For these small schemes, we want to minimise bureaucracy, so the application process will be simple and there will be no formal partnership structure to set up. To help parishes identify and work up proposals, the Countryside Agency will publish guidance on best practice and will support parishes through liaison with Rural Transport Partnership officers. Parishes will also be offered help to install and use IT networks to exchange experience. They will be encouraged to set up joint arrangements where appropriate. The aim will be to focus particularly on small-scale projects which meet very specific local needs such as:

- Purchase of cars or mopeds for community use, including for the use of job-seekers;
- Support for a car club or social car scheme;
- Support for community transport services, including refurbishment and maintenance of existing community vehicles
- Vouchers for taxis for the elderly or other people needing transport;
- Funding for a local bus company to divert a service through a village.

### Concessionary fares

**6.3.7.** Local authorities can offer help towards travel costs through concessionary fare schemes. *The Transport Bill* introduces a national minimum standard for local authority concessionary travel schemes, which will guarantee half fares or better on local buses for pensioners and disabled people. The bus pass will be free of charge. Local authorities with more generous schemes (including those which cover travel by train) need not change them. Some local authorities operate voucher schemes which can be used for taxis as well as

buses. This may be particularly appropriate in remote rural areas where scheduled bus services are more limited. Provided they also offer the standard scheme, local authorities may continue such voucher schemes as an alternative option.

## 6.4.   More responsive public transport

**6.4.1.** Our policy is to support a range of different public transport services, for different needs, and different places. That may mean better conventional, scheduled bus and train services; but in some areas the emphasis may be on less conventional services: buses with flexible routes which respond to passengers' demand, community buses and schemes for sharing taxis. We want to make it easier for people to plan specific journeys which may rely on several of these. There also needs to be good interchange between modes and better facilities for people who need to use private transport to get to public transport options. If it is not easy to switch between modes, people are more likely to stay in their cars for the whole journey.

### Bus services

**6.4.2.** Many rural bus services are subsidised by local authorities because they would otherwise be uneconomic. Over 1,800 new or more frequent services are operating as a result of the Rural Bus Subsidy Grant (RBSG) introduced by DETR in 1998, with nearly 16 million passenger journeys made on the services in 1999–00.

> - **We will continue RBSG until at least 2004 with up to £132m available over the next three years from the funding announced in the 10 year plan. This is an increase of 45% over the spending in the previous three years;**
> - **We will consider changing the rules to allow local authorities to let subsidy contracts for unremunerative services for up to 10 years instead of the five-year maximum which applies at present.**

**6.4.3.** As part of a policy to encourage market towns to serve as a focus for services for a rural hinterland we want to improve services into and around market towns.

> - The criteria for eligibility for RBSG will be broadened to allow services in and around towns up to 25,000 population to be supported. (The current threshold is 10,000 population.)

RBSG enabled Lancashire County Council to develop its benchmark scheme to ensure that, as far as possible, all communities received at least a minimum level of public transport service.
Credit: Lancashire County Council

**6.4.4.** The Rural Bus Challenge scheme is aimed at supporting innovative bus and minibus projects across the country. It has already financed 100 projects at a total cost of £28m.

- **Rural Bus Challenge funding will continue for the next three years with a minimum of £20m available each year, a 25% increase over the previous three years.**

### Case studies – Rural Bus Challenge examples

**The Wiltshire Wigglybus** provides three new hourly bus services in the Pewsey and Devizes areas of Wiltshire. Journeys are booked in advance via a central booking agency up to the time of departure of the bus. The service operates along a core route but the bus 'wiggles' off the route to pick up passengers. Fares can be paid on the bus but these can be much lower for those who are members of a travelclub scheme. Since its launch in mid-1999, passenger numbers have increased significantly (currently about 2,500 per month) and there have been requests for extensions to the service. The Rural Bus Challenge contribution is £0.5m. The rural area around Worksop will benefit from the **Worksop Area Travel Choice** (WATCH) Project which aims to reduce rural isolation and social exclusion. It includes a Travelwise centre (monitoring securing and brokering transport services in advance of use), satellite vehicle tracking providing real-time information and the development of a smart card system for rural residents. The project is already delivering results: satellite tracking equipment has been fitted to 78 vehicles and is passing back information to the Travelwise centre; and bus stops are now in place which show real-time information on bus arrival times. The Rural Bus challenge contribution is £1.1m.

**6.4.5.** The combined effect of these measures should be to offer more people a useful bus service within easy reach. By 2010 we expect to see a one third increase in the proportion of rural households living within about a 10 minute walk of a bus service which is hourly or better.

### Flexible services

**6.4.6.** Scheduled bus services have a vital role to play in rural areas, particularly in linking local centres, and we are funding more of them. But they cannot meet all rural public transport needs. So we need to encourage a network of complementary feeder services to these main routes or cater for situations where potential passengers are few or widely dispersed.

**6.4.7.** The existing law already provides for a range of such services, such as taxis or private hire vehicles, but also small buses operated by small-scale commercial operators or community transport organisations who are not required to meet the full requirements of operator licensing. The particular provisions that apply are summarised in table 6.1 on the next page.

**6.4.8.** There is scope within this framework of powers to offer a wide range of flexible services to meet a variety of needs. But although there are some excellent individual examples of what can be done, there is little evidence as yet that the full range of possibilities is being routinely built in to the planning of an integrated package of services for rural areas. We need to address this.

- **We will launch new guidance on what the law already allows – targeted at taxi and private vehicle operators, bus operators, local authorities and transport partnerships – highlighting examples of how the provisions can be used to open up opportunities for passengers.**

| | A - Z Guide | | Customer Services |
| Best Value | | | Council Offices |
| Rutnet Home | | | About Us |

Rutland County Council

**Rutland Bus Routes**

**600 RUTLAND FLYER**
CORBY - UPPINGHAM - OAKHAM - MELTON MOWBRAY
MONDAY TO SATURDAY
NS: Not Saturdays   S: Saturdays only
R: Stops on request for passengers already on the bus

| | NS | NS | | | | | | |
|---|---|---|---|---|---|---|---|---|
| CORBY Bus station bay 5 | | 07:55 | 09:00 | 11:00 | 13:00 | | 15:00 | | 17:45 |
| Rockingham Sondes Arms | | 08:03 | 09:08 | 11:08 | 13:08 | | 15:08 | | 17:53 |
| Great Easton High Street | | 08:08 | 09:13 | 11:13 | 13:13 | | 15:13 | | 17:58 |

Rutland bus timetable, available on the internet
Credit: Rutnet, Rutland County Council

**Table 6.1: Provisions which can be used to set up flexible local services**

| Service | Description | Benefits |
|---|---|---|
| Shared taxi and private hire vehicles (PHVs) – advance bookings.<br><br>(Section 11 Transport Act 1985) | Licensed taxis and PHVs providing a service at separate fares for up to 8 passengers sharing the vehicle.<br><br>Operator takes the initiative to "match up" passengers who book in advance and agree to share vehicle. | An on-demand, flexibly routed service based on telephone bookings. For example, passengers being picked up at their own homes to go to a common or similar destination, or separate passengers returning home from a popular location (eg a shopping centre).<br><br>Lower fares than for an exclusive hiring.<br><br>Potential for operators to increase their passenger loadings. |
| Shared taxis – immediate hirings.<br><br>(Section 10 Transport Act 1985) | Licensing authorities can set up schemes whereby licensed taxis (up to 8 passengers but not PHVs) can be hired by more than one person at separate fares, from designated taxi ranks or other designated places.<br><br>The decision to establish is for the local licensing authority, but it is required to set up a scheme if the holders of 10% of taxi licences in the area ask for one.<br><br>Sharing schemes identified by special signs at ranks or on vehicles. | Passengers pay only a proportion of the metered fare, and drivers will receive more than the metered fare.<br><br>Consequently, cheaper for passengers to return from, say, the local town to an outlying area, or perhaps to a series of destinations in the same general area, without having to make prior arrangements. |
| Taxibuses.<br><br>(Section 12 Transport Act 1985) | Licensed taxi owners can apply to the Traffic Commissioner for a restricted public service vehicle (PSV – or bus, see below) operator licence.<br><br>A taxi proprietor can then use his cab to provide a bus service for up to 8 passengers. The route must be registered with the Traffic Commissioner.<br><br>Taxibus services must have at least one stopping place within the area of the local authority which granted the taxi licence, but they can go beyond it. | Increased flexibility for taxis operators. They can register services at certain times of the day where they have identified a need (eg going to and returning from school), and then revert to traditional taxi work at other times of the day. Provides passengers with a bus service in circumstances where a larger bus would not be economic.<br><br>When running local bus services, taxi owners will be eligible for fuel duty rebate (subject to meeting certain conditions).<br><br>Taxibuses could be used for local authority subsidised bus services. |
| Bus service provided by an operator with a restricted operator's licence<br><br>(Section 13 of the Public Passenger Vehicles Act 1981) | For bus operators with up to 2 small vehicles. For an operator whose main business is not bus transport the vehicle may be up to 16 passenger seats. Restricted licence holders do not need to hold the Certificate of Professional Competence and they pay lower operator licence fees | Encourages small-scale operators to run bus services, including those doing so as a sideline to another business. |
| Excursions and tours<br><br>(Section 137 of the Transport Act 1985) | Passengers pay separate fares for a bus journey travelling together to, and back from, one or more places. Such services are exempt from the requirement to register a route or timetable unless they are run at least once a week for a period of at least 6 weeks (if they are operated that frequently, there is a registration requirement though less detailed than that for a normal bus service) | Can be used for, say, a shopping expedition to town and back without involving the full route registration requirements. |

**6**

| Service | Description | Benefits |
|---------|-------------|----------|
| Community bus service run by a non-profit making body (Section 22 of the Transport Act 1985) | Minibus service provided for the general public by a community group (a group concerned with social and welfare needs) on a non-profit making basis. A permit, issued by the Traffic Commissioner is required, but not an operator's licence. Services have to be registered as a local bus service. | Enables a voluntary group to run a scheduled bus service without the cost or burden of meeting all of the requirements of operator licensing. Can fill a gap not being met by a commercial operator. |
| Service provided by a non-profit making body for a particular social or community group. (Section 19 of the Transport Act 1985) | Enables voluntary bodies to provide a transport service for the particular group they serve, eg the elderly or disabled (though not for the general public) Permits issued by the appropriate "designated body" or the Traffic Commissioner. No requirement to register the service. | Enables the group to provide, say, a dial-a-ride service for those it serves without the need to obtain an operator's licence or register a route. |

**6.4.9.** Despite the flexibility which already exists, it may well be right to go further, particularly with the needs of rural areas in mind. The bus service registration requirements provide important consumer protection in terms of ensuring reliability and accountability – just as important in rural areas as in urban ones. So we need to make sure that moves to flexibility do not prejudice these safeguards, or discourage conventional scheduled bus services. It may be that in some remote rural areas where there are few scheduled services, more relaxation of the rules will be appropriate.

> • **We will consult on detailed proposals to relax registration requirements covering the specification of routes and timetables, so as to make it easier to run flexibly routed services, especially in the remoter rural areas less well served at present by scheduled services.**

### Community transport and voluntary services

**6.4.10.** Community transport (that is, services run on a not-for-profit basis) has a key role in catering for needs which are difficult to meet through scheduled commercial services, as it can offer a tailored and personalised service. We want to see its expansion, and its greater integration with commercial services in rural areas.

### Case studies – examples of community transport schemes

In **South Gloucestershire**, with a Rural Bus Challenge Fund contribution of £0.6million, a rural community transport co-ordination centre has been established. It provides a brokerage service matching vehicles with needs, minibus group hire, timetable information and research into car sharing and local transport needs. Dial-a-ride services introduced in October 1999 have proved highly successful. Registered users of the scheme have more than doubled in the first six months of the scheme with a similar increase in patronage. On a smaller scale, the Challenge has provided **South Yorkshire** with £30,000 to refurbish two community transport vehicles and the construction of a bus turning circle which has brought a bus service to the village of Thorpe-in-Balne. Funding has also provided for the introduction of radio communication to 30 commercial and community transport vehicles which will enable the development and introduction of flexible and demand responsive services in the area.

**6.4.11.** The relaxation in the rules on registration described in paragraph 6.4.9 above should help some community services, and transport services run by non-profit making bodies already benefit from a 'light touch' regulatory regime. For instance, they are already exempt from the requirements of operator licensing and instead only require a permit issued by a 'designated body' or a Traffic Commissioner. But the PIU *Rural Economies* report drew attention to other barriers, such as the ban on employing paid drivers (under section 22 of the *Transport Act 1985*) – a rule that can prevent communities which have purchased a minibus from making full use of it because of problems finding enough volunteer drivers. Allowing voluntary minibuses to offer services to the wider travelling public (by broadening the ambit of section 19 of the *Transport Act 1985*) could also make these services more viable and provide a more seamless web of commercial and voluntary services to the public. To encourage further development of community transport schemes:

> - **We will provide increased funding for good schemes through the Rural Bus Challenge Fund and the Rural Transport Partnership.** The parishes scheme described in paragraph 6.3.5. above can also be used to help such services;
>
> - **We will consult on proposals to broaden the eligibility for Fuel Duty Rebate, with the intention of having new rules in place for the 2001–02 financial year;**
>
> - **We will review the notice period which community-based services are required to give before starting or withdrawing a registered service;**
>
> - **We will also consult shortly on possible changes to the rules (eg on using paid drivers) so as to reduce the barriers to further expansion of the community transport sector.**

**6.4.12.** We need to make sure that in doing so essential safety standards are retained. It will be important to work with the community transport sector to ensure that quality of service, driver professionalism and safety standards are maintained, and improved where necessary, as the sector expands.

## Rail services

**6.4.13.** Rural areas are now less well served by railways and where rural lines do exist they are unlikely to be profitable. That said, rail access can bring many benefits to rural communities, by making local businesses more competitive; reducing the amount of traffic – passenger and freight – on the roads; and, in some cases such as the Settle-Carlisle line, offering a tourist attraction in their own right. We want to see rail playing its full part in rural transport.

**6.4.14.** The level of franchised passenger services on rural lines is protected by the Passenger Service Requirement (PSR).

> - **The shadow Strategic Rail Authority has announced that replacement franchises will be required to meet at least the existing PSR.** This means that people living in rural areas will have the security of knowing that their trains are protected: operators can run more trains, but they cannot run fewer than set out in the PSR.

**6.4.15.** A study commissioned by the shadow Strategic Rail Authority into *Secondary Rail Lines*, many of which serve rural communities, was published last June. It recommended ways in which such lines could be developed, through micro-franchises. These could involve the main franchise operator subcontracting responsibility for particular branch lines to local rail companies, whose increased focus on promoting the line, the report argued, could bring benefits in terms of increased passenger numbers, better integrated services, reduced costs and a more dynamic and sustainable rural economy. We would like to see this idea taken forward.

**6.4.16.** Rail users also benefit from community rail partnerships: local authorities and local businesses working together to attract more people to rail and to promote rail to visiting tourists.

> - In August 2000 additional funding of £220,000 over 3 years was announced to support **Community Rail Partnerships** – to be provided jointly by the Countryside Agency, the Strategic Rail Authority and the Esmee Fairbairn Charitable Foundation.

### Case study – Devon and Cornwall Rail Partnership

The Devon and Cornwall Rail Partnership, funded by local authorities, has helped establish and promote easier access to Dartmoor, with bus links and the restoration of a freight line to carry passenger trains for tourists at weekends in the summer. Quality promotional literature helps to promote green tourism and reduce the pressure on rural roads in the two counties.

**Looe Valley Line – A case study for micro franchising (see 6.4.15)**
Credit: Devon and Cornwall Rail Partnership

**6.4.17.** The Rail Passenger Partnership (RRP) Scheme resourced at £105m over 3 years to 2002, administered through the SRA, funds projects which promote integrated transport and modal shift to rail.

> • To make the scheme more responsive to local circumstances, a fast track **Rail Passenger Partnership bidding process** has been introduced, which allows for less formal and faster consideration and approval of smaller schemes.

### Case study – Esk Valley Line

RPP funds have enabled the Esk Valley Line in North Yorkshire to operate a Sunday service throughout the year for local people and tourists visiting the North York Moors National Park. Previously trains ran only at the height of the summer.

**Esk Valley line – the afternoon train at Egton**
Credit: Neil Buxton

## 6.5. Better local transport planning and information

### Co-ordinating services

**6.5.1.** A key objective for the Government is that local transport planning should reflect wide consultation and that there should be stronger and more pro-active co-ordination and integration of different transport services and modes. Local Transport Plans are central to achieving this. Our guidance on Local Transport Plans requires local authorities to identify the particular needs of rural areas; to develop targeted measures for dealing with them; and to develop consultation methods which tap into the views of all sections of the community including the use of their community planning powers contained in the *Local Government Act 2000* (chapter 12).

### Case study – Lake District Transport Strategy

In the Lake District National Park, integrated transport planning is part of a wider strategy. The Lake District Transport Strategy aims to promote economic prosperity through tourism, to protect the environment and to combat social exclusion by engaging communities in developing services which meet the needs of local people.

Measures include a coach drivers' handbook about how to avoid unsuitable minor roads; interchange arrangements between trains and buses within the National Park to make it easier for visitors to get to the main sights by public transport; and park and ride schemes at strategic transport routes into the National Park.

**6.5.2.** In our *Transport Bill* we are emphasising and restating the requirement that, in exercising their powers to subsidise bus services, local authorities should co-operate with local education authorities and authorities with social service responsibilities. They also have a duty to take account of the transport needs of those authorities in formulating their general transport policies for their areas. Joint working of this kind – often through transport co-ordination centres – has opened up new opportunities to meet the needs of people in the communities being served and has delivered savings in terms of economies of scale and greater efficiency.

Devon CC's Transport Co-ordination Service, set up in 1986, co-ordinates transport services across the whole of the County's functions – local bus services, school transport, social services transport and the in-house fleet. Over time, working closely with the local Health Authority, public transport operators and community transport groups, opportunities have been taken to introduce more flexibility in the way in which the county responds to the transport needs of people in rural Devon, and to develop new services to meet needs identified in conjunction with local communities. For example, merging education, transport and local bus services on some routes, has given school children more flexibility to stay on for after school activities and provides more travel choice for post 16 students as well as enhanced bus services for the general public. Similarly, through use of accessible minibuses jointly for social service and community transport provision the County has been able to offer an increased level of service to many rural communities.

- The Government will be looking at how **Local Transport Plans** can be used to identify and highlight **best practice in addressing rural transport issues** and we will be examining bids from a number of local authorities for Centres of Excellence status for rural transport in addition to the development of the Centre of Excellence for rural transport in Cornwall;

- The Countryside Agency will launch a good practice guide so that local authorities, operators and community groups can be better informed about what works, and can benefit from lessons learnt elsewhere.

### Better transport information and ticketing

**6.5.3.** Public transport users and potential users often complain that information about services is difficult to access, incomplete or inaccurate or too narrowly focused on one mode or operator. New information and communications technologies offer one means of providing better information and marketing of services. A telephone-based 'Traveline' information service has now been switched on region by region in England and Wales. This is a step towards an internet based comprehensive transport information and retailing service

"Transport Direct" which the Government plans to see established by 2003. In addition:

- New powers in the *Transport Bill* will give local authorities power to require bus companies to provide and display information about their services. In rural areas, these powers may be used to ensure that integrated information is available in villages, for instance displayed in post offices;

- We will look to local authorities to demonstrate in their Local Transport Plans how, working with others, they are achieving improvements in information and other service quality issues, such as through ticketing and good interchange arrangements between modes.

TravelCumbria is an innovative web-based project designed to encourage visitors to the Lake District and the use of public transport by providing an interactive source of information linking accommodation, travel and tourist attractions. The site includes detailed information about public transport in the Lake District.

## 6.6.  Improving rural road safety and reducing the impact of traffic in the countryside

### Road safety

**6.6.1.** Public concern about road safety in rural areas is growing. Levels of traffic are increasing faster on rural roads than on urban roads. Although casualty rates nationally are falling, this is happening at a slower rate on rural roads. Road accidents on rural roads are more likely to be fatal, for all types of road users, than in towns. With the growth in countryside recreation, rural roads also have to cater for an increasing mix of users such as cyclists, walkers and horse riders.

**6.6.2.** The Local Transport Plans which local authorities produce in consultation with local communities will include local targets for reducing road casualties. To support the efforts of local authorities we will be implementing a programme of actions set out in our road safety strategy *Tomorrow's Roads*

- We believe that the national 60mph speed limit is too high for some poor quality rural roads and lanes. We are developing a systematic way of assessing traffic demands on different types of rural road, so that the right speed limits can be imposed on the right roads. We are planning to develop **a simpler system of setting speed limits** which preserves adequate consultation with local people.

- In villages, we believe 30mph should be the norm, supported by traffic calming measures. Some authorities have taken action already. On the basis of experience, we will develop general **guidance** for issue in 2002.

- We are also promoting **traffic calming** more generally in villages – studies have shown that this can reduce all injury accidents by 25% and accidents involving death and injury by 50%. We have published new guidance and expect local authorities to include appropriate measures in their capital programmes from April 2001.

- We are looking for **new types of speed limit** signing for rural areas, which are both effective and fit in with the rural landscape. This will respond to concern that current speed restriction signs are often inappropriate for a rural environment.

- Some predominantly rural authorities are taking part with the police and Highways Agency in our **pilot scheme for funding the operation of speed cameras from fine revenue**. We will have early results of that this year. If they are successful, we will be looking to extend them and it may be possible for parishes to initiate or join partnerships to operate cameras, involving the police, the local highway authority, and the courts;

- On faster rural roads at locations where collisions are most common, such as junctions and bends, **we are developing measures for reducing vehicle speeds** (like vehicle activated warning signs); advice will be available in summer 2001.

**Traffic-calming measure in the New Forest**
Credit: The Countryside Agency – Chris Blandford Associates

### Tackling the problems of too much traffic

**6.6.3.** High volumes of traffic may be relatively uncommon in rural areas but where problems exist they can be acute – for instance where a main road goes through a village or small town. Some 50 new bypasses will take through traffic out of some of the worst affected towns and villages. But by-passes are not always possible and will not solve all problems. In National Parks, these are a variety of other measures that can be taken to alleviate the effects of traffic. The box in Section 6.5 describes the Lake District Transport Strategy; and the box in tourism and transport in Chapter 11 also gives examples.

### Case study – Transport 2000

With Government support, **Transport 2000** is working on a project to develop strategic approaches for leisure based travel. The project's three outputs are: a model for reducing leisure travel by car in a tourist area (pilot in South Downs, East Sussex); a green travel plan for a specific leisure facility (pilot in Harewood House, near Leeds); and a good practice guide (to be launched next year) on reducing car use for leisure trips.

### Reducing the impact of lorry traffic

**6.6.4.** Rural areas need to be protected wherever possible from the environmental effects of heavy lorries. Problems can occur with deliveries in and access to market towns, as well as in larger towns and cities, and when lorries pass through small villages or use unsuitable minor roads. Lorries may have to travel over local roads to access their point of origin or destination but should generally otherwise use the existing network of 'primary routes' comprising all green-signed roads, trunk roads and motorways.

6.6.5. There are a number of initiatives that can assist in reducing the impacts of lorry movements, for example:

- Freight quality partnerships can help by addressing freight traffic issues in sensitive areas.
- Local authorities can use their greater responsibility for traffic management, to produce a vehicle routing strategy and can introduce lorry control plans, which fully consider the needs and impacts of lorry movements.
- We are encouraging businesses to improve the efficiency of their transport operations in ways, which also benefit the environment by reducing the number of vehicle movements.

## Case studies – reducing the impact of lorry movements

In **Ripon**, a **Freight Quality Partnership** – involving local businesses and transport operators, local authorities, the police and local residents – is looking at freight traffic management issues in this historic market town. For example delivery windows for goods vehicles are being controlled on a voluntary goodwill basis to minimise conflict between HGVs and people. **Lorry controls have been introduced to approximately 70% of Leicestershire's roads.** The Plan, developed after a review of the existing road hierarchy, limits access to controlled areas for commercial vehicles over 7.5 tonnes, except for loading and unloading.

**Computerised Vehicle Routing and Scheduling Systems (CVRS)** are increasingly being used by industry to improve the efficiency of their transport operations. By automating the matching of customer locations and quantities and types of goods to be transported, CVRS can bring cost savings and reliability improvements for business and benefits for the environment in terms of reduced lorry mileage. Safeway's use of CVRS for its national delivery operation has resulted in an 18% reduction in km travelled.

### Encouraging cycling and walking

6.6.6. The measures to improve road safety and reduce traffic impacts will make it easier and safer for cyclists and walkers to use rural roads. Increased spending on road maintenance (see paragraph 7.5.6) will also improve conditions for cyclists and pedestrians. In addition, we expect all highway authorities in England and Wales to include cycling and walking strategies in their local transport plans. The Lottery funded National Cycle Network, launched in June 2000, will help to promote cycling in rural areas by linking town and country. Once it is complete, one third of our population will live within two miles of the National Cycle Network. Cycling for leisure can help to boost tourism in rural areas, and better cycling facilities open up opportunities for people living in rural areas. Assistance is being provided for the promotion of integrated and sustainable transport involving combined bicycle and rail, and bicycle and bus journeys.

6.6.7. The **Quiet Lanes project** is an initiative of the Countryside Agency. Pilot schemes are being undertaken in Norfolk and Kent following consultation with local communities, using existing legislative powers. The aim is to make selected country lanes more attractive for walking, cycling, and horse riding in the interests of a more tranquil and attractive rural environment.

- We have added a clause to the Transport Bill which will give legal status to quiet lanes. **Local authorities will be able to designate roads as quiet lanes** and to make orders affecting the way they are used and providing for speed reduction measures in them.

Quiet lanes, Norfolk Pilot project
Credit: Norfolk County Council

Truronian bus/bike rack
Credit: Truronian Ltd

## Case studies – facilitating leisure on rural roads

**Anglia Railways** has recently received Rail Passenger Partnership funding to provide additional cycle parking at stations along its network.

**Truronian Bus** now operate buses serving Helston and The Lizard in South Cornwall, with funding from the County Council, Railtrack and the Rural Bus Challenge, specifically designed to connect with local rail services with an integrated timetable and through ticketing. The buses have been designed with purpose built cycle racks, and the route has become the first bus route in the country to win the National Cycle Marker, an award previously only ever given to rail services.

A Working Group of the National Cycling Forum is looking at examples of best practice in combined bicycle and bus initiatives.

# Part 1

## a *living* countryside
## – objectives and spending

**Objectives:**

- To maintain and stimulate communities, and secure access to services which is equitable in all the circumstances, for those who live or work in the countryside.

- To facilitate the development of dynamic, competitive and sustainable economies in the countryside, tackling poverty in rural areas.

| £m | 1996–7 | 2000–01 | Projected for 2003–4 | Projected 2001/2–2003/4 |
|---|---|---|---|---|
| | | **Spending (£ million)** | | |
| Support for Small Schools | – | 60 | (note 1) | |
| Village Shops Rate Relief | – | 4 | (note 2) | |
| Countryside Agency (services/social exclusion) | n/a | 4 | 4 | 12 |
| Post Office Network improvements (partly rural) | | | £270m over 3 years | 270 |
| Community Services Fund | – | – | 8 | 15 |
| NHS Primary Care facilities in rural areas (capital expenditure including public-private partnerships) | | | up to £100m over 3 years | 100 |
| Police Modernisation Fund (rural) | – | 15 | 32 | 45 |
| Neighbourhood Renewal Fund | – | – | 6 | |
| Housing Corporation Approved Development Programme | 105 | 90 | 120 | 300 |
| Local Authority housing programmes (rural districts) | 245 | 360 | c £400m (note 3) | |
| Rural Bus Subsidy Grant | – | 33 | 48 | 132 |
| Rural Bus Challenge | – | 20 | 21 | 60 |
| Rural Transport Funds (Countryside Agency) | 1 | 6 | 12 | 32 |
| Parish Transport Fund | – | – | 8 | 15 |

*Note 1* Will continue but budget not yet set.

*Note 2* Will increase in light of decisions on consultation (see 3.2.3)

*Note 3* Outcome depends on local authority investment decisions. Central Government support will be increased by 40% nationally over next 3 years.

# Part 2

# a *working* countryside

*We want to see a working countryside, with a prosperous and diverse economy*

# market towns and
## a thriving local economy

**7**

## The issues

- Many rural areas are prosperous with high growth rates, high employment and attractive as a business location. Others – particularly in remote rural, coastal and coalfield regions – have serious economic difficulties with declining towns, loss of younger people, high unemployment, low wages and low investment: seven out of ten English counties with the lowest GDP per head are predominantly rural.
- In places the local economy can be heavily dependent on primary industries, such as agriculture, mining, quarrying and fishing; this can cause social and economic difficulties should there be any large structural changes in those industries.
- For some businesses in rural areas small size and physical isolation can create barriers to growth; it is harder to access markets, transport materials, obtain skilled labour and get business support and advice.

## The future – what we want to see

- Thriving economies in all rural areas which provide good quality employment opportunities and exploit the versatility, entrepreneurial tradition, and, increasingly, local green business potential. A better trained rural workforce. Small rural businesses exploiting ICT and marketing their goods and services well outside their local region.
- Market Towns as a focus for growth in areas which need regeneration, and more generally as service centres and hubs for surrounding hinterland, exploiting their potential as attractive places to live, work and spend leisure time.
- Regeneration of deprived rural areas (the Rural Priority Areas) through development of a broader economic base and regionally comparable skill levels, employment and business development.
- Tourism as an increasingly important business sector as leisure spending on enjoying the countryside and its towns increases. Land based businesses such as forestry and horse enterprises and demand for distinctive rural products and services will be key factors in continued rural prosperity.

### Summary of measures

- Market Towns 'Health Check';
- £37m over three years to fund Regeneration for Market Towns in or near Rural Priority Areas to create a £100m programme with partnership funds;
- Rural areas will benefit from increased resources and flexibility for RDA programmes (from £1.2bn to £1.7bn by 2003-04);
- New rural vision for RDAs to realise potential of rural economy and help it adapt to declining industries;
- Extending ICT access and use in rural areas;
- Tailored business support and training in rural areas;
- 100 per cent capital allowances for creating flats over shops for letting.

# 7

## Contents

---

**Rural Economies**

The Cabinet Office PIU study on *Rural Economies* (see chapter 1) looked at the role of the economy in rural areas and highlighted the following

Strengths

- High quality of life in rural areas attracts relocating businesses and encourages local businesses to stay;
- The value of the countryside as a marketable product, for tourism and recreation;
- Competitive advantage over urban areas for some types of enterprise, such as those dependent on natural resources;

Weaknesses

- Absence of a sufficient pool of suitable labour for some types of business;
- Lack of a critical mass of supporting businesses and services;
- Relatively poor communications, including the infrastructure supporting Information and Communication Technology (ICT).

## 7.1. The economy in rural areas

**7.1.1.** The economy in rural areas is increasingly dependent on regional, national and global business links, rather than the traditional pattern of rural trades. Nevertheless rural areas continue to have certain distinct business features (see box) such as a high proportion of micro-businesses (90% under 10 employees). Land and countryside character are a strong factor in creating new enterprises in tourism, food, country sports and recreation. Also important are professions and trades which support businesses in the hinterland (accountants, surveyors, construction trades) and public services which are often the large employers underpinning the economic strength of a country town. As with conservation, environment and tourism businesses, these act as a focus for other services and new business growth.

## 7.2. Enhancing the role of market towns

**7.2.1.** Market towns play a critical role in helping rural communities to thrive and in regenerating deprived areas. They are small rural and coastal towns many of which serve a rural hinterland whether or not they have ever had traditional agricultural markets. Some may have grown up around a canal or railway junction or as a coastal resort while continuing to be an important commercial and leisure focus for a rural hinterland. There are over 1,000 towns in England with populations between 2,000 and 20,000. Many have suffered from the decline of agriculture, mining, textiles or other industries.

### A changing role

**7.2.2.** The shift of services (both private and public) to larger towns because of economies of scale has further undermined the role of some market towns. Research on the impact of large foodstores on market towns has shown that locating new stores outside the centre of a market town can have a devastating effect on the continued vitality and viability of the town centre and of town centre shops. They may now be further threatened as Internet-based services replace traditional high street activities such as banking, estate agents and travel agents. The businesses and communities in these towns need to respond to their changed circumstances to maintain their physical fabric, economic vitality and a good quality of life for people both in the town itself and the surrounding rural areas. But there is no single solution to meeting the challenges they face.

**Market day in Sleaford, Lincolnshire**
Credit: Countryside Agency – Andy Tryner

**7.2.3.** Our planning policy guidance on town centres and retail development (*PPG6*) already seeks to ensure that new retail and other key town centre uses locate in the centre of market towns to maintain and enhance their vitality and viability. We also stress the need for town health checks and town centre management. We have stopped the drift to out-of-centre or out-of-town sites. We now need to reinforce the role of market towns and their potential to support a more sustainable pattern of development by ensuring that they are the focus for a range of private and public services to which people need access.

**7.2.4.** With vigorous local effort, the fortunes of some market towns have revived, and rural regeneration programmes have already helped many towns, but with rapid change in business, retail and consumer patterns many more are vulnerable. We see market towns as having a crucial part to play in the future development of the rural economy. Prosperous market towns can help regenerate the surrounding area as:

- A focus for economic development and regeneration including markets for local food and other countryside products;
- Centres which meet people's needs for access to a wide range of retail, professional and public services without destroying the character of the area (see chapter 4);
- A focus for properly planned and co-ordinated public transport (see chapter 6);
- Distinctive places to live often with a fine heritage and historic buildings and the potential to act as a centre of cultural activity.

### A new commitment to market towns

**7.2.5.** So we are making a **new commitment to market towns** to help them manage the process of change. We will strengthen market towns which can provide improved services for surrounding rural areas and we will help regenerate the most deprived. We will ensure that both central and local Government bodies explicitly recognise the role of market towns in their strategies. Many of the RDA strategies and recent reviews of Regional Planning Guidance (RPG) already recognise the crucial role of market towns and are identifying action to support this role. It will also feature in our revised guidance to RDAs on rural policy. We will also expect regional planning bodies to take this objective fully into account in future RPG reviews. In addition:

- **We will provide new resources of £37m within the Regional Development Agencies (RDAs) rural programme and the Countryside Agency programme over the next three years to support market town regeneration.** Together with matching support from partners and EU funds we expect to create a £100m Market Towns programme over three years. This will enable:

- A **regional regeneration programme led by the RDAs, with the CA and other regional partners, of around 100 towns across all RDAs,** which will help create new job opportunities, new workspace, restored high streets, improved amenities and transport facilities and help with community needs. These towns will be selected on the basis of:

    - their potential to act as a focus for growth, relieving disadvantage and increasing economic opportunity in the Rural Priority Areas (see paragraph 7.3.4);

    - their potential to act as a service centre, with a broad range of services, and well placed with good transport links to surrounding towns and villages;

    - the ability of local partners to commit resources alongside the RDA programme;

    - the extent to which they have already benefited from regeneration programmes including the rural programme, SRB, European funding and others.

- **The Countryside Agency will identify a national beacon towns network drawing on this experience and featuring 10-20 towns to demonstrate the range of different problems and challenges** which market towns experience and from which other towns can learn. All market towns would be able to draw on a National **Best Practice Programme** – publications, training events, and a web site – led by the Countryside Agency, in partnership with the RDAs and Action for Market Towns. **Health checks** for individual towns – see page 78 – will be a part of this approach.

- We are revising the *Planning Policy Guidance on Land Use Planning and Transport (PPG 13)* which emphasises the role of market towns as the focus for rural jobs and services. The new guidance will advise local planning authorities in rural areas that major public services which need to be accessible to the largest rural population should be located as far as possible in local service centres which may be market towns or large villages with good transport links. At the same time, this does not rule out smaller employment opportunities being located in more remote rural areas (see paragraph 8.4.3).

- **We will be asking public service providers to make Market Town provision a key element in their strategies** (and encouraging the private sector to make a commitment to Market Towns in their service programmes) (see table 7.1).

**The town centre, Richmond, Yorkshire, which has benefitted from a successful regeneration partnership**
Credit: Action for Market Towns

## Case study – Oswestry: town centre regeneration

In 1994, Oswestry, Shropshire, was experiencing the impact of major out of town shopping centres. Many town centre shops were empty; there was a feeling of apathy, particularly within the Chamber of Commerce; the retail markets were hit by recession and the ever extending hours of supermarket trading; bad 1960s town planning coupled with a medieval street pattern made pedestrian and traffic conflict commonplace; Town and Borough Councils were in conflict over supermarket applications and in or out of town siting. At one time, the Borough Council had 11 supermarket applications to resolve. Following a presentation by Boots, the Chemist, to the councils and Chamber of Commerce, a town centre working group was set up involving both the public and private sectors. Partners worked together on tourism, retailing, competition, unemployment and the superstore issue. The Oswestry Town Centre Partnership drives forward the strategy, and oversees the special task force of 14 council officers who carry out the work and apply for project funding.

Much has been achieved by the Partnership, including a facelift of shop fronts, cycleways, new bus station, steam railway centre, visitor signing, shopper loyalty scheme, customer care training, community safety audit, living over the shop and a workway arts scheme. Over £7m has already been raised from the Lottery, businesses, European funding and local authorities. Within five years, the Town Partnership aims to reduce crime by 20%, create 200 new jobs, attract £16m investment and train 250 people in customer care.

## Case study – Ibstock: community led regeneration

The village of Ibstock in Leicestershire is on a former coalfield and the 5,000-strong community was hard hit by the closures of the surrounding pits in the 1980s. When the village's only bank closed in 1995, local traders fought hard to install a cashpoint machine in the defunct bank, and turn the building into a community resource centre. They persuaded the Co-operative Bank to provide the cashpoint machine, and the benefits have been felt by residents and businesses alike. The campaign has boosted village morale and rekindled a sense of pride in the town.

**Saltburn-by-Sea: where heritage has a future**
Credit: The Countryside Agency

**Table 7.1: A Market Town Template for the East Midlands – facilities to be available (edited extract)**

| | Larger Market Town (10,000-25,000 people) | Smaller Market Town (2,000-10,000 people) |
|---|---|---|
| Retail | Basic comparison shopping, including local traders and national multiple retailers. Post Office. Farmers market and/or other retailing of local produce. Existing livestock markets. | Convenience shopping (including Post Office) and some weekly specialist needs provided for. Farmers market and/or other retailing of local produce. Existing livestock markets. |
| Financial services | Main High Street banks and building societies. 24 hour cash provision. | At least one bank and one building society agency. 24 hour cash provision. |
| Healthcare | Large Health Centre including dentist and pharmacy and Ambulance Station. | Small Health Care Centre or large doctors surgery, dentist and pharmacy |
| Education, community and social services | Adult education facilities, youth centre, Further education provision and full access to remote learning. Secondary school. Dedicated IT facility. | Secondary school, base for youth services, access centre for further/adult education. Remote learning and ICT links available to public in business hours. |
| Cultural facilities (sports, arts and leisure) | Permanent library, range of cultural facilities, leisure centre (with swimming pool), local cinema. Pubs and restaurants. Facilities for teenagers other than youth clubs. | Permanent library facilities. Cultural events/local Arts venue. Sports pitches with changing rooms, sports hall, weekly cinema. Pubs and restaurant. Recreation park. |
| Natural environment | Trees/woodlands in the built environment. Habitat and open space linked. Watercourse corridors and floodplains enhanced. | Trees/woodlands in the built environment. Habitat and open space linked. Watercourse corridors and floodplains enhanced. |
| Employment sites | Wide range of sites/premises available including workspace and serviced sites. Re-use of existing buildings and brown field sites. | Adequate range of sites/premises available plus the provision of workspace and serviced sites for employment opportunities. |
| Employment opportunities | Full time Job Centre or equivalent. Information for the individual on jobs/training. | Part-time Job Centre or equivalent. Information for the individual on jobs/training. |
| Business support/advice | Support base providing access to Small Business Service and Citizens Advice Bureau. | Visiting support including access to Small Business Service and Citizens Advice Bureau. |
| Childcare | Range of facilities and holiday clubs. Permanent nursery and out of hours childcare. | At least one facility and holiday club available including out of hours childcare. |
| Public administration | Permanent Local Authority presence and/or Town Council office. A town centre manager. | Access to a District/County Council sub-area office. Shared town centre management. |
| Tourism | Tourist Information Centre and a wide range of overnight accommodation. | Tourist Information access in a multipurpose centre. Range of overnight accommodation. |
| Police, fire, courts | Magistrates Court, main police station, fire station and/or links via multi purpose centres. | Part-time police office and fire station and/or integrated emergency services centre. |
| Public and community transport | Daily town and rural public transport, including evening and weekend services. Bus station with coach services interchange. Taxi services. | Regular daily public transport to surrounding villages/towns. Evening and weekend services to major towns. Local taxi service. |
| Town centre environmental uplift | Comprehensive approach to historic buildings. Traffic management and pedestrian access plan. | Proposal to identify individual buildings or groups of buildings for environmental uplift. |
| Housing | Range of housing for purchase and rental. Local point to advise on housing availability. | Range of housing for purchase or rental. Access point to advise on housing availability. |

This template has been compiled by East Midlands Development Agency, The Countryside Agency, Government Office for the East Midlands, Council for the Protection of Rural England, Civic Trust, Heritage Lottery Fund, East Midlands Regional Local Government Association, Lincolnshire Tourism, Ministry of Agriculture Fisheries and Food, East Midlands Arts, Employment Service, Heart of England Tourist Board, English Nature, English Heritage, Action for Market Towns, and the Forestry Commission. These partners are committed to providing a positive response wherever possible to the provision of any facilities shown in the template.

### The Market Towns Health Check

Some market towns and their centres need particular support to regenerate themselves. The evidence suggests that the key ingredients for success are:

- Business, local authority, voluntary group, residents and other partners coming together as a steering group for each town;
- Appointment of suitably qualified project officers, answering to the steering group for each town (or a group of very small towns). These will sometimes be secondees from local authorities and sometimes outside appointees;
- Intensive and systematic consultation of communities with data being gathered via surveys;
- On the basis of the findings, a range of specific proposals for change to be drawn up by the group and put to the community;
- On the basis of consultation feedback, a way forward will be agreed and an action plan drawn up. This will include agreeing any applications for funding from outside sources;
- Action in accordance with the plan will be carried out, co-ordinated by the project officer who will report regularly on progress to the Steering Group.

This is not intended to be a precise blueprint, and the ordering of events may differ in different towns, but it sets out the main steps. The outcome will take advantage of each town's comparative advantages of location, physical inheritance, human capital and both local and outside financial resources. The results should be a variety of physical improvements as well as in renewed local pride, with the community taking and keeping control of its town's destiny.

Individual town programmes will help local authorities and community partners with the consultation process; the employment of project officers; some individual projects; and training, eg to help local businesses to use modern retail practices, and put ICT to best use. The Countryside Agency will encourage the application of best practice health check methods across all of England.

### Opportunities for business funding

**7.2.6.** If market towns are to become the busy hubs that we want to see, they need to be attractive places with good buildings and good open spaces. The maintenance of historic buildings in a good condition and their continuation in use makes an important contribution to this. We see the achievement of this quality and **area improvement** as very much a matter for partnership between the local authority and the local businesses, in whose interest it will be to help improve the attractiveness of the town as a whole to help to attract more custom. To help achieve this we are consulting in the Green Paper *Modernising Local Government Finance* on:

- **Proposals that will allow local authorities to raise a supplementary rate** providing that representative partnership arrangements have been agreed with their local business community. The funds raised could be used for local projects chosen with the agreement of the affected ratepayers. The proposals would allow councils to raise a local supplement of no more than 5% of the national rate, phased in at 1% per year, with high performing authorities able to raise a further 5%. This may be a local authority wide supplement or locally targeted (for instance on one market town);

- **Town Improvement Schemes (TISs)** (as described more fully in the companion White Paper *Our Towns and Cities: The Future – Delivering an Urban Renaissance*) These could be funded by the supplementary rate. The Green Paper *Modernising Local Government Finance* also invites views on alternative funding arrangements.

**7.2.7.** Empty or under-used space above commercial premises in the centres of market towns can have an adverse impact on their appearance and attractiveness as well as being a waste of space that can be used to provide more homes.

- As announced in the November 2000 Pre-Budget Report, we plan to introduce a **100% capital allowance for creating 'flats over shops'** for letting to encourage better use of vacant and under-utilised space above shops and other commercial premises.

**Towcester Mill: Part of Heritage Economic Regeneration in the market town of Towcester**
Credit: English Heritage

- Building on local identity, culture and character particularly in leisure related businesses, as in the success of market towns such as Ludlow, Hay on Wye, Wareham, and Romsey.

## 7.3. Widening the economy in rural areas

**7.3.1.** If market towns and their hinterland are to thrive, their role needs to complement that of neighbouring towns and cities. A thriving countryside means being part of a successful regional economy. That helps rural areas achieve a wider base so as to maintain and create good quality jobs. Some rural areas do well in attracting new business but others suffering job losses in farming, mining or through defence base closures fail to do so. Similarly, some areas are more successful than others in growing small and medium-sized companies, establishing business clusters and encouraging the formation of start-ups. It is from activities such as these that much of the future prosperity of rural areas will spring. Our objective is to promote growth which is in tune with its surroundings and builds on countryside strengths, for example through:

- Developing local advantage in particular trades or specialisms, such as vegetables and food processing in the Fens or small scale engineering in the Midlands;
- Promoting ICT based business potential as in East of England Development Agency's strategic Innovation corridors linking new economy businesses in the rural hinterland of its major industrial and research centres such as Ipswich and Cambridge;
- Supporting local business clusters based on links with higher education or local networks in creative or media businesses;
- Supporting and building up local business groups through sympathetic development planning, purchasing local speciality products (for example by local authorities) and supply chain initiatives;

Raku Pottery from Chan Abbott Studios – part of the Brigantia association which brings together art and craft workers in the North York Moors, Wolds and coastal areas
Credit: Philip Chan

### Regional Development Agencies

**7.3.2.** To achieve a successful **economic strategy** which will benefit towns and rural areas as well as cities, requires partnership and leadership at a regional level. We have created **Regional Development Agencies** (RDAs) to drive forward economic performance, development and competitiveness, skills development, encourage inward investment, and deliver regeneration within a sustainable development framework. This means working with regional and local partners including the Regional Chamber (who will have endorsed the Regional Sustainable Development Framework) and the Regional

Planning Body if it is not already the Chamber, County and District Authorities, Learning and Skills Councils (see 7.5.8.) and the Small Business Service (see 7.6.2.).

## Rural regeneration

**7.3.3.** Rural, as well as urban, regeneration is one of the key objectives for the RDAs and their programmes will bring substantial benefits across the region through work on training and skills, on ICT and business support, on improving regional infrastructure and on competitiveness generally (see box). Each Regional Development Agency published a **Regional Strategy** in October 1999, analysing the strengths and weaknesses of their region and these take account of the needs and strengths of rural areas and of their differing regional priorities and character (in the south west over 65% of the population in the RDA live in largely rural districts).

This map is based upon the OS map by the Countryside Agency with the permission of Ordnance Survey on behalf of The Controller of Her Majesty's Stationary Office, © Crown Copyright. All rights reserved. Unauthorised reproduction infringes Crown Copyright and may lead to prosecution or civil proceedings. Licence Number GD272434.

**Rural Priority Areas in England**

---

> **How RDA regional priorities benefit rural areas:**
>
> **East of England Development Agency** have identified skill shortages and gaps in the construction sector across the region, but also that much of the sector is rural and as demand continues to grow it has become an increasingly practical alternative to agricultural employment. But to meet projected demand of 8,000 vacancies a year will require an integrated approach to training, mobility and recruitment.
>
> **The North West Development Agency** has adopted a strategic approach to tourism in Cumbria to encourage visitors away from the major honeypot areas such as parts of the Lake District. The development of the major and innovative earth covered 'Rheged' Upland Kingdom Discovery Centre in North Cumbria will create up to 300 jobs in an area suffering from unemployment as a result of upland farming's decline. Visitors are also being encouraged to the western coastal resorts in Cumbria by infrastructure improvements.
>
> **The East Midlands Development Agency**, introduced the concept of creating the East Midlands Food Campus (formerly known as the University for Food) as a means of enhancing the competitiveness of the food industry within the East Midlands through greater collaboration between the educational sector and industry. The East Midlands Food Campus will be a mechanism for delivering the key parts of the Regional Strategy relating to education, skills, research and technology transfer. This will provide the opportunity for business and institutions to influence the profile of the region and may also provide the potential impetus for the region to become recognised internationally as a centre for excellence for the food and related industries. A model has been developed and the Agency along with its partners are currently developing an action plan to take the project forward.

---

> **Rural Priority Areas**
>
> At present the RDAs' rural programme spending is concentrated in the **Rural Priority Areas** (RPAs) defined in 1994 as being the areas of greatest need. 1991 Census figures were weighted together with unemployment statistics to create measures reflecting poverty and social exclusion. The RPAs cover about a third of rural England, as shown in the map above. Work will shortly begin to review the areas to ensure they remain a valid guide for spending priorities, and both the RDAs and the Countryside Agency will be involved in the review.

**7.3.4.** A specific task for the RDAs is to help regenerate **deprived rural areas**, focusing currently on the Rural Priority Areas (see box) – the most seriously deprived rural areas. Problems vary from area to area, and each must develop its own solutions. The RDAs presently operate **Rural Development Programmes** in each Area in partnership with local authorities, Rural Community Councils and other key local players depending on the nature of the area covered by the partnership. The partnerships generate projects dealing with a wide range of issues ranging from job creation to workspace, renovation of buildings and better local infrastructure, support for tourism and combating the various aspects of social disadvantage found in rural areas. Together these programmes spend £29m a year. Within this programme we have expanded the **Redundant Building Grant** scheme to included an extra £4m for farmers. This has been heavily oversubsribed and will continue for another two years.

**7.3.5.** The challenge for the RDAs on rural regeneration projects has been to combine a range of different funding streams to the best effect. For example EEDA's **rural programme** of £1.4m in 1999–00 has leveraged a total programme of £12.8m for Rural Priority Areas in Eastern England. Rural areas have benefited substantially from other RDA programmes. 5–9% of the **Single Regeneration Budget** is currently required to be spent for the benefit of rural areas. (In SRB Round 5 this meant some £70m being directed to rural areas over the programme period and in SRB 6 some £60m). The **Land and Property Programme** funded, for example, work in market towns such as Great Torrington in Devon where, led by a Community Development Trust, refurbishment of a listed pannier market and conversion of a disused hotel has provided a new visitor attraction, 'Torrington 1646', tourist centre, ICT training suite and a better library. The **European Structural Funds** (see annex) will also continue to be a major source of support for rural as well as urban regeneration, and to which the Government – both directly and via local authorities – will contribute considerable match funding during 2000–06. For example this will generate around £300m for rural areas under Objective 2 over this period.

Ripon's historic waterfront showing restored Grade 2 listed warehouse
Credit: British Waterways

### EU funds for rural community development

The EU initiative LEADER+ will involve local communities in developing and testing innovative approaches to integrated and sustainable rural development. MAFF has been working closely with national, regional and local partners in developing and implementing this initiative. Following consultation, an England Programme, which will receive about £35m during 2000–06, will shortly be submitted to the European Commission.

## Case study – waterways-led regeneration

Inland waterways can make a major contribution to rural regeneration. Restoring canals and redeveloping derelict waterside land can provide scope for waterways based rural enterprises and an attractive environment for new development. *Waterways for Tomorrow* sets out the Government's vision for our inland waterways.

An example is the Ripon Canal and waterfront. British Waterways, along with partners including the local authority, private companies, canal society and Environment Agency, have successfully regenerated Ripon's historic waterfront and breathed new life into this area of the historic Yorkshire market town.

A successful restoration of the Ripon Canal in 1997 allowed boats to reach the canal terminus basin for the first time in many years. Sensitive redevelopment of the area around the basin has led to new housing and four business units being established on the site, bringing new jobs and additional prosperity to the local community.

A former gravel pits site has also now been turned into an 80-berth marina.

Widening Participation – Higher Education Experience. A joint project between Boston College, De Monfort University and Lincolnshire's Education Business Partnership Team has proved popular with pupils, students and staff alike and has resulted in pupils considering higher education
Credit: City Graphics Partnership

### Working in Partnership

Partnership working is at the heart of rural spending. **In each Rural Priority Area a Rural Development Programme Committee** involves a range of core partners – the RDA, local authorities, TECs, English Partnerships, Rural Community Councils and others as appropriate, such as the Countryside Agency, Tourist Boards, Business Links, and FRCA. Together they are responsible for developing a strategy for the area which identifies needs, opportunities and resources and sets objectives and a framework for action. These strategies are translated into action via three-year rolling operating plans and funding bids which set out specific projects or proposals for tackling issues.

Partnership working is of course not confined to the RPAs, and an example of a wider partnership is provided by the recently created **South Holland Rural Action Zone in Lincolnshire**. This focuses on the local RPA and adjacent rural areas, and aims to attack rural problems in the broad via an approach similar to that used in urban areas by New Deal for Communities programmes. Work will therefore tackle a wide range of issues from poor transport and other infrastructure to low wage levels, skills deficits and agricultural diversification. The breadth of the aims is reflected in the range of partners, who include South Holland DC, Lincolnshire CC, Government Office East Midlands, East Midlands Development Agency, the Countryside Agency, MAFF, Lincolnshire TEC Group, Lincolnshire Health, South Lincs Community Health NHS Trust, De Montfort University, Foodnet and voluntary sector groups.

In the heart of the South Lincolnshire horticultural growing area, Gosberton Bank Nursery has been transformed into the largest supplier of freesias in the UK. Increasingly selling via the internet, their award-winning website – www.freesia.co.uk – has opened up global markets
Credit: City Graphics Partnership

**7.3.6. Regional Development Agencies** have agreed a new rural remit as set out below.

> • **We are asking the RDAs to take forward the implementation of the policies set out in this White Paper** as a key component in the updating and development of their Regional Strategies and Frameworks for Action.

### A new rural vision for the Regional Development Agencies

The RDAs' primary aim for rural areas is to ensure a dynamic local economy and vibrant communities able to respond to changes in traditional industries such as agriculture and mining and to contribute positively to the regional and national economy. RDAs will work with local and regional partners to:

#### Help rural business through

- Raising the level of new business formation in remote rural areas and diversifying the economic base by stimulating innovation and competitiveness;
- Increasing the number of rural product and speciality food businesses; stimulating rural tourism and adding value to rural products and services through further processing or via regional and sub-regional branding, marketing and promotion;
- Developing better business to business links by stimulating the use of Information and Communications Technology.
- Ensuring that the Small Business Service (SBS) providers are equipped to respond to the specific needs of rural small business.

#### Create viable rural communities and better links between town and country through

- Identifying and taking action to address rural deprivation
- Delivering a programme of strategic market towns regeneration;
- Improving service delivery, encouraging multiuse facilities and innovative service delivery;
- Working to remove barriers to business creation and survival;
- Providing improved access to education, training and retraining opportunities to enable rural communities to update their skills and adapt to change;
- Improving transport links between urban and rural areas.

#### Encourage sustainable development through

- Recognising the value of the environment as an economic asset to be used sustainably;
- Ensuring development is appropriate and occurs in areas which are able to support it;
- Supporting sustainable best practice through funding, example and guidance.

## Future funding of Regional Development Agencies

**7.3.7.** The RDAs are now being given even more scope to boost their regions economies. In the *Spending Review 2000* we have announced a commitment to boost their overall funding over the three years from April 2001 and give them much greater freedom on how to achieve their regional strategies. A single budget will now be created for the RDAs from 2002. **The RDAs currently receive £1.2bn a year. This will rise to £1.7bn a year by 2003–04.**

**7.3.8.** Following the *Spending Review 2000*, the RDAs will also operate the **Regional Innovation Fund** which will benefit rural as well as urban areas. The RDAs will have £50m per year between them to promote innovative activity in their regions. This will encompass the existing **Innovative Clusters Fund (ICF)** which aims to help business do better as part of a cluster of interdependent firms, particularly through transfer of ideas and sharing a common labour pool.

> • **We are supporting several clusters which focus wholly or partly on rural areas.** For example, a Food Technology Transfer Centre and an Organic Demonstration Farm, both in Cornwall, are featured in the South West of England Development Agency's business plan for cluster development, submitted in response to the DTI's initiative. The allocation for the second year is now under discussion with RDA chairmen, and we expect further rurally-based proposals to come forward, in accordance with the priorities identified in the RDAs' Strategies.

**7.3.9.** We have created a **new Phoenix Fund** of over £100m. The Fund is aimed at helping promote enterprise in disadvantaged neighbourhoods and groups, including those in rural areas. Financial assistance is going to the Business Volunteer Mentoring Association (BVMA), Community Finance Initiatives and a wide range of innovative projects which encourage entrepreneurship as a means of tackling social exclusion.

**7.3.10.** Financial assistance for small businesses with growth potential at the lower end of the risk capital market will be boosted through the Government's provision of £180m to the **Enterprise Fund**, which included continuation of the Small Firms Loan Guarantee Scheme, and the development of the new Regional Venture Capital Funds in each of the English regions. A further £100m to develop the risk capital market was announced in the March 2000 Budget.

---

## Case study – DALE – Dales Action for Local Enterprise

This pilot project looks specifically at the issue of rural disadvantage faced by young people in remote areas who lack job and business opportunities and, as a result, find it hard to either remain in rural areas, progress within them, or find a voice or role in the wider community.

### The Project

- The project builds on a Prince's Trust model to provide outreach and support for a new initiative in the Yorkshire Dales National Park, targeted at 18-30 year olds, and providing grant and loan support for business start-up.
- The emphasis is on industry/business that is particularly suited to or sustainable in rural areas, and on businesses that grow out of rural area activity.
- Reflecting its remote rural base, the project includes local and non-Dales business mentors, and setting up a Dales Youth Business Forum and providing a virtual business park.
- There is a bespoke training package focussed on the business problems encountered in rural areas and IT support and facilities provided to each new business.

### The Objectives

- To pilot approaches to tackle underemployment and unemployment for 18-30 year olds in remote rural areas.
- To reduce the drift of population away from the area.
- To address the lack of local access to information about, and support for, new employment/business initiatives.
- To provide peer group support
- To provide capital for micro-business start-up.
- To raise possibly low aspirations about ability and potential of business sector.

### Funding and Outputs

- The project has been set up for five years from 2000, with the first three years funded by the Prince's Trust, the Countryside Agency, Yorkshire Forward, European grant aid and private sector support from Lockheed Martin and Scarborough Property Group.

A sketch of Semerwater from above Ellerkin, North Yorkshire by
Tim Slatter, a young artist helped by the Prince's Trust Dales Project
Credit: © Tim Slatter

## 7.4. A key rural industry: tourism

**7.4.1.** Tourism income is fundamental for the rural economy
and has played a central role in revitalising many small towns
and their surrounding areas and there is considerable potential
for further growth. In its report PIU noted that expenditure by
visitors to the countryside supported 380,000 jobs across rural
England and underpinned 25,000 usually small, tourism
businesses, including around 40% of England's total
accommodation stock. Day visitors are estimated to spend
£8bn in the English countryside in a year.

St. Elgin, North Frodingham, East Riding of Yorkshire. One of
rural England's 10,000 medieval churches – outstanding art and
architecture which attracts visitors worldwide – as well as a vital
base for community services. The Government is acting to reduce
VAT on repairs and maintenance (3.2.4).
Credit: The Countryside Agency

**7.4.2.** The benefits of tourism, however, are spread unevenly
across the country and through different seasons. In a few
popular areas there are adverse effects from the high number
of visitors. Future potential is likely to reflect growing demand
for taking more short breaks (of less than four nights), seeking
distinctive experiences rooted in local and regional culture,
enjoying more specialist activities and demanding higher quality
accommodation and tourism services. Tourism can also help
other rural industries. Businesses who provide eating and
catering services for tourists are well placed to promote regional
food and drink products, benefiting local food producers,
as well as improving the interest of an area to visitors.

**7.4.3.** As set out in *Tomorrow's Tourism* our strategy is to:
provide the right policy framework for sustainable tourism to
flourish – for example, by creating the English Tourism Council
to provide strategic leadership for the industry; to support
promotional activity to develop and spread quality – for
example, by launching new harmonised quality ratings for
hotels, guest accommodation and holiday parks; and to
encourage sustainable growth in tourism through a wider
spread of tourism related development and projects
including developing a new strategy to regenerate traditional
seaside resorts.

**7.4.4.** We are looking to **the Regional Development
Agencies and Regional Tourist Boards to develop joint
tourism and recreation strategies**. Many are already doing
so. For instance, Yorkshire Forward and the Yorkshire Tourist
Board have jointly led the development of the new Yorkshire
brand, which was launched in June. Regional Planning Bodies
also have a role to play in helping to ensure that these
strategies are sustainable and in their subsequent
implementation. To follow up the national strategy in
*Tomorrow's Tourism* we think there is a need for a strategy
in rural areas. We believe that such a strategy is necessary
to improve the quality of the visitor experience and increase
income and employment, while at the same time enhancing
the quality of the environment and spreading the benefits of
tourism throughout rural communities.

- **The English Tourism Council and the Countryside
  Agency will produce a joint rural tourism strategy
  in 2001**, to provide a clear focus for national,
  regional and local action. It will consider:

  - Creative promotion of rural tourism products
    and destinations, to increase awareness of
    what rural England has to offer amongst
    overseas and domestic visitors.

  - Action to bring out the distinctiveness of
    different rural areas and encourage more visitor
    spending to be retained locally, such
    as through the promotion of local produce.

- Better advisory services and training, backed by research, to help existing and potential businesses understand more clearly the market opportunities and avoid over supply.

- Greater co-operation between rural tourism businesses, to assist joint marketing and the sharing of good practice.

- Sound management of rural destinations, including improving visitor information, encouraging alternative means of transport, and reflecting the special roles of market towns and protected areas.

**7.4.5.** We are considering the extent to which our current **planning guidance** that affects rural tourism needs revision. We are about to consult on revisions to our *planning guidance on sport and recreation (PPG17)*. We will shortly be publishing a research report on planning for leisure and tourism and in the light of the debate on its findings we will decide whether our planning guidance on tourism needs revision.

---

### Tourist charges

A more difficult question raised in the *Rural Economies* PIU report is whether tourists should be asked to contribute directly to local economies through some form of tourist tax or other payment, particularly in the so-called 'honeypot' areas which attract large numbers of tourists. **Voluntary charge schemes** are already used in hotels and restaurants around the country. For instance, almost 100 Cumbrian hotels and caravan parks raise money for the Lake District Tourism and Conservation partnership by adding an optional £1 to tourists' bills. The partnership funds local environmental protection projects such as footpath repair and woodland management. The PIU report suggested extending visitor charging schemes on a voluntary or mandatory basis. The Government considers it right to maintain the present voluntary approach, rather than introducing new legislation which could be complex and burdensome.

---

## 7.5. Dealing with distance and raising skill levels

### Information and Communications Technology (ICT)

**7.5.1.** ICT is already playing a central role in widening the economic base in rural areas, enabling the smallest business to market globally with potential environmental benefits as travel needs are reduced. But the ability of rural businesses to take advantage of the new opportunities is currently limited by poorer communications infrastructure in rural areas and particularly the absence of broadband (see box) together with a low level of awareness and lack of relevant skills. There is also a need to manage potentially undesirable **impacts** of ICT such as the need for new radio masts to deliver mobile telephone coverage.

---

### What is Broadband?

Broadband is a service or connection allowing a considerable amount of information to be conveyed. It is generally defined as a connection capable of delivering data at speeds of 2 megabytes per second (2MB/s) or faster, the minimum bandwidth necessary to deliver real time video. Consumer services needing broadband connections include high speed internet access and video-on-demand. Businesses may need broadband connections for a variety of data transfer functions. Broadband communications networks will increasingly become available through land based cables (BT and cable), wireless access, and third generation mobile telephones. Satellite systems are also being developed and terrestrial and satellite digital TV systems will provide certain types of interactive services at high speed.

---

**7.5.2.** The Government will stimulate and promote industry investment in higher bandwidth services so that as many people as possible can get faster access to the internet and other information services. But the market alone will not deliver affordable high-speed connections to all rural areas. We will therefore work through the development agencies in the regions, and in Northern Ireland, Scotland, and Wales to develop effective strategies for the rollout of higher bandwidth services in rural areas, taking full advantage of public sector investment and the opportunities, in some regions, to obtain EU funding. Other stakeholders will also be involved, to ensure that access to broadband services reaches as widely as practicable. **We will ask the Countryside Agency to monitor the rollout of broadband in rural areas, and we will take this into account in developing policy.**

**7.5.3.** We are also examining the case for requiring the communications industry to make higher bandwidth services available universally, as they already do for telephone services. The case for such a Universal Service Obligation (USO) to ensure that everyone has access to more rapid digital services may become more compelling as rollout of these services accelerates and as more of the services necessary for full participation in modern society, particularly public services, are delivered electronically. However, neither we nor the European Commission think it would be right to take such an initiative at such an early stage in the rollout of higher bandwidth services. **If the market fails over time to deliver a reasonable level of broadband in rural areas, then we will revisit our position on the Universal Service Obligation in this light.**

- We will encourage **RDAs** to include plans within their **ICT strategies** to ensure that rural businesses have adequate access to training and business advice on ICT (perhaps through rural ICT access centres) and that the rural workforce has the requisite skills drawing on work of the new Small Business Service and Learning and Skills Councils;

- We aim to provide an **Electronic Rural Portal** for farming (as announced at the Farming Summit at No 10 Downing Street on 30 March 2000). This will provide a first-stop shop access to information and interactive advice for farmers, the public and businesses generally. The design will be sufficiently flexible to broaden the service to become a full rural portal in due course. Subject to the outcome of the current feasibility study, expected shortly, it is anticipated that a prototype will be developed by early-2001. A fully interactive site, enabling farmers and others in the rural community to undertake a range of electronic transactions with government and private sector bodies, is expected to be developed by end-2002. MAFF has committed to making all CAP scheme forms available electronically by 2002. The study will draw upon experience gained from the CLICK Project.

## Case study – connecting up farmers

**CLICK** (Connecting to the Local ICT Centre at Kington) is a pilot project in Kington, Herefordshire, to link farmers and their families to existing IT facilities which was announced as part of the Farming Summit package. The pilot scheme targets around 100 farmers, some with and some without PCs, and aims to encourage farmers and their families to gain access to ICT and the necessary skills training in its use. By electronically integrating all the information already held by MAFF about the farm, farmers are beginning to reap the benefits of time saving in making claims. It is hoped that this will expand with further marketing initiatives for farmers in the near future. The project is being developed by MAFF in partnership with Advantage West Midlands (RDA) and the Kington Connected Community Company (www.kc3.co.uk) which has IT facilities in Kington, and has the support of the Government Office West Midlands and the Countryside Agency.

More information about the project and a chance to see how it works can be found on www.click.maff.gov.uk

David Forbes of the Titley Court Farm, who has benefited from the CLICK scheme
Credit: KC3

### Transport Infrastructure

**7.5.4.** Physical isolation and poor access can be a barrier to the growth of rural economies. Chapter 6 describes the measures we are taking to improve transport within rural areas. But the Government's new £180bn *10 Year Plan* for transport will also help improve the links between many rural areas and other parts of the country. The substantial increase in funding to modernise our national transport networks will improve road and rail access for both passengers and freight, bringing direct benefits for rural economies.

**7.5.5.** Among the benefits we expect to see as a result of the 10 Year Plan are:

- A major programme of investment in the road network, with targeted improvements at bottlenecks and junctions, widening schemes, by-passes and better maintenance and traffic management, resulting in reduced congestion despite traffic growth;
- Increased capacity and improved services on our railways, resulting in a 50% increase in passenger numbers and an 80% increase in rail freight volumes;
- Improved access to ports and airports, and to areas in need of regeneration.

**7.5.6.** Past under-investment has brought **local roads** to their worst condition for 30 years. Sufficient additional resources have been provided through the 10 Year Plan to halt the deterioration by 2004, and eliminate the backlog by the end of the Plan period. This will be of particular benefit to rural roads where condition has been below standard for long periods.

**7.5.7.** Funding will be directed to regional and local priorities through the new Regional Transport Strategies and statutory Local Transport Plans. The 10 Year Plan will also provide the resources to implement the findings of the programme of Multi-Modal Studies, which is currently looking at some of our most important transport corridors, such as the links between London and the South West (see box).

## Road haulage

**7.5.8.** Businesses in rural areas including farmers face higher
transport costs and will benefit from the measures affecting
hauliers announced in the Pre-Budget Report 2000, reducing
Vehicle Excise Duty, introducing a freeze on fuel duties and
cutting the duty on ultra low sulphur diesel. For example, the
reforms to lorry VED will generate around £265m benefit to the
haulage industry this year and around £300m from next year.

- The measures announced in the Pre-Budget
  Report 2000 represent a cost reduction of £750m
  annually for the road haulage industry and this will
  benefit the competitiveness of rural economies.

## Action to raise the skills base

**7.5.9.** Education and training are one of our major priorities
for the country as a whole, rural as well as urban, and we are
establishing a national network of Learning and skills Councils
in April 2001 (see annex) to streamline the delivery of post 16
education and training. Our aim will be to ensure that the new
councils (which will work closely with the RDAs) take full
account of rural needs and the special problems of rural areas.

- **We will ensure that rural users are included in
  rural Local Learning Partnerships** in which local
  organisations and individuals help to meet the skill
  challenge, improve standards and increase
  participation;

- **The plans of Local Learning and Skills Councils will
  consider the needs of those who have difficulty in
  accessing learning opportunities (including travel
  difficulties).** This will be particularly important for rural
  areas. Resources for access funds have been greatly
  increased. LSCs will have discretionary funds to support
  new initiatives and pump-priming for small projects.

**7.5.10.** Farmers will be eligible for training through the
England Rural Development Programme (see 8.3.4).

## 7.6. Helping rural businesses to succeed

**7.6.1.** Small businesses continue to be the main enterprises
in rural areas and we will support them and the start up of
new businesses through better advice and support; cutting
unnecessary red tape; and other initiatives to encourage
enterprise and innovation such as rural rate relief and RDA
enterprise funds (see paragraph 7.3.9.). **The annex sets out
additional sources of funding and advice for small
business in rural areas.**

## Improving business advice and support

**7.6.2.** The new **Small Business Service (see annex)** is setting up a new network of customer focused Business Links which will place a greater emphasis on micro-business than before. The Countryside Agency has taken part in the process to set up the network, in particular, looking at how the organisations which are running outlets with rural areas in their catchment give access to their customers. New communications technology will help provide advice in the remoter rural areas, and the Small Business Service, along with the Regional Development Agencies and Learning and Skills Councils will work to encourage educational institutions to develop the take up of IT.

- **The Small Business Council (SBC)** has been established to advise on the needs of small businesses and the effect of the activities of Government on existing and potential SMEs. **The SBC is considering setting up a Rural Issues sub-group.**

- **To help farmers and growers respond to changing market demand and changes in their industry the government is providing, through Business Links, tailored business advice.** The service will include an initial health check of their business and the production of an Action Plan. This will help them develop better business practices and take strategic decisions about the future of their business which could include diversification or leaving the industry. They will then be helped to access other sources of advice and support. The service was launched on 10 October 2000 and will continue until 2004 providing up to **£21m of advice allowing 15,000 farmers to benefit.**

### Case study – North and Western Lancashire Personal Business Adviser

A rural Personal Business Adviser (PBA) is working with agricultural and non-agricultural clients in North and Western Lancashire to enable them to develop opportunities for diversification and growth. In addition to building a continuing client working relationship the Rural PBA acts as a central point of contact for all Partner services such as the North West Tourist Board, European Assisted Initiatives and Local Authorities as well as the services available from the Business Link. Through the work of the Rural PBA a Business Support Centre is being set up in Garstang to offer counselling for start-ups and for farmers wishing to diversify. Particular success has come from working with planners and rural businesses through planning surgeries.

North and Western Lancashire Rural Business Advisor Beryl Smith with client Neil Anderton
Credit: Business Link – North and Western Lancashire

## Better regulation and less red tape

**7.6.4.** We are committed to minimising regulatory burdens on small businesses in order to help them realise their potential. For example we are preparing legislation to modernise our liquor and public entertainment licensing laws and considering how to streamline the fire safety legislation. Both should help rural business. Chapter 8 (section 5) sets out the action we are taking on regulation of the farming industry including a review of environmental legislation

**7.6.5.** One of the key tasks of the Small Business Service will be to focus on cutting red tape – eliminating unnecessary regulation, minimising the burdens imposed by necessary regulation, such as encouraging higher standards of enforcement and, making sure that the interests of small firms are properly considered. **We have also set up a panel which will call Ministers to account for their performance on minimising regulation.**

## Rate relief

**7.6.6.** Many small businesses in market towns and other rural areas occupy premises with lower rateable values, including non-agricultural businesses on farms. These would all benefit from our proposals for rate relief for all small businesses.

- **We are consulting on proposals to reduce the rating burden on small businesses in the Green Paper *Modernising Local Government Finance.*** We propose that relief of 50% would be available to small businesses occupying properties with rateable values less than £3,000. This would be gradually reduced so that 20% relief would be available to small businesses occupying properties with a rateable value of £6,000 and no relief would be given to properties with a rateable value above £8,000. In the current year this would amount to a saving of £624 for a business with a rateable value of £3,000; and a saving of £492 for a business with a rateable value of £6,000.

# a new future
## for farming

## Key issues

- Farming is going through its most difficult period since before the Second World War. Farm incomes have fallen by around 60% over the past five years. No sector of farming has been unaffected.
- Some pressures common to all sectors of the economy: the problems of competing in an increasingly global and more competitive market; the need to meet ever more sophisticated consumer tastes and preferences; and the challenge of new technology and new ways of buying, producing and selling.
- Other pressures specific to farming: a long and deep international slump in commodity prices; falling sterling support payments due to the weakness of the Euro; and the devastating impact of the BSE crisis, not only for the beef industry but also for other parts of farming.
- Growing demands to manage the countryside so that its beauty and richness are enhanced rather than damaged.

## The future – what we want to see

- Farming's main task will still be to produce the food we eat.
- But farming will be more forward-looking, competitive, and flexible, more capable of responding quickly to market changes and new consumer demands.
- An increasing recognition of the role which farmers and land managers play in maintaining an attractive and diverse countryside and in sustaining the wider rural economy.
- Many more farmers will turn a positive approach to the environment to their own economic advantage, with payments for environmental 'goods' that the nation wants – flourishing wildlife, living landscapes, a protected heritage and opportunities for leisure.
- The growing market opportunities for sustainable products will enable the production and environmental functions to be combined via the marketplace for an increasing proportion of the industry.
- There will still be room for large and small farms, full-time and part-time businesses. But farms – including entrepreneurial family farms – will be more diverse in terms of structure, business organisation and the mix of agricultural and non-agricultural activities.
- Farmers will take up opportunities to learn, develop and exploit new skills and new techniques.
- Government and industry will continue to work closely together to meet these challenges: to get away from the cycle of short-term crises and become again what farming should be – a world-class industry in a world-class setting.

---

### Summary of measures

The *New Direction for Agriculture* includes:

- Pressing for further reform to the Common Agricultural Policy

- Help for specialist abattoirs

- Launch of joint government/industry taskforce to look at the costs of inputs to farming

- Joint studies of efficiency of key sectors

- The launch of the £1.6bn, 7 year England Rural Development Programme which includes:

  - More help for marketing, skills and enterprise;

  - Additional funding for agri-environment schemes;

- More help for farm business diversification, including:

  - Clearer planning guidance and advice

  - Consulting on rate relief for diversifying farmers

  - Grants for non-food crops, woodland and diversification

- An additional £4m Redundant Building Grant for farm diversification;

- Removing unnecessary regulatory burdens.

# 8

## Contents

## 8.1. Introduction

**8.1.1.** Farming is important. It supplies most of our food. It directly employs around 600,000 people (including seasonal and part-time workers). It contributes £7bn each year to the UK economy. It is and will continue to be the bedrock of a UK food chain worth £57bn each year and 3.3 million jobs. Farming has defined most of the landscape and shaped its diversity.

**8.1.2.** Farming communities have created the fabric of our rural life over centuries, and in many areas still maintain it. Our countryside and the environment we cherish still depend on our farmers. Farming is not the same as the countryside, but rural life and the rural environment as we know it would not exist without farming.

*"There's also the countryside and the issue of who is going to look after this vast area if people are not actually making a living out of it. And that concerns me greatly, because it's a very beautiful country that we live in, and on the whole pretty well maintained."*

**8.1.3.** The economic crisis in farming has been very painful and it is not over yet. It is bringing about major restructuring in the industry. Many farmers have left the industry. The number of workers employed in farming has fallen significantly. The trend towards bigger farms has accelerated.

*"We have five farms within the village and each farm has one or two people, but it's all father and son – there isn't a single employee now from outside."*

**8.1.4.** We believe that farming must emerge stronger from this crisis. We accept that the industry cannot achieve this by acting alone. But nor would it be right for the Government solely to direct and manage the way forward. For the past year, the farming industry and the Government have been working together on a new direction for farming which meets the challenges the industry faces, and which defines the right roles for industry and for government. At the heart of this new direction is a vision of agriculture for the future. It is set out above, and in more detail in our *New Direction for Agriculture*, published in December 1999, and the *Action Plan for Farming* launched by the Prime Minister in March 2000.

**Nettleton Top, Lincolnshire Wolds**
Credit: Countryside Agency, Simon Warner

**8.1.5.** The Action Plan identified more than £200m of new aid, directed not only to short-term relief, but also to industry restructuring and other longer-term action on marketing, diversification, training and removing regulatory costs and burdens. It was a new partnership between the Government and the farming and food industries. A majority of its 60-plus measures have already been implemented by the Government.

**8.1.6.** As well as implementing the March *Action Plan*, we are committed to to identifying new action to achieve the farming strategy and vision drawn up with the industry. The recent Spending Review will provide a further £300m over the next three years to continue and develop the measures in the Plan. An Industry Forum chaired by the Minister of Agriculture, Fisheries and Food is giving strategic direction to this work.

**8.1.7.** To maintain momentum on the farming strategy:

- Our aim remains radical reform of the Agricultural Policy;

- We will undertake national strategic initiatives to make farming fit for the future;

- We will put new emphasis on marketing, skills and innovation;

- We will support new opportunities to diversify;

- We are committed to regulate only when it is really necessary, and to remove burdens that are not justified.

## 8.2. Strategic action

### Reform of the Common Agricultural Policy

**8.2.1.** The Government pays £3-3.5bn in the form of EU and domestic support to UK agriculture each year.

- **Over the period 1997–01 farmers will have received a total of £629m in aid to offset the effect of exchange rate movements.**

- **On top of this, we have in the past two years agreed additional aid packages worth £235m.**

**8.2.2.** The industry recognises that subsidy and aid by themselves are not the answer. Indeed, much of the EU Common Agricultural Policy (CAP) still acts against the new vision and direction we are seeking. Subsidies which simply reward production have damaged the countryside and have stifled innovation. A complicated bureaucracy has created expensive surpluses of basic products and has prevented farmers from responding to what consumers really want.

**8.2.3.** The Government will therefore continue to lead the drive to reform the CAP. Last year's *Agenda 2000* reforms were a substantial step forward. Its price reductions will reduce the annual food bill for a family of four by around £65 a year. Its reforms will further direct agricultural support away from production subsidies towards measures which deliver environmental benefits.

**8.2.4.** But more still needs to be done. The CAP must be further deregulated so that agricultural production can adapt to a competitive world market. Production quotas which prevent farmers from responding to the market must be removed. The CAP must respond to external pressures too. In a few years we will have an expanded EU with up to twelve more member states and a total population of 500 million people. Without CAP reform, the budgetary consequences would be unsustainable. Negotiations have also begun on liberalising agricultural trade in the World Trade Organisation. This will open up new markets as well as exposing us to greater competition. An unchanged CAP will simply hand the advantage to our competitors outside Europe.

**Our aim is progressively:**

- **To move towards a CAP which encourages farmers to be more competitive and responsive to market signals so that they can make a good living while at the same time following practices which conserve and enhance the landscape and wildlife; and**

- **To move environmental and social goals closer to the heart of agricultural policy alongside its economic objectives.**

### Re-directing agricultural support to improve, not damage, the environment

**8.2.5.** The Government recently secured EU approval for the England Rural Development Programme (ERDP) which includes a major switch of CAP funds from production aids to support for the broader rural economy. We will spend £1.6bn by 2006 – around 10% of total support for the agriculture industry – on measures to advance environmentally beneficial farming practices as well as on new measures to develop and promote rural enterprise and diversification, and better training and marketing.

- **Within the ERDP, the Government is more than doubling the amount to be spent on agri-environment schemes, including the Countryside Stewardship and Organic Farming Schemes, and Environmentally Sensitive Areas.**

**8.2.6.** These schemes, together with farm woodlands schemes, are vital to biodiversity. They also provide important income-generating opportunities for farmers. The additional resources will mean that many more farmers can participate over the coming years. Part 3 of this White Paper provides more on farming's role in our landscape and biodiversity objectives.

*"What we get to walk on and play with, that made us move here, is what farmers have managed."*

*"Down our way they've started setting hedges again"*

## Case study – integrated sustainable rural development

**The Bowland Initiative** aims to test **how agriculture, business and environment objectives can be made to work together** as a potential model for the future of rural policy in the uplands. It is one of two such experiments – the other is in Bodmin, Cornwall. Bowland is an Area of Outstanding Natural Beauty (AONB), and most of the area is designated as a Special Protection Area under the EC Birds Directive, being very rich in wildlife.

The project combines business and environmental planning, provided by a dedicated project team and supported by a broad partnership of Departments, agencies and NGOs. Farmers and others receive expert help and aid for business developments, on condition that they also have an environmental audit of the holding, with a view to taking up appropriate environmental or woodland schemes, and to dealing with any environmental problems identified. In return, the project staff offer the farmer a streamlined package, preparing application forms on their behalf and negotiating funding from various sources. Schemes might include redundant building conversion, woodland planting, diversification into livery or accommodation (with associated training), hedging and walling, meadow management, river bank protection, upgrading farm pollution control equipment, and training for off-farm employment. One-third of all farms in the area (150) have become involved. Broader initiatives to help develop the Bowland economy and meet environmental and social goals at the same time have been developed: farmers, local abattoirs and auction marts are collaborating in a **Bowland Beef and Lamb** marketing Initiative. There is also a project by which local hotels and guesthouses will collect visitor contributions to a '**Bowland Environment Fund**', to support small-scale environmental work on farms and in villages.

**Bowland Fells**
Credit: Countryside Agency – Mike Williams

### Strategic action at national level

**8.2.7.** Although much of the economic and regulatory framework is European, we will tackle key strategic issues affecting the structure and efficiency of the industry. These include developing a clear vision of how key sectors, such as the dairy industry, will develop in the future, and can exploit likely changes to the CAP. We also need to ensure that we protect essential infrastructure which will support farmers diversifying and expanding into new and added-value markets.

- **We will target help for small and medium sized abattoirs**. Many small and medium-sized abattoirs are threatened by over-capacity and competitive pressures in the industry. We recognise that some of these abattoirs play an important role in remote rural areas, and in preparing meat for specialist markets (eg organic meat, specialist breeds and farmers' markets). **We are providing new, additional aid (worth £8.7m in 2001–02) in respect of meat inspection costs to help secure the future of small and medium-sized abattoirs.**

- **We will establish a new government/industry task force to look at inputs to farming.** This will examine the industry's concerns about the costs of key inputs (eg of machinery, agro-chemicals and labour), review their impact on farming businesses, and identify measures to ensure their optimum use and reduce costs.

- **We will set up joint government/industry studies of efficiencies in key sectors.** A working group comprising government, producer, processor, and retailer representatives will be set up to explore how to improve efficiencies in the milk and dairy supply chain. It will look at reducing the wide differences in performance within the sector, and how the industry can best prepare for a market beyond EU quotas. It will also explore ways of ensuring that the UK better exploits the strong demand for value-added products. If the initiative is a success, other sectoral studies will follow.

- As set out in chapter 13, we will introduce **new regional rural sounding boards** in which farmers and other rural interests will be able to make government better aware of their concerns, ideas and proposals.

- We will **provide the resources required to offset the EU reduction in support for the School Milk Scheme.** This will be worth about £1.4m in a full year.

- The Government announced in the **Pre-Budget Report 2000** that subject to consultation, particularly with the National Farmers Union and the police about ensuring that controls over insurance, maintenance and theft will remain, **Vehicle Excise Duty on tractors** will be abolished, saving farmers £40 a year on each vehicle. Farmers, for whom haulage and motoring costs are also a key input, will benefit from measures on VED and fuel duty as referred to in 7.5.8 and 6.3.1.

---

### Climate change and farming

In March 2000, the Ministry of Agriculture, Fisheries and Food published a review of the potential long-term impact of climate change on UK agriculture.
It concluded that:

- For arable crops, the range of current crops will move northward and marginal crops such as maize and sunflowers may increasingly penetrate southern UK; new crop varieties may need to be selected;
- In horticulture, crops will be more susceptible to changing conditions although beans, onions and sweetcorn production will benefit;
- Livestock production is unlikely to change significantly, although increased heat stress and disease transmission may be a problem for intensive systems;
- Weeds will be able to evolve more rapidly in the higher temperatures and the type of pests and disease confronting farmers may alter and pests such as colorado beetle may become a problem.

---

## 8.3. Marketing, skills and innovation

**8.3.1.** Many farmers are already taking advantage of better marketing, new skills and innovation. They are making use of integrated crop management and organic farming, and are getting closer to their customers through farmers' markets and other channels.

**8.3.2.** The Government believes that there are still huge opportunities for agriculture in better marketing, training and innovation. For example, the UK applies animal health and welfare standards that are among the highest in the world. We must make these a point of distinction and market on quality. Similarly, on training, there are also huge opportunities for farming in the knowledge-based economy. And new methods of co-operation between farmers and others in the food chain can bring various benefits. The resulting economies of scale can generate lower costs, of production, inputs and professional expertise. Co-operation can also help farmers to guarantee the continuity and quality of products to their suppliers.

**8.3.3.** The Government can help in various ways on marketing, training and innovation. It can bring different parts of the food chain together and can provide financial aid to kick-start initiatives.

**8.3.4.** Our help will include:

- **Marketing grants:** the *ERDP* will provide both capital grants to develop new processing and marketing facilities for farmers, and non-capital grants to encourage the marketing of high-quality agricultural products. The Vocational Training Scheme under the ERDP will include grants for training in marketing and improving business skills, information and communication.

- **Tailored business advice for farmers** (see 7.6.2). Farmers are also eligible through the ERDP vocational training scheme to help them modernise and improve their agricultural, horticultural and forestry holdings. There will be an emphasis on sustainable and environmentally-sensitive practices. The onus will be on farmers, where appropriate in groups, to put forward projects designed to meet their own needs. We are is also funding £1.8m of advice through LANTRA (the national training organisation for land-based industries) to help farmers identify how they can best make use of this ERDP support.

- A stakeholder seminar on **e-business** in the countryside. This will help bring together progress on a number of e-business initiatives driven forward by MAFF since the farming summit in March 2000.

- The Countryside Agency will be taking forward its new **'Eat the View'** programme to increase consumer awareness of the links between the products they buy and the countryside they value, to improve the marketing of local and regional products, and to enhance the environmental quality and diversity of the countryside while delivering real benefits to the rural economy. The Agency's aims include, by 2004, doubling consumer awareness of the impact of their purchasing decisions on the countryside, and helping 300 producers find new markets for local produce through direct selling and trade partnerships.

- **MAFF's organic farming scheme** increases the help for farmers to convert to organic production – see 10.3.12.

In addition:

- Around £5m has been allocated this year under the new **Agriculture Development Scheme** (ADS) to help farmers and growers improve their marketing. Examples include projects to help farmers meet the specifications set by the major caterers, and establishing Assured Food Standards to co-ordinate and drive forward farm assurance schemes.

- **MAFF is working with the NFU to encourage farmers to come together to market their produce.** MAFF and the NFU have mounted joint exhibits at five major agricultural shows this year.

Single Gloucester cheese is under EU legal protection: Gloucestershire farms producing the cheese must have a herd of registered Gloucester cows on the farm. Single Gloucester is sometimes known as 'hay cheese' because in years gone by the cheese was made in the winter months when the cows were feeding on hay. It is now produced all the year round in an effort to satisfy the ever increasing demand
Credit: The Countryside Agency

- **Promotion of speciality and regional foods. Through Food from Britain we are helping to develop the speciality food industry,** including regional food groups such as 'A Taste of the West' and 'North West Fine Foods', so that local speciality food producers can maximise opportunities to market their produce. A new e-commerce 'shopping mall' for speciality food businesses: www.speciality-foods.com has been established.

- **Direct selling.** Many farmers are now selling direct to consumers via farmers' markets, farm shops, box schemes, mail order and the internet. The number of farmers' markets has expanded from one in 1997 to around 250 now. MAFF and the Countryside Agency have helped to fund a new National Association of Farmers' Markets and to reach a new target of 400 farmers markets.

**8.3.6.** We continue to believe that the farming and food industries can only prosper if they work together. We therefore support the creation of Assured Food Standards to bring the main existing assurance schemes within a single structure and have offered grant aid to help its establishment. We welcome the move to use the British Farm Standard red tractor logo on a wide range of produce, enabling consumers to identify those products that have been produced to the exacting standards of assurance schemes.

- **We also welcome the Competition Commission's report into the supermarkets** and the recommendation that there should be a code of practice to put relations between supermarkets and their suppliers on a clearer and more certain basis. The relevant supermarkets will have to give legally binding undertakings to comply with the code.

- **Fruit and vegetables.** We are committed to introducing a National School Fruit Scheme, which will make a free piece of fruit available to school children aged four to six each school day by 2004 – **equivalent to around 40% of the British apple market.**

- As part of the new *NHS Plan*, we will work closely with the food industry and other key stakeholders to increase access to fruit and vegetables. Pilot schemes will start this year.

**8.3.7.** These positive campaigns for health will, together with DfEE action on school meals, be of significant benefit to producers through increased demand for good quality fruit and vegetables. The challenge to the industry, including farmers, is to work with us to increase provision and access to fruit and vegetables, for example through local initiatives such as Farmers' Markets.

## 8.4. Farm diversification

**8.4.1.** We will help farmers diversify, to strengthen their core business of providing the food we eat. Over the past twenty years, many farmers have decided that diversification can give their farming incomes some protection against market fluctuations. Often the whole family are involved in setting up and running new enterprises such as bed and breakfast facilities, or farm shops. Sometimes new businesses may be established solely by one partner within the farm. Research undertaken by the National Farmers Union in 1999 showed that one third of all women on farms questioned were involved in some form of diversification to bring in additional income.

### Case study – Farm diversification 1

Mrs Alice Bennett farms in partnership with her husband Christopher on their 200 acre tenancy in Madresfield. Alice has supported the dairy enterprise establishing an efficient farm office, computerised records and accounts and has raised four children. In 1994 she opened a nursery school on the farm which has grown rapidly to cater for over 100 children daily, creating local employment. In April 1999 she further utilised redundant buildings to develop a small riding school which employs five people. This year has seen the expansion of the school into infant education, up to the Key Stage 1 (age 7 years).

Alice Bennett of Madresfield Early Years Centre, Haysward Farm
Credit: NFU

### Case study – Farm diversification 2

Richard Dix and his father are pig farmers based at Heacham in north Norfolk. In 1999 following the problems in the pig sector Richard decided to develop his hobby of helping other people to solve their IT problems into a business. Richard, whose family have been farming at Heacham for over 150 years, took the difficult decision to sell the breeding herd, releasing capital to pay off most of the farm's overdraft and simplifying the farm's activities. This change also reduced the workload on the farm enabling Richard's father to manage the farm on a daily basis and allowing Richard to concentrate on making a success of his IT support business, which specialises in helping small businesses and private IT users. He has now been joined in the venture by his wife, Angela, who has brought skills in marketing and administration into the business.

Looking to Pastures New
Credit: Anglia Newspapers Ltd © Donna Semmens

**8.4.2.** We believe that, if it is pursued intelligently and realistically and with the right encouragement and support, diversification can play an even greater role in the future in strengthening UK agriculture. Section 7.6 describes the measures we are taking to provide better business advice to farmers and others running small businesses. We are also taking other steps to make this vision a reality:

- Introduced under the ERDP, **the Rural Enterprise Scheme will provide £152m in aid over the next seven years to help farmers re-direct their businesses,** for example by marketing quality agricultural produce, or by moving into rural tourism and craft activities. It also provides funding for measures to help the wider rural community.

- MAFF will publish before the end of the year a free guide 'New Directions – Farm Diversification' providing fresh up-to-date advice, illustrated by a number of recent case studies, for farmers wishing to diversify to get alternative or additional sources of income. The guide will include advice on planning issues and would be of help to farmers considering applying for funding to diversify under the Rural Enterprise Scheme.

## The Planning Environment

**8.4.3.** Surplus farm buildings can provide suitable accommodation for diversified businesses. The Government is determined that the planning system should be sufficiently flexible to enable this to happen.

**8.4.4.** Advice for planning authorities on sustainable rural development, including the re-use of rural buildings, is set out in *The Countryside – Environmental Quality and Economic and Social Development (PPG7)*. A DETR/MAFF seminar in May 2000 identified the need to ensure that this guidance was implemented more consistently at local level. There is evidence of good practice by many local planning authorities, but it needs to be spread more widely. Planning officers and councillors in local authorities must recognise the crucial role that diversification can play in sustaining and developing farm businesses.

**8.4.5.** The May seminar also found that most farmers were unfamiliar with the planning system. This results in many poor-quality applications. There is also anecdotal evidence that farmers may sometimes be discouraged by local authorities from submitting and pursuing worthwhile diversification proposals. Another concern was that planning guidance on transport *(PPG13)* is often being interpreted in a way which undermines other policies designed to encourage rural diversification.

**8.4.6.** The Government is taking steps to address these problems through:

- **Free consultancy advice** on planning is available to farmers who pursue diversification projects under the Rural Enterprise Scheme.

- We will issue **a planning policy statement** clarifying the positive approach we expect local authorities to take towards farm diversification proposals.

- **We are revising** *Planning Policy Guidance 13* to clarify the framework for considering the transport implications of rural development proposals. We are confident that this will lead to more diversification proposals being accepted by planning authorities.

- The Countryside Agency and RDAs issued a joint statement in September explaining how their organisations will work together to promote the right kind of development to meet the needs for rural businesses.

- DETR has commissioned fact-finding research on how local planning authorities deal with farmers and their proposals for diversification. This research will be completed in early 2001.

- DETR will publish a revised Farmer's Guide to the Planning System. This will be a user-friendly handbook on how the planning system works.

- **The Redundant Building Grant Scheme**, which previously operated only in Rural Priority Areas, has been extended in 2000–01 with an additional £4m, for farmers only, to cover the whole country. We are making available a further £4m of funding to meet demand before similar measures funded under the Rural Enterprise Scheme come on stream. (See also section 9.2 on planning policies)

## Diversification and the rating system

**8.4.7.** Farmers are already exempt from business rates. In its March 2000 *Action Plan*, the Government set out proposals to stimulate diversification into small-scale horse enterprises, such as stables for trekking or livery. We have since consulted publicly on proposals to introduce transitional rate relief for farmers diversifying into farm-based horse enterprises and in the light of that consideration we shall be consulting further on extending rate relief to farm diversification generally.

- **We will consult shortly on proposals to provide time limited rate relief for farmers diversifying into other non-farming activities.**

- **We will also consult on extending the agricultural exemption from rates to a range of flexible farming business arrangements,** including contract and share farming, and machinery pooling.

## Diversification into non-food crops

**8.4.8.** Agriculture has for centuries provided a wide range of materials other than foodstuffs. These include fibres (flax and hemp), oils (linseed and rape), dyes (woad and madder) medicines (willow and foxglove) and energy (coppice wood). Modern technology has expanded the range of products which can be produced from plants and the yields which can be obtained. Non-food crop products include automotive components, lubricants, nutritional supplements and feedstocks for speciality chemicals. These uses contribute to sustainable development, both in environmental terms by reducing greenhouse gas emissions, and in economic terms by boosting farm diversification and rural incomes. They also have the potential to create new jobs in rural areas. We are launching the following initiatives to stimulate these developments further:

- In response to a recent Foresight panel recommendation, **we are creating a new Government/Industry Non-Food Forum to give strategic advice on developing non-food applications of crops other than energy crops.** Too often, those promoting non-food uses complain that they run up against legislative and other bureaucratic barriers, and point out that the necessary industrial infrastructure is inadequate or non-existent. The forum will provide clear advice to Government and industry on what needs to be done – for example on research and infrastructure – to develop these non-food uses.

- A new **Energy Crops Scheme** under the ERDP launched by MAFF in October will provide planting grants for short-rotation willow or poplar coppice and for miscanthus, an energy grass. £30m in aid over seven years will enable 20–25,000 hectares to be planted, as a first tranche towards a national target of around 100,000 ha in the longer term. This will enable agriculture to begin contributing towards the Government's targets on reducing greenhouse gas emissions. Hundreds of jobs could be created in rural areas in the energy plants and supporting industries which use these crops.

- Under the ERDP, we are increasing the funding for both the **Woodland Grant Scheme** and the **Farm Woodland Premium Scheme** (see section 9.7).

Lavender – a non-food crop
Credit: ACTIN

## 8.5. Regulating only when it is really necessary, and removing burdens that are not justified

**8.5.1.** We underlined in our *Action Plan* in March 2000 a commitment to regulate only when it was really necessary. The *Action Plan* also explained that our policy on implementing EU obligations relating to farming would be to avoid all 'gold plating' of legislation, both in its implementation and enforcement; to regulate in the least bureaucratic and burdensome way; and to avoid implementing legislation ahead of specified EU deadlines.

**8.5.2.** The *Action Plan* contained a number of specific commitments to review and remove regulatory burdens affecting farmers. All of these have since been acted upon, and most have been completed. Progress reports are set out in a regular *Action Plan for Farming Bulletin* issued by MAFF. We are currently considering the recommendations of the Better

Regulation Task Force Review of environmental regulations and their impact on farming, and will respond shortly. The Food Standards Agency is also due to report in the coming months on its separate reviews of the current main measures to protect the public against BSE/vCJD in relation to the food chain, and of the Meat Hygiene Service's efficiency.

**8.5.3.** We believe it vital to maintain momentum in this area. To this end, in addition to the steps set out in the *Action Plan*, we will take forward the following new initiatives:

- We will increase the number of **overseas students** allowed to work on UK farms in the summer. The farming industry finds it increasingly difficult to find harvesting labour in order to meeting growing consumer demand. At present, some of the labour requirement is met through a seasonal agricultural worker scheme. This long-established youth mobility scheme enables a quota of non-EEA students to enter the UK each year to do seasonal work in agriculture and then return to their studies. Following discussion between the industry and the Home Office, it has been agreed that the present annual quota of 10,000 will be increased to 15,200.

- We will ensure that the recently announced review of **the UK organic food standards regulator** – UKROFS – includes within its scope an examination of the regulator's role in setting standards for organic produce, both where there are no EU standards and by supplementing EU standards.

- We will come forward with specific proposals within the next six months to **integrate on-farm inspections**. This will include proposals to reduce the number of on-farm cattle inspections, both by combining subsidy and cattle identification inspections and by better co-ordination between inspection authorities.

- We will introduce electronic data transfer in the **Cattle Tracing System**.

**8.5.4.** **Hygiene controls** are an essential protection for the public but they can impose unnecessary burdens. For example EU legislation lays down detailed requirements for slaughterhouses, including a high level of official inspection and supervision that is not related to the risks to consumers, and bears especially heavily on small and medium-sized slaughterhouses which are important to farmers seeking to diversify into new markets.

- As part of the *Action Plan for Farming* we are pressing for an early agreement and introduction of EU Commission proposals – produced under UK pressure over a number of years – to modernise food hygiene controls and replace unnecessarily detailed requirements with control measures based on risk assessment which will maintain high standards of food safety for consumers.

- An independent Task Force set up by the Food Standards Agency to review the burden of food regulations on small businesses, including farms, will report by the end of the year. It will seek to identify any unnecessary or disproportionate burdens and recommend solutions.

**8.5.5.** There is a wide range of advisory services available to farmers and land managers on the various schemes and activities covered in this chapter. We will look further at whether we can improve the accessibility, quality and relevance of this advice, and better integrate economic and environmental messages.

## 8.6. Farmers and the wider community

### Farming on the urban fringe

**8.6.1.** Farming on the urban fringe has its own special attributes and problems. Its landscape is vitally important in its own right and as a bridge to the wider countryside. Demand for access and amenity is high. Crime and vandalism can be problems. The Urban White Paper recognises the importance of agricultural and horticultural businesses in and around cities and towns and sets out our policies for dealing with problems such as crime and antisocial behaviour.

**8.6.2.** But urban fringe farmers also face the same challenges as the rest of farming. Our measures will help these farmers too. For example, the ERDP has a separate London chapter, programming group and budget for rural economy measures. And our initiatives to improve the planning environment will achieve a better dialogue and awareness between farmers and urban authority planners.

Yorkshire Coalfield Urban Fringe at Baildon, West Yorks
Credit: MAFF

- **The Fly Tipping Forum which brings together the Government, the Environment Agency, local authorities, the NFU and the Country Landowners Association is addressing the problem of fly tipping on farms.** It is assessing the scale of the problem, and will look at how the enforcement agencies can work more effectively together, including the pursuit of offenders and more effective deterrence.

## Measuring the public benefits which farming and land managers provide

**8.6.3.** Most of our landscape is the result of farming and other rural land uses, such as forestry. As the following chapters indicate, these land management activities – often through private investment and without any direct public support – can provide very significant public benefits through maintaining landscape features including hedges and other field boundaries and watercourses, and the wildlife they support. A fuller understanding of the implications of the challenges facing agriculture and land managers for the delivery of public benefits of this sort could be useful. It would also help to have more quantified information on the environmental and other public benefits provided by land managers, through a range of different land management approaches and their costs, to help in assessing whether public policies generally need adapting to encourage such benefits in the future.

- We will set up a **DETR/MAFF Review Group**, with representatives from other interested departments, the Countryside Agency, as well as farmers, land managers and conservation bodies, to advise on **how the public benefits which managed landscape and land-based enterprises provide can be better assessed**, including independent evaluation, across the full range of rural land uses and to advise on how these benefits can be sustained and increased. The work of this Group would also inform the European debate on action to sustain and increase benefits arising from land management and help to shape our approach to aspects of future negotiations on CAP reform.

---

### Land Management Initiatives

The Countryside Agency's £6m, seven year experimental Land Management Initiatives are seeking ways to encourage more sustainable land management by involving and bringing local communities and farmers closer together. The nine projects cover upland, arable, lowland pastoral and urban fringe landscapes across the English regions. The objectives for each project reflect the problems facing farming and rural communities within the different areas. Local people are therefore involved in highlighting the issues of concern and identifying solutions. Project activity will include:

- Helping land managers to identify and meet the needs of local communities;
- Whole farm appraisals – identifying all the natural and capital assets of the farm and skills of the farmer
- Adding value to farm produce by promoting links between quality products and a quality farmed landscape;
- Promoting the uptake of new ideas and technologies, such as integrated farm management and novel crops;
- Payments for the delivery of defined environmental goods;
- Investigating new ways of delivering support and advice to farmers bringing togther business and conversation advice.

Both existing and new forms of support will be used to deliver the projects. Lessons learned will help us to understand how to deliver a wider range of benefits from land management and will help in the shaping of future UK and EU policy.

# Part 2

## a *working* countryside – objective and spending

**Objective:**

- To facilitate the development of dynamic, competitive and sustainable economies in the countryside, tackling poverty in rural areas.

| £m | 1996–7 | 2000–01 | Projected for 2003–4 | Projected 2001/2–2003/4 |
|---|---|---|---|---|
| **Spending (£ million)** | | | | |
| Regional Development Agencies (urban and rural) | n/a | 1,250 | 1,700 | 4,700 |
| of which: | | | | |
| *Single Regeneration Budget (rural)* | n/a | 50 | *(Note 1)* | |
| *Rural Development Programme* | 25 | 29 | *(Note 1)* | |
| *Market Towns (RDA)* | n/a | – | 13 | 32 |
| Regional Selective Assistance | 10 | 9 | n/a | |
| Countryside Agency (enterprise) | n/a | 5 | 7 | 20 |
| EU Structural funds | 64 | 89 | 96 | 270 |
| CAP payments (UK) | 4,100 | 2,500 | 2,900 | 8,600 |
| England Rural Development Programme | 137 | 194 | 261 | 697 |
| of which: | | | | |
| *Agri-Environment* | 67 | 97 | 153 | 409 |
| *Forestry* | 12 | 24 | 32 | 88 |
| *Less Favoured Areas* | 28 | 44 | 35 | 113 |
| *Other* | 30 | 29 | 41 | 87 |
| Action Plan for Farming (Farming summit March 2000) | – | 200 | 80 | 303 |

Note 1. The constituent parts of the RDAs' new single budget, including rural, have yet to be determined

# Part 3

# a *protected* countryside

*We want to see a restored countryside in which the environment is protected and enhanced, and which all can enjoy*

# conserving and
## enhancing our countryside

## The issues

- Development pressures on the countryside have grown as the number of households has steadily increased and businesses and homeowners have moved out of urban areas to the country or rural fringe.
- Although the English landscape generally has been well protected through our planning system, particularly in Areas of Outstanding Natural Beauty and National Parks, continuing greenfield development is causing progressive loss of countryside.
- Too often the development that does occur in the countryside fails to respect its character and quality.
- Changes in agricultural practices have also affected the landscape and archaeological features.

## The future: what we want to see

- Reduced pressures for greenfield development through more successful cities and making the best use of recycled land. A planning framework which continues to safeguard our countryside while allowing rural communities to thrive. Landscapes will continue to evolve but in ways that strengthen their character and value.
- There will be stronger protection for our most valued landscapes in National Parks and Areas of Outstanding Natural Beauty through improved funding and management; and better understanding by all decision-makers of the distinctiveness and diversity of the wider countryside. Local village design statements will ensure that development is sited and designed to conserve and enhance valued landscape and heritage features of the countryside.
- Increased measures will be taken to promote tranquillity.
- Trees, woods and forests will have a more prominent place in the countryside. This will include an increase in the role of forestry in the rural economy, more woodlands on derelict and former industrial land, more woodlands available for people to visit and enjoy as well as an increase in the extent of semi-natural and native woodlands.

### Summary of measures

- Tackling development pressure through improving the attractiveness of urban areas and strong controls on building on greenfield sites;
- A more holistic approach to take better account of all landscapes in planning decisions;
- Consultation on applying environmental impact assessment procedures to major new agricultural activities which could affect landscape or wildlife;
- More funding for National Parks and AONBs, and stronger planning and management arrangements for AONBs;
- Doubling the number of new Countryside Stewardship Scheme agreements to enhance wildlife and landscape.

# 9

## Contents

**Mendips landscape**
Credit: The Countryside Agency, Jim Hallet

## 9.1. Introduction

**9.1.1.** Rural landscapes, green spaces, wildlife and the heritage features created by man's interaction with them lie at the heart of why people value the countryside so highly. They are a most precious asset, providing enjoyment, refreshment of body and mind, cultural inspiration, opportunities for improved health and expanding potential for recreation. The English countryside is, however, largely man-made and has evolved over thousands of years of settlement and agricultural use. For it to retain its vitality, we must allow for necessary change. Both the evolution of society itself and wider global trends such as climate change will, as in the past, continue the process.

**9.1.2. Our aim** is to manage this change in a way which recognises and where possible enhances the diversity and distinctiveness of the countryside and its amenity value for society as a whole. Our policies elsewhere in this White Paper emphasise our commitment to economic prosperity and social progress in the countryside. We also need to exercise good stewardship of our natural resources and to protect and enhance our environment.

*"Don't be in such a hurry to make the villages towns"*
*"Keep the rural areas rural, support the farming, support the communities which are the rural areas"*
*"Yeah, support the farmers, don't put pressure on them so that they end up having to sell to building concerns"*
*"Farming's one of the most important things in this area of course, because these are the people who look after the countryside"*

**9.1.3.** There will sometimes be hard choices, and not everyone will agree as to what should and should not be conserved. Ensuring that good decisions are taken for our descendants is one of our most difficult challenges. We also recognise that the conservation both of landscape and of wildlife often go hand in hand. Measures to help one will tend to help the other as, for instance, with hedgerows which are both a valued traditional landscape feature and are also the home of many forms of wildlife.

## 9.2. Tackling development pressure in the countryside: planning for rural areas

**9.2.1.** A key challenge is to get right the relationship between our towns and cities and the countryside. That is why we are publishing the Urban and Rural White Papers together. The Urban White Paper sets out how successful urban regeneration with its emphasis on higher quality design, improved services and better and more efficient use of urban land will help to stem migration from towns to the countryside. That will reduce the pressure on our countryside.

**9.2.3.** Development on farms and in villages will still be needed to provide homes and to support living and working communities. Where development does take place, we want this to be good quality and well planned. This means minimising land take, fully utilising existing buildings and previously developed land where possible; locating new building as far as possible where it will reduce rather than increase the need for transport; and respecting local character and environment. This needs commitment and imagination on the part of local authorities, local communities and developers alike. To help them achieve these objectives:

**9.2.4.** We are modernising our planning system so that it strikes a balance between protecting our countryside, providing for economic prosperity and promoting social inclusion.

- **Housing:** Our new planning guidance gives priority to the development of sustainable brownfield sites before building on greenfields. We have set a national target that, by 2008, 60% of additional housing should be built on previously developed land or reuse existing buildings. That will help prevent the unnecessary loss of countryside to development.

- We are encouraging **rural housing to be increasingly concentrated round market towns**, but with some small developments in villages where there is a particular need for affordable dwellings (see chapter 5).

- **Green belts:** We are committed to retaining green belt policy. Our record speaks for itself: during this Government 30,000 hectares of new green belt has been designated or proposed.

- **Town centres:** We have strengthened our planning guidance to protect town centres from out of town retail and leisure development. We want to put the heart back into our market towns.

- **Countryside:** We will continue with our policy of safeguarding the open countryside against inappropriate development, protecting our best landscapes and conserving our wildlife. We will be updating our planning guidance *(PPG7)* to take account of the needs of the living, working countryside.

- **Redundant farm buildings:** farm diversification projects can often make use of existing farm buildings. We are in favour of ensuring that good quality existing buildings are reused to provide jobs in the countryside and we are going to make this clear in planning guidance. Not all farm buildings are suitable for reuse – some, for instance, are unsightly and were never designed to be permanent – and we will have safeguards to ensure that a proper balance is struck between helping the rural economy and protecting the environment.

**Very derelict barn converted to provide design/office space**
Credit: Countryside Agency

- **Planning for transport:** we will be issuing new planning guidance which implements our policy of strengthening market towns by making them the focus for development of new jobs, housing and services. Our new guidance will make it clear that new employment opportunities – such as jobs in redundant farm buildings – should not be ruled out simply because they are in less accessible locations, especially where they can be reached by walking, cycling or public transport.

- **Open space:** open spaces like parks and play areas are especially important to quality of life in towns and villages. We will be issuing a new planning framework which will help safeguard existing recreational open spaces and create new ones where necessary.

- **Speeding up planning applications:** nearly 500,000 planning applications are made each year, 38% in rural districts. Decision-making needs to be efficient. We are using the new Best Value regime to raise performance and we are considering setting statutory performance targets to drive up the performance of the poorest authorities.

- **Village design statements:** we want local people to have a role in the planning process. We have set out (chapter 12) our intention that more villages and towns should prepare village design statements which can be adopted as a supplement to the main development plan of a local authority.

- **Planning obligations:** these are the arrangement by which contributions from developers can be used to offset the negative consequences of development or to secure positive benefits that will make development more sustainable by, for example, providing new infrastructure or money for local environmental improvements. **We will consult shortly on a range of options, including impact fees (see box) and broadening the range of local improvements which can be requested under a planning obligation.**

**9.2.5. New buildings in the countryside need to be well thought out and designed to fit in with their surroundings.** Our agenda for good architecture and for better urban design and planning skills applies equally in rural areas. The Commission for Architecture and the Built Environment, described in the Urban White Paper, is concerned with settlements of all sizes and will seek to involve communities in the future of their environment.

---

*Rural Economies* Report: planning provision

This report by the Performance and Innovation Unit (PIU) discussed the impacts that granting planning permission can have: positive for the value of land and buildings, but often negative for the local community (eg increased traffic and demands on local services). Under planning obligations a developer may agree to provide services or amenities (for example, an element of social housing, or a children's play area) to the local community as part of the approval process. However the PIU noted that (amongst other problems) this generally fails to address directly the off-site effects it is intended to compensate for. The PIU suggested that we examine two ideas in more detail:

- **Offsetting** involves developers being required to offset the external or off-site effects of the development. For example, the loss of an area of greenfield habitat might require the establishment of a nature reserve in its place.

- **Impact fees** involve an explicit schedule of charges for the various external and off-site effects of development. This can directly capture the costs to the local authority (or indeed the economy or society more widely) of some of these off-site effects, such as increased demands on public services; and could provide the funding for local authorities to offset other effects, such as replacing lost habitats.

**Award-winning new development – Offices (BI useclass) at Broughton Hall in CLA Farm and Country Building Award scheme 1999**
Credit: Gerry Passman

*"You don't want to walk into the countryside and see these modern boxes littering fields … Some fit in, but the majority don't, and I think if you have a rural setting then you want a rural style of property rather than a little concrete box"*

### Flooding in Rural Areas

As recent events have indicated, both rural and urban areas can suffer flood damage as a result of extreme weather conditions. Whilst individual extreme weather events cannot be attributed purely to climate change, **climate change** is expected to lead to more extreme weather, such as heavy rainfall, becoming more frequent and this, together with sea level rise, is contributing to more flooding. We intend to enhance and speed up the research at the Hadley Centre and the UK Climate Impacts Programme to improve our prediction and assessment of the effects of climate change. In particular this will look at the link between climate change and the severe floods we have had in recent years.

The Government is looking at **long term action** to deal with the effects of climate change generally, and flooding in particular. Land use and land use management practices, for instance, can have a significant impact on the capacity of the land to retain water and reduce the severity of flooding.

**Our approach** is one of flood alleviation, that is to reduce risks to people and the developed and natural environment. It will never be possible to protect every piece of property against all flood risk. In some cases flood defences work to protect the environment but in every case they must take account of the environmental impact. MAFF works in partnership with operating authorities – the Environment Agency, Internal Drainage Boards and local authorities – who are responsible for determining the works programme locally within the policy framework established by MAFF. We will explore the potential to bring other partners into discussions, where they have particular expertise in this area.

An effective **flood defence** infrastructure is in place as evidenced by the performance in the recent floods. A total of around 1.8m properties in England are at some risk of flooding and in the recent events only some 6000 have been flooded. Current national spending on flood defence is some £380m annually and will rise to £430m annually by 2003–4. Additional funding of £51m was announced on 4 November 2000. As part of this we will be looking to make further significant improvements in flood warning, to carry out whole river catchment area assessments to improve our ability to plan flood management, and to look at factors, such as land use, that have affected the most vulnerable areas. The answers may require significant re-thinking of our land use priorities. The major part of the additional funding will be targeted on investment in an accelerated programme of river flood defence works.

### Flooding in Rural Areas – continued

We also need to discourage further **housing development** in areas of high flood risk.

We consulted earlier this year on draft planning guidance in relation to areas at flood risk. The new guidance will emphasise the need to take a precautionary and sequential approach in minimising the amount of new housing in high-risk areas. When development occurs, developers need to fund provision and maintenance of adequate defences as part of the development and ensure a sustainable design, minimising water run off. We will issue revised guidance shortly.

We have also asked the water regulators to look at a **more sustainable water management** and in particular at how integrated management approaches can help to reduce both the incidence and the impact of flooding. (see 10.3.14-15)

Looking over Upton-on-Severn
Credit: Richard Findon

## 9.3. Understanding, evaluating and protecting countryside diversity and character

**9.3.1.** Rural landscapes are changing as landscape features such as hedges and dry-stone walls lose their economic functions. Historic features have also been in decline with over 22,500 or 16% of recorded archaeological monuments lost since 1945, a rate of over one a day. We need to find ways of ensuring that the valued features and attributes of the whole countryside are conserved and enhanced.

**9.3.2.** Our aim is to ensure that the things people value about the countryside are properly taken into account in planning and similar decisions; and that local communities have the opportunity to play a part in shaping the landscape around them.

## Countryside character

To raise understanding of what gives the different areas of our countryside their diversity and distinctiveness, the Countryside Agency, English Nature and English Heritage have collaborated in developing the countryside character approach. Following the national mapping project, more detailed descriptions of each of the 159 English character areas have been published. To help those interested in carrying out character assessment at sub-regional or more local level, the Countryside Agency will publish shortly revised landscape character assessment guidance and has carried out county demonstration case studies for Durham and Oxfordshire. The Agency has also established an information exchange and support service, with its own newsletter (Countryside Character Network Update) reporting the latest developments in the application of the countryside character approach, and highlighting regular workshop training opportunities (details can be found on the Countryside Agency website at www.countryside.gov.uk).

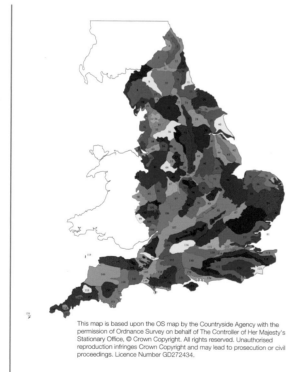

This map is based upon the OS map by the Countryside Agency with the permission of Ordnance Survey on behalf of The Controller of Her Majesty's Stationary Office, © Crown Copyright. All rights reserved. Unauthorised reproduction infringes Crown Copyright and may lead to prosecution or civil proceedings. Licence Number GD272434.

**The Character of England – Major landscape characteristics – see box above.**

### Safeguarding the landscape

**9.3.3.** It has been long-standing Government policy to protect 'best and most versatile' (BMV) farmland from development, as a national agricultural resource. This is land (about a third of all farmland in England) which can be used for the widest range of farming uses and is the most productive. The Minister of Agriculture has been able to intervene in decisions over development of such land.

## Rural Economies report: BMV land

The PIU report questioned whether there was a continuing national interest in protecting BMV land, and suggested that removing such protection would facilitate economic adjustment in rural areas. Instead, decisions about the protection or development of BMV land should be entirely matters for local authorities. But in order to improve upon the present arrangements, the PIU suggested that removing protection for BMV land should be dependent on the introduction of a new national framework for protecting areas of high environmental value. This new framework should be based on the principles of sustainable development, and flexible enough to take account of the possible consequences of future changes to local circumstances and priorities; but it should take account of local distinctiveness of the land and give stronger protection to land of exceptional environmental value. The PIU envisaged a mechanism to draw all the elements together so as to inform planning processes and decisions at both national and local levels.

**9.3.4.** We believe that planning decisions should consider the **overall value of the land** in deciding what countryside should have the greater protection. Agricultural quality should be treated only as one factor. The quality of landscapes, wildlife and habitats, recreational amenity and our historic and cultural heritage are equally important and must be weighed in planning decisions. We need effective ways to identify which are important to any particular decision and how they should be taken into account. It would be wrong to protect an area simply because of its agricultural quality at the expense of another that offers much greater countryside character.

- The Government's policy is that the countryside should be safeguarded for its own sake, and we will continue strict controls over development in the open countryside;

- We will continue to give the highest level of planning protection to our very best landscapes, in National Parks and Areas of Outstanding Natural Beauty;

- But we want local authorities to seek ways to enrich the countryside as a whole, not just in the protected areas, and maintain its distinctive local features. The box above describes an approach to the assessment of **countryside character** and sources of advice on its use. To help local decision-makers, we will provide **good practice guidance** on evaluating in a more integrated way factors such as landscape quality, local character, biodiversity and soil quality. We accept as a long term goal the PIU's suggestion of a single evaluation framework.

- To achieve **a more holistic approach**, decisions about proposed development affecting the best and most versatile agricultural land will be made locally through the planning process. National best practice guidance and advice provided by Government will ensure no diminution of protection for the countryside overall.

- The powers of the Minister of Agriculture to intervene in decisions on **BMV land** will be repealed.

- For the time being, the Agricultural Land Classification will be kept up to date to assist local planning authorities in making decisions affecting BMV land. **MAFF technical expertise** will be available to advise local planning authorities about agricultural land quality issues;

- To further assist decisions on agricultural land we will publish for consultation a draft **Soil Strategy** for England which will identify the need to manage the extent, diversity and quality of soils.

## Quarrying and minerals extraction

**9.3.5.** It is not just new development which can affect communities and the local landscape. Quarrying and minerals extraction can have intensive and sometimes long-lasting effects on rural environments. We need mineral extraction to provide for the needs of society and the economy. But we need to take account of the environmental costs of aggregates extraction when deciding how much society needs. And when there is extraction, modern techniques for working and restoring sites should be used to protect the soil and return the land to an agricultural or alternative use such as nature conservation, woodland or amenity. The Government has already announced a number of measures to achieve this:

- From 2002 we will place **a levy of £1.60 per tonne on sales of primary aggregate**. This measure, announced in the last budget, will ensure that the quarrying of aggregates (which go into concrete and other materials used for road building and maintenance and for the construction of buildings) carries a price tag that will encourage the use of alternative products made from recycled construction materials or from wastes;

- The Budget 2000 announced that the revenues raised from the levy would be recycled to business partly via a new Sustainability Fund aimed at delivering local environmental benefits to areas subject to the environmental costs of aggregates extraction. The Government has recently consulted on how this fund could best be used and has decided **to allocate £35 million to the new Sustainability** Fund that will be introduced alongside the Aggregates Levy in April 2002. In the run up to Budget 2001, the Government will hold discussions with the devolved administrations on whether there is scope for setting up a UK-wide Fund with shared objectives that maximise the environmental benefits of the fund and complement the aggregates levy.

- We will issue **new planning policy guidance on aggregate supply in 2001**, with the aim of getting away from the present mechanistic 'predict and provide' approach by making more realistic estimates of future requirements, and providing a greater opportunity for these estimates to be tested at a local and regional level. We also want to find better ways of ensuring that environmental issues are built into the decision taking;

- We are applying the European Directives on Environmental Impact Assessment to the periodic statutory reviews of conditions at existing sites, with effect from November 2000. This will ensure that the remaining programme of work at long-term quarries will be subject to the same environmental scrutiny as would be a proposed new quarry.

**Quarry at Leinthal Earls, Herefordshire**
Credit: The Countryside Agency, Archie Miles

**Stone wall restoration**
Credit: The Countryside Agency, Simon Warner

### The influence of agriculture

**9.3.6.** Some of the unwelcome changes to our countryside have resulted from modern agricultural practices and the intensification of farming encouraged by the Common Agricultural Policy. The length of managed hedgerows fell sharply up to 1990, although since then there have been more incentives for new hedge planting and there are new tougher regulations – introduced in 1997 – on when hedgerows may be removed. Cultivation is the main cause of loss of archaeological monuments in the countryside. New intensive agricultural activities, for instance when farmers plough up hitherto uncultivated land, or drain such land as part of improvements to the grazing, can have a major impact on landscapes and on wildlife.

- Under the ERDP we are doubling the number of new **Countryside Stewardship Scheme agreements** offered each year to bring about a significant increase in the area and range of habitats, species, landscapes and historic features covered. Through such agri-environment schemes we have already paid for the restoration of more than 1400 kilometres of traditional stone walls. These are the schemes under which farmers are paid subsidy to take measures which conserve and improve the landscape, wildlife and historic heritage of the countryside. Such schemes can also contribute indirectly to sustaining countryside skills and extending employment opportunities;

- MAFF will shortly be going out to consultation on the application of **environmental impact assessment procedures** to projects intended to make more intensive agricultural use of uncultivated land. The proposed procedures, which derive from obligations contained in European Community legislation, will seek to minimise the regulatory burdens on farmers and will apply only in cases where projects are likely to have significant environmental impacts. In such cases, the farmer would be asked to submit an environmental statement so that the impacts could be fully assessed.

### Historic heritage

**9.3.7.** We are currently reviewing our policies for **the historic environment**; the first stage is being conducted by English Heritage. The outcome will be announced next year, and the need for further measures in rural areas considered. MAFF already funds and will continue to fund research to help develop management strategies for archaeological sites on arable land, concentrating on where damage is most serious and looking at ways of minimising or remedying damage.

### A role for everybody in looking after our countryside

**9.3.8.** We also want to encourage the community as a whole to care for their landscape and historic heritage.

In this Local Heritage Initiative project children from Brigstock Village School recorded their observations about the village and influenced action plans for landscape change.
Credit: The Countryside Agency

- **The Local Heritage Initiative**, devised by the Countryside Agency and supported by the Heritage Lottery Fund, provides a national grant scheme that helps local groups to investigate, explain and care for their local landscape, landmarks, traditions and culture;

- We will continue to support the **voluntary sector**, through grants for specific projects and through the provision of core funding to key partners, in the invaluable work they do to conserve and enhance our environment, and we allow volunteers' time to count towards match funding for grant proposes. We want to encourage as many people as possible to join voluntary organisations such as the BTCV (British Trust for Conservation Volunteers), the Wildlife Trusts and Community Service Volunteers which offer volunteers the help and experience they need to get things done.

## 9.4. Promoting tranquillity

**9.4.1.** It is not just its physical features which gives the countryside its unique character; there are also less tangible features such as tranquillity and lack of noise and visual intrusion, dark skies and remoteness from the visible impact of civilisation.

### Noise

**9.4.2.** There will always be sources of noise in the countryside, and many of these – such as noise from harvesting and livestock – are themselves representative of activities which have long been central to the rural way of life. But protecting the countryside from further intrusion of noise is not a luxury. It is about preserving and promoting a feature that is genuinely valued by residents and visitors alike. Noise can also disturb the breeding of vulnerable species, and thereby undermine biodiversity.

- **We will consult next year on a national noise strategy**. The strategy will include mapping the main sources and areas of noise – a major new exercise for which we have put aside £13m. In rural areas, this will involve major road and rail links. We aim to complete the mapping by 2004. The maps will enable policy to take account more accurately of the implications of noise sources for rural areas, including major reservoirs of rural tranquillity and valued local pockets of tranquillity.

**9.4.3.** In the meantime, we are taking a number of specific measures to reduce noise pollution, particularly from traffic and quarrying operations.

- We will be putting **low noise surfaces** on 60% of the trunk road network, including all concrete roads, over the next 10 years. This, together with other new techniques of road building and repair, can cut road noise by half – bringing significant relief to the many rural areas affected by road noise on busy roads. Our policies for road safety and reducing the impact of traffic in rural areas, including the 'quiet roads' initiative, described in section 6.6, will also contribute to promoting greater tranquillity in rural areas;

- We will introduce revised planning guidance next year to enable local authorities to apply suitable **low noise limits to new or extended quarries**. They will also be able – subject to payment of compensation where necessary – to apply lower noise limits than at present when existing permissions to quarry are reviewed.

### Light pollution

**9.4.4.** 'Light pollution' of the night sky is an increasing intrusion into the countryside at night, and it is an issue that we want all rural local authorities to take into account in their planning and other decisions. Local planning authorities have powers, for instance, to control many external lighting installations.

The adverse effects of lighting can be reduced or prevented by using the right technology, design and installation. Road lighting is one of the main problems, and the Highways Agency is now using lighting that focuses the light onto the road surface – as here on the M62 over Saddleworth Moor.
Credit: Highways Agency

## 9.5.  Measuring countryside quality

**9.5.1.**  We have recently completed **Countryside Survey 2000**, a major survey of the English countryside. The results will be published shortly, and will provide extensive information on changes to the countryside during the 1990s. In the light of this information, we will be considering what further action needs to be taken to protect and enhance countryside features such as hedges.

**9.5.2.**  The variety of the things we value in the countryside means that we do not yet have an agreed way of measuring whether, overall, the quality of the countryside is being maintained. But it is important for us to be clear about the nature and overall direction of change, to see whether our strategy is working.

- We will publish **a measure of change in countryside quality**, including issues such as biodiversity, tranquillity, heritage and landscape character using analysis of the results of Countryside Survey 2000 and based on the Agencies' character areas map.

## 9.6.  Enhancing the protection of our most valuable landscapes

### National Parks and AONBs

**9.6.1.**  Our most valuable landscapes have long been designated and administered as National Parks and areas of outstanding natural beauty (AONBs). We are bringing in new powers, administrative and funding changes to improve their protection and management.

**Peak District National Park**
Credit: The Countryside Agency, Mike Williams

**National Parks** cover 7.6% of the land area of England. They attract over 100 million visitors annually, and have led the way over the past 50 years in making the countryside accessible to people. The Parks are designated as areas of national importance both for their landscape and wildlife and for open air recreation. Most of the land in National Parks is in the hands of farmers and other private landowners. Some areas are managed by public bodies such as the Forestry Commission, the National Park Authorities or English Nature and some are managed by voluntary conservation organisations such as the National Trust.
**AONBs** are also some of our very finest and special landscapes, designated by the Countryside Agency under the same legislation as the National Parks. Like the National Parks, they are areas considered as a national asset, but principally for their natural beauty rather than opportunities for open air recreation. Nevertheless, many AONBs attract a considerable number of visitors and face considerable pressures due to their popularity. There are 37 AONBs in England, covering some 15.6% of the territory. Government funding for AONBs is channelled through the Countryside Agency.

**Fovant Down, Cranborne Chase and Wiltshire Downs AONB**
Credit: The Countryside Agency, Jim Hallett

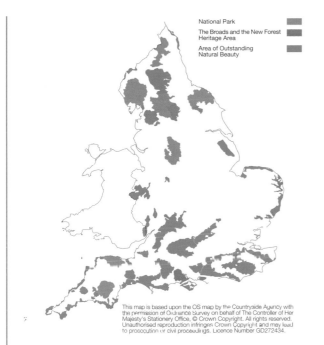

This map is based upon the OS map by the Countryside Agency with the permission of Ordnance Survey on behalf of The Controller of Her Majesty's Stationery Office, © Crown Copyright. All rights reserved. Unauthorised reproduction infringes Crown Copyright and may lead to prosecution or civil proceedings. Licence Number GD272434.

**National Parks and Areas of Outstanding Natural Beauty**

- We will continue to increase the Government's direct **grants to the National Parks** over the next decade and implement a system to ensure that the grant is distributed more equitably among the Parks, using an approach based on an objective assessment of needs. Our aim is to bring the management of all the Parks up to the standard of the best. We have already shown the importance we attach to the National Parks by increasing their funding by 13% from £23m in 1998–99 to £26m in 2000–01;

- The Countryside Agency has begun the process of designation of **new National Parks in the South Downs and the New Forest.** The current eight National Parks (including the Norfolk and Suffolk Broads) were established between 1951 and 1989. We think that there should continue to be a distinction between National Parks (as areas where opportunities to enjoy their special qualities should be promoted by an authority established for that purpose) and AONBs, and by and large we think that the right decisions have been made on which areas should be National Parks and which should be AONBs. But it has been strongly argued that there is a case for creating new National Parks to include the New Forest and the South Downs. The designation process will involve extensive local consultation to ensure the best arrangements, and is likely to take some two to three years. The final decisions will take account of what emerges from this consultation.

- **Stronger planning protection for AONBs.** We formally confirmed in *a Parliamentary answer, June 2000* that, in terms of landscape beauty, AONBs were equivalent to National Parks and that planning policies for the protection of the landscape should also be equivalent. This removed an anomaly which could be perceived as giving AONBs less protection than National Parks from unsuitable development;

**New Forest – traditional pony round-up (or 'drift')**
Credit: The Countryside Agency, Tony Heathcote

- **Stronger management arrangements for AONBs.** The Countryside and Rights of Way Bill, currently before Parliament, requires local authorities to adopt, within three years, a statutory management plan for each AONB. Management plans will provide the clear strategy and particular targets needed to improve conservation and enhancement of AONBs. Grants will be available from the Countryside Agency. In addition, the Bill will allow **Conservation Boards to be created for individual AONBs** where there would be particular benefit and there is local support for doing so, for example in the larger AONBs which cross a number of local authority boundaries. Our aim is to establish satisfactory management arrangements in all AONBs by 2005;

- **We have increased the funding for AONBs almost threefold over the last three years and will be increasing it further.**

113

**9.6.2. Planning in National Parks** can be a contentious issue with policies and decisions criticised on the one hand for being too restrictive, and on the other for giving insufficient weight to conservation purposes. The Countryside Agency is setting up training seminars for National Park Authority Members to help them assess the different priorities. This complements a wider initiative, as part of Modernising Planning, to encourage better training in planning for councillors in local authorities.

**9.6.3.** Particularly if new National Parks are established in the New Forest and South Downs, some changes may be desirable to allow regimes better tailored to the circumstances of individual Parks. We intend to undertake a policy review beginning in 2001 which will look at a range of issues: governance, policy remit, the distribution of funding and the legislation affecting the Parks.

## Commons

**9.6.4. Commons** are a particular and valued feature of the English countryside which cover 370,000 hectares or 4% of the land area of England and are appreciated by all for their special open and uncultivated character. Traditional farming activities have maintained this valued character and handed it down through the centuries, and the commons are vital to the viability of many upland livestock farms. Many are valued for their wildlife and plant life.

> ### What are commons?
> Though their ultimate origins are obscure, commons are generally taken to have emerged from the medieval manorial system. The least agriculturally productive land, or the "waste of the manor", was often used for communal grazing, cutting of peat, gathering firewood or bracken and other activities now recognised as rights of common. Often misunderstood as land belonging to or free for the use of all, most common land is privately owned and rights of common are for the most part exercisable only by owners of specific properties in the vicinity of the common – these are the commoners. General public access is not at present a right on most commons (although it is tolerated on many). The Countryside and Rights of Way Bill, currently before Parliament, will introduce a new right of access for open air recreation to all commons.

**Common at East Runton, Norfolk**
Credit: The Countryside Agency, David Burton

**9.6.5.** Although the ancient regimes covering common land have worked well over the years, there are now pressures which mean that a review is needed. For example, when too many commoners graze their sheep on a common, this can cause real environmental damage. Moreover, rights of common can be bought out by the owner of the land, and the common deregistered, losing its special protection. 65% of common land has no remaining rights of common over it and as a consequence is at risk of de-registration.

- We have been consulting on possible **improvements to the law on commons** in *Greater Protection and Better Management of Common Land in England and Wales*. We plan to legislate as soon as Parliamentary time allows to provide for the protection of all commons for the benefit of future generations; we want to increase our ability to tackle overgrazing wherever it occurs and to provide fairer and more effective systems of registration and management. We will also look to improve the arrangements for town and village greens.

## 9.7. Woodlands and forestry

**9.7.1.** It is often assumed that trees are planted just for their timber. But woodlands and forests are also immense assets in terms of landscape, nature conservation and recreation. We want forestry in future to be an investment in the beauty and prosperity of the countryside, as well as a commercial asset.

**9.7.2.** In medieval times, large parts of England were covered by forests, many protected from clearance for farming because they were royal hunting forests. The New Forest is now one of the few remnants of the royal hunting forests, and over the centuries there has been massive deforestation as agricultural activity has increased. With 8% of the land area under woodlands, England is one of the least forested areas in the European Community.

- **We are determined to reverse this decline.** We want a significant increase in woodland cover across England; and we want to encourage tree planting whose main priorities are visual, environmental and recreational as well as commercial.

**The Forestry Commission** is the Government Department responsible for forestry policy. It regulates forestry activities in England, provides grant aid to woodland owners, and – through its Forest Enterprise Agency – it manages the Government's forest estate. It is:

- the largest land manager (265,000 hectares);
- the largest timber producer (1.5m cubic metres a year);
- the largest provider of informal countryside recreation with about 50 million vists a year)

It is financed through its commercial activities, including sales of timber from its forests, and through the Forestry Fund voted annually by Parliament.

### Forestry: a true multi-use activity

**9.7.3.** Our forestry strategy *A New Focus for England's Woodlands*, published in December 1998, represents a quiet revolution in forestry policy. Gone are the days when forestry policy largely consisted of encouraging the planting of serried rows of conifers. Generating an economic return will still be important, but it will sit alongside other objectives. In future, our aim is to use forestry for rural development and economic regeneration, and for the environment and conservation.

### Forestry for rural development
The Forestry Commission will harvest four million cubic metres of timber from the nation's forest estate between 2001 and 2004, thus helping sustain rural employment and reducing our dependence on imported supplies. Over 19,000 people work in the forestry and wood processing industries in England. Recent research carried out for the Forestry Commission shows that over 90% of economic benefits of these jobs accrue locally. Our aim is to ensure that new and existing woodlands are managed in a way that brings continued benefits to local economies, creating jobs and wealth.

Extraction of oak and hornbeam logs from the National Trust's Hatfield Forest in Essex
Credit: Forestry Commission

### Forestry for economic regeneration
Woodlands can be very effective in improving the environment in and around towns, particularly through planting on formerly derelict land. Forestry Commission research has shown that trees can often be successfully planted on land such as ex-landfill sites and derelict coal pits which frequently have few alternative uses. £9m has been have been made available from the Government's Capital Modernisation Fund to plant on damaged ex-industrial land in the Mersey, Red Rose and Thames Chase Community Forest areas.

New woodland being established on a former landfill site in the Ingrebourne Valley, Thames Chase Community Forest.
Credit: Forestry Commission

**Picknickers at Symonds Yat Rock in the Forest of Dean**
Credit: Forestry Commission

**Learning about red squirrel conservation in Thetford Forest, Norfolk**
Credit: Forestry Commission

**9.7.4.** There are a range of grants and incentives to support woodland creation and management. The main ones are the Forestry Commission's Woodland Grant Scheme which provides variable incentives for people to create and manage woodlands depending on the type of planting and the extent of public benefit conferred; and MAFF's Farm Woodland Premium Scheme, which encourages the creation of new woodlands on farmland.

- Under the England Rural Development Programme we are increasing the budget of the **Woodland Grant and Farm Woodland Premium Schemes** bringing total expenditure to £216m over the seven years of the programme.

### The National Forest

**9.7.5.** In addition, the Government finances the **National Forest Company**, a public body set up specially to create greater woodland coverage over a large area of the East Midlands, much of it scarred by the legacy of coal mining. It has the task of increasing afforestation in its area from its original level of 6% to 30%, and has so far succeeded in planting over 1,500 hectares of new woodlands.

### Working in Partnership

**9.7.6.** A vital role is played by the voluntary sector and public/private sector partnerships in promoting woodlands. Bodies pursuing shared forestry goals include the Woodland Trust (which by acquiring woodland sites brings them into care and protection in perpetuity), the RSPB, the National Trust, and many small but committed bodies such as the National Small Woods Association and individual Groundwork Trusts. A substantial proportion of England's woodlands is owned by private landowners. Our aim is to continue to work with them to increase the area of England's woodlands that are managed in a sustainable way. We will also encourage local planning authorities and others to use trees and woodlands to the full for the benefit of the local population.

**Tree planting – part of South West Forest's training programme**
Credit. South West Forest

## Case Study – South West Forest

The South West Forest is pioneering a new approach to integrated rural development in parts of Cornwall and Devon. A broad partnership of aims to reinforce the links between people and rural land by using woodland planting and management as a catalyst for the sustainable regeneration of a remote rural area. In the process it will:

- Double the woodland cover by planting 30,000 hectares over two generations;
- Provide a supplement to farming incomes and jobs;
- Provide other small scale rural employment;
- Enhance landscape and biodiversity;
- Stimulate employment opportunities for instance in tourism and recreation.

Opportunities include the establishment of forestry skills and adding value to rural businesses, wood products and craft industries, country sports, coppicing for energy biomass, rural tourism, and hopefully larger scale economic developments.

An important part of the initiative will be arranging for training in the new and wider skills needed.

A new Forest Centre will act as a gateway for visitors and educational establishments wishing to explore and understand the surrounding countryside.

The initiative is being supported by the Forestry Commission through a special locational supplement and challenge fund, as well as by European funds, MAFF, local authorities, other countryside bodies and individuals.

# restoring and
## maintaining wildlife diversity and the natural environment

**10**

## The issues

- Loss of wildlife habitats due to changes in agricultural practices (including intensification, with its greater mechanisation, fertiliser and pesticide use) and a general loss of biodiversity – for example numbers of farmland birds declined by 36% between 1970 and 1998.
- The number of wildlife species has also been declining, particularly since the 1970s, and many species are now at risk of disappearing from this country.
- Many of our important wildlife sites need restoration or enhanced management, for instance only about 60% of sites of special scientific interest are estimated at present to be in a favourable condition.
- Wider impacts on the natural environment for example on water management from development and changing agricultural practice.
- Over the longer term, climate change is likely to bring new challenges, and preparing to meet these will be an important preoccupation.

## The future: what we want to see

- Better protection for wildlife. Expanded agri-environment schemes and more promotion of best practices in agriculture will help reverse the long-term decline in farmland birds by 2020. 95% of nationally important wildlife sites will be brought into favourable condition by 2010, with increased funding both through English Nature and through agri-environment schemes, and through the new measures, in the Countryside and Rights of Way Bill to improve the management and protection of SSSIs.
- A new strategy and targets for the 400 species and habitats identified in the UK Biodiversity Action Plan for priority action. There will be more rational policies on imported species; and heavier sanctions against wildlife crime. The need to preserve biodiversity will increasingly be accepted as automatically to be taken into account in both government and private sector decisions.

- More sustainable water management and an approach which safeguards environmental capital.

> ### Summary of measures
> - Government targets to reverse the decline in farmland birds by 2020 and to bring 95% of nationally important wildlife sites into favourable condition by 2010;
>
> - New national guidelines for the identification and management of local wildlife sites;
>
> - New planning guidance on nature conservation and biodiversity to ensure that they are better taken into account in local decisions;
>
> - A new biodiversity strategy for England to carry forward the action plans which have already been developed for species and habitats identified as particular priorities;
>
> - A new area-based Hill Farm Allowance Scheme.
>
> - Fundamental review of policy on alien and invasive species.

# 10

## Contents

## 10.1. Introduction

**10.1.1.**  Because the overwhelming majority of land in England has been actively managed – largely for farming – for hundreds of years, the pattern of habitats and species of wildlife that has emerged is especially sensitive to changes in the way that the countryside is used and managed. This has resulted over the centuries in a richer and more varied wildlife than climate and geography alone might have produced, but also in a vulnerability, well illustrated over the last 50 years. Changes in agricultural practices have been linked to a serious decline in farmland wildlife, exemplified by the 36% fall in the populations of farmland birds since 1970. One of the Government's Public Service Agreement targets is to reverse this decline.

**10.1.2.**  Our aim over the next 10 years is to:

- Provide better protection and management of the network of specially designated wildlife sites;
- Achieve – or at least move significantly towards achieving – sustainable populations of species at risk;
- Restore and enhance disappearing habitats.

### What is Biodiversity?

Biodiversity is the amazing richness and variety of life. It includes all living things from the tiniest insect to the mightiest oak tree. Biodiversity is found everywhere, in window boxes and wild woods, roadsides and rain forests, snow fields and the sea shore.

We, too, are part of biodiversity and depend on it for our quality of life. Our essential goods and services depend on the variety and variability of genes, species and habitats. They feed and clothe us and also provide housing, medicines and spiritual nourishment. Nor do we exist in isolation. Our interdependence with other species is essential to the healthiness of the planet as a whole and we should hand on to future generations an evironment no less rich than the one we inherited.

**Muker Meadows SSSI, North Yorkshire – A traditional upland haymeadow**
Credit: English Nature, Peter Wakely

**10.1.3.**  We will do this by promoting agricultural practices which enhance biodiversity; ensuring that the adverse effects on wildlife and its habitats of other necessary activities are avoided or minimised; making sure that everybody is conscious of their responsibilities towards maintaining biodiversity; pursuing action plans for priority species and habitats; and addressing future threats such as alien and invasive species and climate change.

## The economic benefits of wildlife conservation

Wildlife conservation benefits rural economies in different ways:

**Employment** in nature conservation in England was estimated to total 8,000 full time equivalent jobs in 1991–92. Recent surveys by the RSPB estimate that the natural environment sector employs 1,400 people in South West England and a further 1,400 in North West England;

**Expenditure** by nature conservation organisations on goods and services provide jobs and incomes in local businesses. For example, more than £57 million is spent annually in managing the South West's natural environment, including over £1.2 million spent on managing heathlands in Dorset;

**Agri-environment and woodland management schemes** offer land managers opportunities to gain revenue and employment by managing wildlife habitats in the wider countryside. ESAs, Countryside Stewardship, organic farming and woodland management schemes such as the Wessex Coppice project have all been shown to benefit wildlife and support rural jobs and incomes.

**Wildlife tourism** brings also growing benefits to local economies. RSPB reserves in the UK are estimated to bring additional visitor spending of at least £11m to local economies each year, supporting more than 300 FTE tourism jobs. A recent survey of visitors to six sites on the North Norfolk coast found that people attracted to the area mainly by its birds and wildlife spend more than £6m annually in the local economy.

## 10.2. Designated sites

**10.2.1.** At the heart of our policy to conserve and enhance wildlife is the network of nationally designated wildlife sites, the sites of special scientific interest (SSSIs). But biodiversity is not just a national matter, as wildlife does not recognise international boundaries. The UK is therefore co-operating actively in European Community measures to set up a European network of wildlife sites, known as Natura 2000 (see box on page 122).

- **We have set ourselves an ambitious target of ensuring that 95% of the nationally important sites (SSSIs) in England are in favourable condition by March 2010**, and we are taking a number of measures to help achieve this target and to meet our obligations in respect of the Natura 2000 network and other internationally important sites in England.

- We are taking legislation through Parliament in the Countryside and Rights of Way Bill to **increase the protection and enhance the management of SSSIs** by:

  - Giving English Nature a new power to refuse consent indefinitely for damaging operations;

  - Providing better tools for English Nature to address problems of neglect, including a power to serve notices to enforce management practices to enhance the quality of sites;

  - Increasing penalties for people who damage SSSIs and introducing a new offence of intentional or reckless damage to an SSSI;

  - Placing duties on all public bodies to further the conservation and enhancement of SSSIs in the course of their normal activities.

- We will aim to complete the land based elements of our contributions to **the Natura 2000 network** before the end of 2001, and to put in place effective systems for managing these sites to ensure their conservation in favourable condition. By the end of 2002, we will also have identified further marine sites both within the 12 mile territorial limit and beyond;

- We will review our contribution to the Ramsar Convention's list of internationally important wetlands, with a view to designating additional necessary sites by 2005 (for details of Ramsar see box on page 120).

Limestone grassland at Barnack Hills and Holes NNR Cambs. Pyramidal Orchids
Credit: English Nature, Peter Wakely

**Different kinds of wildlife site**

- **Sites of Special Scientific Interest** (SSSIs) are the main nationally important wildlife sites. The first SSSIs were established in 1949. There are currently some 4,000 in England covering 7% of the land area. English Nature, the Government's statutory advisory body on nature conservation, designates SSSIs on the basis of scientific criteria to represent our most valuable wildlife and geological sites.

- Some SSSIs have also been designated as **Special Protection Areas** (SPAs) for birds under the EU Birds Directive. These are the sites which are judged to be of EU-wide importance for the conservation of birds. We have currently (as of October 2000) designated 84 SPAs in England and aim to complete the network of terrestrial SPAs early next year.

- Under the Habitats Directive, all EU member states have also proposed **Special Areas of Conservation** (SACs). Together with SPAs, these sites will form the NATURA 2000 Network. This network is still being developed, but when in place will provide the fundamental basis for biodiversity conservation in the European Union. We have so far proposed 148 areas in England to the Commission for inclusion in the network and are currently consulting on the submission of a further 81 sites. All of these potential SACs are already SSSIs or are being designated as such.

- Under the Convention on Wetlands of International Importance, we have designated 71 sites in England as **Ramsar sites**, after the place where the convention was signed. These are SSSIs which are particularly important for the conservation of wetlands species and habitats. Many are also SPAs or SACs.

- Many SSSIs are also **National Nature Reserves (NNRs)**. These are exceptionally important sites designated under the 1949 National Parks and Access to the Country Act, and normally under the ownership or management of English Nature, or other approved managers' bodies, including voluntary conservation organisations or local authorities. The sites are those which are of particular interest for research and for visitors wanting to see how nature conservation works in the field. English Nature has just designated the 200th NNR.

- Outside the SSSI network there are **Local Nature Reserves**. These are designated by local authorities, who have bylaw-making powers to prevent damaging activities from being undertaken on these sites.

- Many local authorities also identify areas of particular interest for their flora and fauna as **Local Wildlife Sites**. This is not a statutory definition, but helps local authorities to take account of these areas in their planning and other policies.

## Local wildlife sites

**10.2.2.** There are many sites of importance for nature conservation at the local level, often managed or owned by conservation organisations such as the RSPB, the Wildlife Trusts and the Woodland Trust. We see as one of our major priorities the encouragement and better management of these non-statutory local wildlife sites. We established a Local Sites Review Group in 1999, and their recommendations have convinced us of the need for further action to increase the protection and effectiveness of the network.

- We will develop and issue **national guidelines** for the identification and management of **local wildlife sites**. This will meet the concern expressed by the Review Group about the absence of national guidance to ensure a consistent approach;

- We will issue for consultation next year a revision of **planning policy guidance on nature conservation** and biodiversity (PPG9) which will emphasise to local planning authorities the need to take account of local wildlife sites and biodiversity action plans (see below) in their planning policies and proposals;

- We are commissioning research on how to avoid damage to local sites from activities outside the planning system.

**10.2.3. Minerals workings, especially peat workings**, can be a particular threat to the value of wildlife sites. We are already reviewing existing minerals workings in cases where they are damaging to an unacceptable extent the scientific interest of internationally designated sites. In the longer term we will be considering how best to protect statutorily designated sites from the effects of such workings.

## 10.3. Biodiversity Action Plans and species at risk

**10.3.1.** The second leg of our biodiversity policy is based on action plans aimed at individual species and habitats which are particularly at risk. In 1999 the UK Biodiversity Group (a partnership between government, the statutory agencies and voluntary conservation and land management organisations) completed the publication of fully costed and targeted action plans setting out the measures to be taken over the next 5-10 years to restore some 400 priority species and over 40 habitats. Each plan involves a number of partners in the public, voluntary or private sectors, with a Lead Partner responsible for co-ordinating implementation. In addition, Country Groups have been set up in England, Northern Ireland, Scotland and Wales to oversee the implementation of the plans.

---

### Case study – Species Action Plan

**The stone curlew**. Likes open places with short vegetation and they used to nest among open crops. But modern intensive farming methods mean that most crops now grow too tall or cover the ground too quickly; and nests were often lost as a result of operations such as mechanical hoeing. As a result, stone curlews were becoming an increasingly endangered species. The Action Plan involves measures to maintain short downland and heathland through grazing; create bare, open ground for nesting sites on farmland in summer; and protect nests and chicks from accidental destruction on arable farmland. RSPB is the lead partner, but many other partners such as English Nature, MoD, Wildlife Trusts and MAFF have played an important part. For instance, MAFF has used the Countryside Stewardship Scheme to pay farmers to undertake agricultural practices which provide suitable nesting areas for Stone Curlews. As a result, the target in the action plan of raising the population to 200 breeding pairs by the year 2000 has already been exceeded.

---

**Stone Curlew**
Credit: Chris Knights

**10.3.2.** Furthering these plans and ensuring that they are all implemented and their targets met is a major part of the Government's biodiversity policy over the next decade. The UK Biodiversity Group will be issuing a **Millennium Biodiversity Report** in spring 2001, assessing the successes of the process so far, and setting out the main challenges for the next five years. In the light of that report:

- **In 2001, we will establish new objectives** for the biodiversity action plan process over the next 5 years and working with the England Biodiversity Group **we will produce a Biodiversity Strategy for England** which will identify the objectives, mechanisms and players for the delivery of biodiversity conservation. We see this as a major initiative, essential to maintaining the vitality of the action plan process. The strategy will also co-ordinate the implementation of the national species action plans with action on biodiversity at the local level;

- **We are giving greater encouragement to local authorities to have their own local biodiversity action plans.** Local Biodiversity Action Plans are a way of involving all sectors of the local community in identifying what can be done and making choices about priorities. At present some 50% of local authorities in England already have such plans. We will expect all local authorities to incorporate planning for local action on biodiversity in the integrated community strategies which they are required to prepare under the *Local Government Act 2000*.

**10.3.3.** We also propose through the *Countryside and Rights of Way Bill*:

- To introduce a duty on DETR to keep permanently under review the species and habitat types which require priority action.

**10.3.4.** All action to conserve wildlife should be based on accurate and up-to-date **information** about biodiversity trends. Countryside Survey 2000 (see section 9.5) will provide much valuable information about general trends, and we will be putting in place arrangements to continue the monitoring of the state of our national biodiversity using the latest technology. **The Government is contributing £500,000 over two years to help the establishment of a National Biodiversity Network**. This major project, with contributions from both public and voluntary sectors, will create a comprehensive web-based biodiversity information system, bringing together existing local and national records.

## Case study – species recovery programme

**English Nature's species recovery programme** already addresses 286 species in England which are rare or threatened with extinction and co-operates with over 100 organisations, businesses and charities, making a significant contribution to the delivery of BAP species action plans.

As well as well-known species such as otters and red kite, the programme has also had many other achievements in direct species conservation. For example, *Calcium corynellum*, a church yard lichen, has been saved from extinction; the blue ground beetle has been re-established at six former sites; the UK population of *Carex muricata*, a rare sedge species, has been doubled; and there have been significant increases in the national populations of greater horseshoe bats.

**10.3.5.** To supplement the species and habitat action plans, we are taking a number of other measures to ensure that species and habitats at risk have better protection:

- We are reviewing the provisions in Part I of the Wildlife and Countryside Act 1981 with a view to rationalising the identification and protection of rare and endangered species, and will bring forward amending legislation where necessary and as Parliamentary time permits;

- **Bigger penalties for wildlife crime offences,** including prison sentences of up to six months and fines of up to £5,000, have been included in the Countryside and Rights of Way Bill. This is in response to the increasing threat which wildlife crime is posing in both rural and urban areas – including the poisoning of birds of prey and the digging up of large numbers of wild snowdrop and bluebell bulbs;

- **We are also proposing the establishment of a National Wildlife Crime Unit** bringing together intelligence and information on wildlife crime so as to help the investigating and prosecuting agencies to carry out successful operations against such criminals;

- **We will carry out a fundamental review of the policy on alien and invasive species.** Grey squirrels and rhododendrons show the impact that introduced species can have – and the well nigh impossibility of controlling these species once well established. Climate change will create a greater likelihood of natural invasions which it may prove difficult to distinguish from human introductions. Our review will look at ways of improving the early warning of problems, and at establishing criteria for when action should be taken and by whom. We hope that the review's findings will be available at the end of next year. We have already made two orders under the Import of Live Fish Act 1980 to try to prevent the further spread of non-native fish and crayfish, requiring a licence before most non-native fish species are kept in fish farms or other waters such as ponds, and introducing tough measures to restrict non-native species of crayfish in England and Wales.

**Otters are now recolonising former areas as water quality and habitat improve**
Credit: English Nature, M J Hammett

Spraying invasive rhododendron with herbicide at Bramshill Forest, Hampshire
Credit: Forestry Commission

## Habitat restoration

**10.3.6.** Wildlife is not limited to habitat 'islands' in our landscape; most has to survive and breed in the wider countryside – in its fields and field margins, hedges, copses, small patches of less improved grassland and the 'matrix' of farmland habitats. Habitats in the wider countryside have become more fragmented, making wildlife like butterflies more vulnerable to external pressures, such as climate change, and natural variations in population dynamics.

Scrub clearance: without grazing or cutting, rare heathland will be invaded by scrub, reducing its wildlife (and amenity) value. Restoration involves removal of scrub and young trees and re-introduction of grazing management.
Credit: English Nature, Nick Michael

**10.3.7.** As part of the Biodiversity Strategy for England, we will be setting targets for re-creation and enhancement of the main habitats which are being lost. Re-creation can be expensive. But there are a number of funding sources such as the National Lottery that can be tapped. And much can be achieved by sensible prioritisation and co-ordination of existing public sector programmes – those for instance of English Nature, the Environment Agency, the Forestry Commission, and of course MAFF's Agri-Environment programme.

### Case study – habitat recreation

An example of what habitat recreation can achieve is provided by **the lowland heathland action plan** under the UK Biodiversity Action Plan which aims to re-establish 5,400 hectares of heath by 2005. Lowland heath is an example of an important and characteristically English habitat that has suffered large losses. England has 32,000 hectares of lowland heath – 20% of the area of two hundred years ago, as a result of increased ploughing up of heathland, afforestation, and building development. Recreating lowland heath offers great opportunities to reverse wildlife losses and to provide open space for people to enjoy wildlife and outdoor recreation in some of the most congested areas of Southern England.

**Tomorrow's Heathland Heritage**, a 10-year £25 million programme will help reverse the decline of lowland heath. It is led by English Nature and made possible by grant aid from the Heritage Lottery Fund, and has already enabled 10 separate projects to begin the task of restoring and re-creating nearly 16,000 hectares of heathland for the benefit of wildlife and people. In June 2000, English Nature announced 4 new projects in Norfolk, Dorset, East Sussex and Devon which will restore, maintain and re-create nearly 11,000 more hectares of heathland. Overall, the programme will make a major contribution to the Biodiversity Action Plan target to restore and manage 58,000 hectares of lowland heathland (an area larger than the Isle of Wight). Rare species like the silver-studded blue, ladybird spider, sand lizard and woodlark will also benefit.

## Case study – the South Downs

The South Downs is one of the most popular English landscapes (with 30 million visits every year) and its chalk grassland is one of the richest habitats of Western Europe, but its survival depends on sheep grazing. The positive management of the majority of the downland is supported by MAFF under the Environmentally Sensitive Areas (ESA) scheme, and this will be helped if more **value is put on the farming product** – lamb – through helping people to make the essential link between farming and the landscape it supports, through 'eating the view' (see 8.3.4).

The Sussex Downs Conservation Board has built a partnership with the various players in the supply chain (from producer through to retailer) and is now establishing a business operation to develop awareness, confidence and the demand and supply for a genuine local product so that people can really support their local landscape and ensure its conservation. The aim is to have the system self-financing within two or three years, and expanding with increasing awareness and demand.

The Countryside Agency is launching a new study to explore additional mechanisms for bringing about **restoration of the South Downs** to open downland, building on existing environmental schemes such as the South Downs ESA. The study will explore new and closer ways of working with local people and the different organisations involved in a sustainable economy and environment for the South Downs, including English Nature (given the precious downland habitats to be found there) and MAFF.

**The South Downs: ancient downland still exists on the steeper slopes (escarpment)**
Credit: Sussex Downs Conservation Board

**10.3.8.** These initiatives illustrate the growing recognition that our policies must be applied on a larger scale if they are to tackle the wider issues of habitat and species loss. English Nature is therefore developing a new concept, '**Lifescapes**', which will provide an integrated approach to nature conservation at a wider scale than traditional site management. They intend to trial this approach in specific areas in concert with other organisations – such as local authorities, the Countryside Agency, MAFF, the Farming and Wildlife Advisory Group and the Environment Agency. We welcome this initiative to maximise the opportunities for the better delivery of policies and the integration of landscape, wildlife, and general environmental, social and economic objectives at a wider scale.

**Lifescapes will help the conservation of wildlife by:**

- Enhancing the sustainability of designated sites through the creation of buffer zones and connections between sites;
- Improving the pattern of habitats within the landscape to restore the ecological health of the countryside as a bufffer against climate change;
- Creating the pattern of habitats needed for the 20% of species covered by action plans that rely upon general action outside designated sites.

### Agriculture

**10.3.9.** Agricultural practices and water management are perhaps the two most important influences on our wildlife. More intensive agricultural practices have been the major contributor to the decline over the past 50 years in farmland birds, wild flowers and insects. Even where land has not been ploughed up, intensive stock-rearing and greater use of fertilisers has led to the loss of meadows rich in wildflowers and wildlife, and over-grazing of upland moors has had similar effects. In other areas, traditional management practices such as the grazing of lowland heaths have changed or ceased, with a loss of species dependent on short grass.

**10.3.10.** Paragraph 8.2.5. describes the shift of emphasis away from subsidies which increase farm production towards payments to farmers under agri-environment schemes which give them incentives to farm in ways which enhance and preserve our wildlife and its habitats. As described in section 9.3, under the ERDP we have already doubled funding for agri-environment schemes. Support for the Environmentally Sensitive Areas scheme (which focuses on 22 areas of particularly high landscape, wildlife or historic value) will continue at broadly current levels.

Overgrazing and inappropriate supplementary feeding has resulted in severe damage to moorland vegetation and loss of heath on Long Mynd. The Long Mynd Common ESA agreement aims to prevent further damage and to restore the moorland vegetation
Credit: English Nature, Andrew Hearle

- **We will undertake a major review of the agri-environment schemes** with a view to reshaping and simplifying them in time for the mid-term evaluation of the ERDP in 2003, and will be seeking a further shift of the Common Agricultural Policy in the longer term towards support for farmers to farm in ways that positively enhance our wild fauna and flora;

- **better advice to farmers will also play a role in promoting more environmentally-friendly agricultural practices.** MAFF already has Codes of Good Agricultural Practice covering the protection of soil, water and air and the use of pesticides. The Codes have recently been revised and a summary leaflet produced in order to make them more user-friendly. MAFF also publishes specific advice on subjects such as fertilisers, manures and waste minimisation.

In February 2000 MAFF published a pilot set of 35 **indicators of sustainable agriculture** – *Towards Sustainable Agriculture* – to provide a means of measuring the economic, social and environmental impacts of agriculture and to help assess the effectiveness of policies and the sustainability of the agriculture sector. The set complements the Government's Sustainable Development Strategy. Our aim is to use these indicators to raise awareness of the environmental impacts of agriculture and of its contribution to sustainable development. A first review of the pilot set will take place in 2003. MAFF also undertakes a major research programme to find ways of reducing the adverse environmental effects of agriculture. Current MAFF projects are looking for instance at the best ways of restoring priority habitats such as – uplands, wetlands and heathlands; minimising pollution from agriculture; and encouraging the best use of mineral and organic fertilisers for both environmental and economic benefit.

## Case study – Integrated Farm Management

Integrated Farm Management is a whole farm policy aiming to provide the basis for efficient and profitable production, which is economically viable and environmentally responsible. It is an approach to farming which combines beneficial natural processes (such as biological predation on crop pests) and traditional practices (like crop rotation) with modern technology and selective targeted use of agri-chemicals. The result is to minimise pollution, and avoid the unnecessary use of chemicals and energy, whilst maintaining profit margins. Measures such as retaining hedges and the vegetation at their base (to help predators like ladybirds which control aphids) and avoiding ploughing stubble (to save fuel, reduce soil erosion and leaching of nitrogen) also provide better habitats for birds and other wildlife. We are working closely with the Integrated Arable Crop Production Alliance and LEAF (Linking Environment and Farming) to develop and promote this approach. In particular, an independent Working Group has been set up to make recommendations by the end of 2000.

**10.3.11.** Hill farming, and especially extensive beef and sheep grazing, is the major influence on upland landscapes and biodiversity. It is also a significant (and in remoter areas very significant) part of the rural social fabric. The ERDP therefore includes an area-based Hill Farm Allowance Scheme, to help offset the natural disadvantages faced by farmers in these areas and maintain sustainable livestock systems. The Scheme will be directed towards sheep and suckler cow producers with more than 10 hectares of forage land (mainly permanent grassland including rough grazing) who undertake to continue farming for at least five years. Basic payments will be enhanced by 10% or 20% for producers following specified practices which favour the environment. Conversely, payments will be conditional on on adherence to Good Farming Practice, detailed in the ERDP. **We have set a target to maintain extensive grazing on 1.4 million hectares in the Less Favoured Areas.** To help hill farmers use their Hill Farm Allowance support to build sustainable businesses:

- We will fund a programme to develop business skills and training, and establish demonstration farms where farmers can look at what others have done, so that they can use it as a basis for their own planning;

- We will commission work to explore ways of improving land classification systems so that HFA payments can be better targeted;

- We will review the operation of the beef and sheep regimes to ensure that – insofar as it is within our control – regulatory controls are reduced and the schemes do not inhibit enterprising farmers from developing their businesses as they see best;

- We will review future options for supporting hill farming in consultation with key interests.

**10.3.12.** The intensive use of fertilisers has been one of the main agricultural practices causing a decline in wildlife. We have already taken measures to tackle this problem and intend more in the future. Pesticides have also harmed animal and plant life. Regulatory action against pesticides has already led to a reversal in the declines of populations of some birds of prey and the successful reintroduction of others such as the red kite, and the growing market for organic products is also reducing the use of agri-chemicals.

- **We will increase the rate of grant payable under the Farm Waste Grants scheme from 25% to 40%.** Under this scheme, farmers in Nitrate Vulnerable Zones can apply for grants for farm slurry storage facilities to help them comply with restrictions on manure use;

- **We propose to extend a pilot scheme run by the Farming and Wildlife Advisory Group to promote nutrient budgeting to farmers in the new nitrate vulnerable zone areas.** This initiative helps farmers to manage their use of fertilisers, both to save money and protect the environment.

- Better use of inputs will also be addressed by the Inputs taskforce described in chapter 8.

- **The Government is committed to minimising the adverse environmental impact of pesticide use,** consistent with effective crop protection. The main vehicle for carrying forward this policy is the Pesticides Forum and we intend to raise the profile of this body and enhance its effectiveness. We have also invited the agricultural pesticides industry to develop a package of voluntary measures aimed at acheiving the Government's objective and will be holding discussions with the Crop Protection Association on how their current proposals can be further improved.

- **We are increasing the assistance to organic farming** under the ERDP by increasing the resources to help farmers to convert their land to organic use (a process which normally requires two years). Organic farming is a successful example of policy and public preference marching in step – it has benefits for wildlife, landscape and pollution control; high standards of animal welfare; and can provide more employment. Resources will rise from £12m in 2000–01 to £23m by 2006–07. This will enable around 45,000 hectares per year to be converted. Our target is 430,000 hectares of land converted or converting to organic farming by 2007.

Scrag Oak Farm – Organic vegetable boxes
Credit: Soil Association

## Water

**10.3.13.** The quality of rivers and waterways especially has suffered from phosphorus and nitrogen leaching from fertilisers and animal wastes. Some rivers and lakes have suffered from silt from agricultural land, and over-grazing and cultivation close to river banks has caused erosion of the banks. A lot has already been done. Otters are also returning to our rivers, largely as a result of reduced pollution levels. But more action is needed.

- By 2005 we will improve our rivers by developing and implementing a programme of measures to improve compliance with **river quality objectives** from 82% in 1997 to at least 91%. As part of the package of agreed price increases by the water companies for the 2000-05 period, the water companies are financing schemes to deal with water abstraction related problems affecting nearly 100 stretches of river or wetlands.

- Some especially sensitive areas are designated as **nitrate vulnerable zones** within which restrictions apply on the use of fertilisers. We will be consulting farmers fully about detailed proposals in the New Year, with a view to making further nitrate vulnerable zone designations following consultation.

### Pulling sustainability into practice – better water management

**10.3.14.** Rivers and streams face a range of pressures – water abstraction to meet the needs of a growing population, and for industry and agriculture; land drainage and river 'improvement' to speed up the flow of water downstream; reduced ability of the land and vegetation to absorb water, due to agriculture and forestry changes; pollution and damage to fisheries and water supplies. But we often address the consequences piecemeal. Vital connections, such as between changing the capacity of the land to soak up water and the flooding of towns way downstream, are not being made. This makes it more difficult to develop long-term solutions to these problems, which can be serious – as shown graphically by the recent floods with their great social and other costs.

**10.3.15.** We want to find ways of tackling these issues better, by working together towards more sustainable management. This will mean strengthening tools like the *Environment Agency's Local Plans*, which engage with industry, rural interests and local communities to work out how the environment can be better protected and enhanced. For example, this might mean EA encouraging farmers or foresters to follow simple and cheap changes to cultivation practices, for better water management. It will also mean more 'joining up' between major policies impacting on water:

- We will encourage the water regulators to take a broader and longer-term view in encouraging more **sustainable water management schemes**, which tackle problems at source rather than through major engineering, where this will be effective and economic.

- As part of the current inter-departmental review of funding mechanisms for flood and coastal defence (due to report September 2001) we will examine the scope for better integration between spending on flood defence and that for environmental and water resource management.

- We will also continue to protect undeveloped flood plains against inappropriate development and to look for environmental gains as part of a coastal and flood defence policy including flood plain management and including environmental considerations in the cost-benefit analysis for new schemes.

## 10.4. Integrating biodiversity considerations into everybody's actions and decisions

**10.4.1.** Our aim is a situation where both every public authority and every private body automatically takes account of the implications for biodiversity in all their policies and programmes. We want to make concern for biodiversity part of the furniture for everyone. Specific measures and activities include:

- **Green Ministers biodiversity check-list**. We want to be a Government that practices what it preaches. We have started on ourselves, therefore, by ensuring that each Government Department has a Minister with specific responsibility for green issues. These 'Green Ministers' have drawn up a biodiversity check-list which all Departments are asked to observe when they decide on new policies. Our aim is both to encourage the development of Government policies which are sensitive to potential biodiversity impacts and to help promote the policy changes which are required to make a real difference across the board;

- **Business:** In partnership with the UK Round Table on Sustainable Development and Earthwatch UK, advice to businesses has been published on how to integrate biodiversity into their environmental management systems. We are also helping to fund Earthwatch to set up a biodiversity resource centre which aims to provide a one-stop-shop for biodiversity advice to business;

- Introduction through the Countryside and Rights of Way Bill of a **new duty** for Government Departments **on biodiversity**.

- **Local communities:** everyone in their local community can play a part in biodiversity conservation, for example in schools, in their gardens and in managing local wildlife sites. Many people are members of conservation organisations and wish to participate actively in conservation work. Local Biodiversity Action Plans are a way of involving all sectors of the local community. Local communities can also benefit themselves through building demand for environmental tourism – eg bird watching holidays and conservation activities such as hedge laying, coppicing and pond digging.

**Wylam, Northumberland: volunteers planting trees**
Credit: K Webster/D Petrie

### The voluntary sector

The Government relies heavily on its partnership with the voluntary conservation sector, including the Biodiversity Challenge Group, to help deliver its biodiversity strategy. They play a strong role in the partnership structures established to pursue the UK Biodiversity Action Plan. They continue to be knowledgeable and provocative advocates for greater progress as well as being tireless workers in the field. Voluntary conservation organisations including Plantlife, the RSPB, Butterfly Conservation and The Wildlife Trusts are the lead partners for some 278 Action Plans, and voluntary organisations manage many SSSIs as well as local wildlife sites.

**The Green Ministers' biodiversity checklist,** published in March 2000, shows the actions that Government Departments can take to promote biodiversity, including:

- Making a commitment to conserve any SSSIs on their land and developing management practices which conserve biodiversity across the whole estate;

- Screening policy areas for changes which could have significant effects on biodiversity;

- Building biodiversity into grant-aid or funding programmes and policy advice.

- Building biodiversity into staff training and development eg awaydays and teambuilding.

Green Ministers will monitor progress and account for their actions in the Green Ministers Annual Report.

### Case study – business action for biodiversity

English Nature and Hanson Quarry Products Europe signed an agreement in February 2000 that will bring many benefits to the 54 SSSIs controlled by the company and help to meet national nature conservation targets. Hanson has agreed to:

- Make no new planning applications on land currently designated as a SSSI unless an over-riding national need for the mineral is clearly identified or it can be demonstrated that the scientific interest will not be significantly adversely affected by the Company's operations;

- Achieve the highest state of conservation management, described by English Nature as favourable, on all land designated as a SSSI under the control of the company with agreed Site Management Statements and necessary action underway within two years;

- Incorporate biodiversity targets, English Nature's Natural Area objectives and the defining local character within all company restoration schemes and afteruses.

Hanson's Clee Hill quarry in Shropshire won a Civic Trust Award in 1999 for work to restore the old quarry workings and other derelict areas to a semi-natural upland landscape, allowing the land to be returned to grazing and wildlife
Credit: Hanson Aggregates

**10.4.2.** In seeking a more effective role for Government Departments, other statutory agencies and the business and voluntary sectors on the biodiversity agenda, an especially important issue will be the benefits to be gained from adjusting investment programmes. There will be many instances in which investment initially generated by other demands, including other environmental pressures, can be designed to secure biodiversity benefits at the same time. An example is the pressure to continue the clean up of rivers and other water courses where biodiversity benefits elsewhere in the system may be secured at the same time.

---

**Business action for biodiversity**

Around 40 companies in 15 FTSE sectors own and/or control land within more than 1300 Sites of Special Scientific Interest in England. Business action for biodiversity makes sound commercial sense because:

- Biodiversity provides direct and indirect economic services to business – many businesses depend, for instance, on biological resources;
- Better biodiversity performance can give companies competitive advantage (compliance with regulation and mitigation of risks) and benefits in terms of reputation

Business can help make biodiversity happen by adopting a company policy on biodiversity; developing a company biodiversity action plan; and ensuring high quality environmental management on all land under the company's control. Where a company owns land designated as an SSSI, its aim should be to achieve "favourable condition" as defined by English Nature.

---

## 10.5. Climate change

**10.5 1.** One of the most serious challenges for the future will be the likelihood that **climate change** will force species to migrate northwards or to higher ground, whilst low-lying coasts will be at risk of flooding and wetlands will become drier. Such natural responses will have to take place in a countryside where agriculture is also adapting to new climatic conditions and extra demands are being placed on water and renewable energy resources. It may not be feasible to strive to keep every species where it is now or every habitat in the same condition, nor to prevent 'new' species from moving in and habitats responding naturally.

---

**Climate change and UK nature conservation**

Because climate change is a key consideration in planning the future conservation of biodiversity, DETR and MAFF have funded a study on climate change impacts on priority habitats and species and on how climate change may affect the achievement of current nature conservation policies.

The DETR is also contributing to the MONARCH and REGIS projects. MONARCH is funded by a consortium of 11 governmental and non-governmental nature conservation organisations in the UK and Ireland, led by English Nature. The study uses modelling approach to evaluate impacts on a broad range of species and geological features in diverse environments in both Britain and Ireland.

REGIS has been commissioned by DETR, MAFF and UK Water Industry Research and is assessing climate change impacts on water resources, agriculture, coastal defence and biodiversity in two regions: North-west England and East Anglia. It involves developing a methodology for conducting integrated impact assessments at the regional scale, including a new model for forecasting changes in species distribution (SPECIES).

---

**10.5.2.** We will need to look ahead to see which species are likely to be supported in the future climatic conditions and think carefully before investing in conserving species or habitats that may eventually be lost from a site. We will need to ensure that our approach to biodiversity conservation is flexible enough to react to climate induced changes and that climate change is explicitly considered in policy development and appraisal. New opportunities such as the increasing expenditure on agri-environment schemes will give scope to enhance the conditions for particular species/habitats in particular places.

## Case study – recreation on coastal marsh: Abbotts Hall, Essex

In the Essex estuaries some 60% of salt marsh and 90% of coastal grazing marsh in Essex have been 'squeezed' out due to sea level rise, expansion of arable cropping and building development. Essex Wildlife Trust have led the purchase of a 700 acre arable farm on the Blackwater Estuary, to be used to demonstrate techniques for enhancing the wildlife value of a commercial arable farm. A major element is the proposal to breach the seawall over a 2.5km length, allowing the flooding of some 300 acres to recreate lost salt marsh – making this the largest such project in England. This will show other landowners how to re-create the habitats lost due to rising sea levels in South East England. MAFF agri-environment schemes are supporting this initiative.

**Essex salt marsh**
Credit: English Nature, Peter Wakely

# increasing
## enjoyment of the countryside

**11**

## The issues

- How to make it easier for in particular urban dwellers to visit the countryside, and to help everybody benefit from the potential for enjoyment which it offers.
- How to reconcile increasing opportunities for people to visit the countryside with the interests of those living and working in the countryside.

## The future: what we want to see

- The public will have, for the first time in recent history, access for recreation on foot to open country – mountain, moor, heath, down and registered common land, with appropriate safeguards for landowners.
- An improved network of rights of way, with improved legal remedies to secure the removal of obstacles.
- Opportunities to visit and enjoy the countryside increased for disadvantaged groups and for town dwellers, for example through better management of the countryside around towns – where the pressures are strongest and the need for green spaces greatest.
- Traditional countryside sports will continue to play their important role in the countryside.

---

**Summary of measures**

- A new right of access for walkers by 2005 to mountain, moor, heath, down and registered common land;

- New powers (in the Countryside and Rights of Way Bill) for landowners to dedicate their land as permanently open to walkers and other users;

- The rights of way system brought up to date through the new legislative measures in the Countryside and Rights of Way Bill and new finance from central Government;

- Codes of practice, a national access database and other readily available sources to inform people of the opportunities available to them in the countryside;

- A review on how to provide more opportunities for all groups of people to enjoy countryside recreation;

- New guidance on revitalising country parks and special funding to improve the country around towns

**11**

## Contents

## 11.1. Introduction

**11.1.1.** The countryside is an enormous recreational asset, with its high quality landscapes, fresh air, open space and tranquillity. Recreation can improve the mental and physical health of participants and the revenue from millions of visitors to the countryside every year is an important component of the economy of rural England. Part of what makes our countryside alive and vibrant is the enormous number of activities created chiefly by and for the residents – agricultural shows, point-to-points, pony shows, game fairs, village fetes, carnivals, etc.

---

**Revenue from visitors**

Total spending by all visitors to the countryside is estimated to be around £11.5bn in 1998, of which 77% is associated with day visitors from home, 17% with UK holiday makers and 6% with overseas tourists. Total employment directly supported by recreation and leisure visitor activity in the countryside is estimated to amount to some 290,000 jobs in 1998 and a further 50,000 indirectly in other sectors of the rural economy.

---

**11.1.2.** Our strategy to increase enjoyment of the countryside involves:

- Legislation to make it easier for people to enjoy recreation in open countryside and to use footpaths, bridle ways and other rights of way;
- Making sure that all sections of society can enjoy the countryside by:
  - making it easier for disadvantaged communities to enjoy the countryside;
  - finding out more about what minority groups would like to do in the countryside;
  - ensuring that there is proper provision for a full range of recreational interests.
- Seeking to ensure that recreation is managed in a way that benefits local communities and protects the environment that people come to visit.

## 11.2. Walking in the countryside

### Walking in open countryside

**11.2.1.** Walking is by far the most popular activity in the countryside. The UK Day Visits Survey showed that 35% of countryside visits and 27% of seaside visits had walking as the main activity. For over a century people have sought the right to explore open countryside. Our manifesto promised that we would give greater freedom to them to do so. In the *Countryside and Rights of Way Bill* we are introducing new statutory rights of access on foot to 1.1 million hectares of open countryside in England and Wales.

---

- **We aim to ensure that by 2005 people in England and Wales will have a right of access for recreation on foot to mountain, moor, heath, down and registered common land. The right will be limited in scope and take account of the interests of land managers and others in the land. The Countryside Agency and the Countryside Council for Wales will be mapping the land concerned. There are provisions for all interested parties to comment on the maps and for landowners to appeal against the boundaries.**

---

Soar Mill Cove, Devon
Credit: Countryside Agency, Graham Parish

**11.2.2.** There is also considerable public interest in better access to woodlands, canal sides, riversides and coastal land. Much of such land is owned by public authorities such as the Forestry Commission and British Waterways; or by non-profit-making bodies such as the National Trust and the Woodland Trust who already open most of their land to the public. We believe, therefore, that a statutory right in respect of woodlands, canal sides and riversides is unnecessary. But the public bodies concerned are looking at ways to improve the access that they provide to walkers and horse-riders, and we have aimed through the Countryside and Rights of Way Bill to make it easier for all landowners, whether public bodies, charitable or non-profit-making organisations or private landowners to dedicate their land as permanently open.

- The Bill introduces **new powers for landowners to dedicate their land** as permanently open to walkers, and to other users such as horse-riders if they wish. This means that the land will remain open even when it passes to another owner. We shall be encouraging landowners to make full use of this new power;

- The Forestry Commission will continue to encourage landowners to provide **access to their woodlands** through incentives under the Woodland Grant Scheme. The Forestry Commission will also consider the scope for dedicating its own woodlands, so that they will remain open to the public even if they are sold on. The Commission will seek to increase the area of woodlands under its control open for public access by purchasing the freeholds of leasehold properties where opportunities arise;

- British Waterways, which manages most of the navigable **canal network**, has instituted a programme – Access to All – to promote access to the canal network;

- The Ministry of Defence has committed itself in the Strategy for the **Defence Estate** to providing public access wherever possible. It will seek to increase the amount, quality and certainty of access overall, and ensure that maximum advance notice is given of access opportunities. The existing presumption of access to its estate will continue wherever consistent with operational, safety and security considerations, and the interests of conservation;

- The Countryside and Rights of Way Bill provides for the statutory opening of **coastal land** if appropriate in the future. We shall review this in the light of experience with other types of land open for statutory access, and consult fully on any proposals.

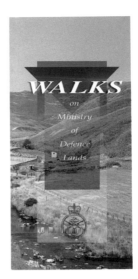

*Walking guide for MOD Estate*
Credit: Defence Estates

### Rights of way

**11.2.3.** The new rights of access to open countryside will open up new possibilities for many millions of walkers. Nonetheless, our historic rights of way network are likely to remain the most important means of access into the countryside for walkers, as well as for the several million horse-riders and cyclists in England. Although much of the rights of way network reflects the day-to-day working needs of a bygone age, it now offers many opportunities for countryside recreation. There are 147,000 kilometres of footpath, 32,000 kilometres of bridleway, 6,000 kilometres of roads used as public paths/restricted byways and 4,000 kilometres of byways open to all traffic in England.

**11.2.4.** However, the current legal regime makes it difficult to remove obstructions, to divert routes or to be certain where some routes exist. The Countryside and Rights of Way Bill aims to provide an improved network and a fairer system for both landowners and users.

Credit: Countryside Agency, A Seth

- Through the *Countryside and Rights of Way Bill*, we will:

  - Provide a new right to require **removal of obstructions**;

  - Require local highway authorities to produce **rights of way improvement plans**;

  - Give a right to landowners to appeal to the Secretary of State if local highway authorities do not deal with **requests for diversions** promptly; and make it possible for farmers to make temporary diversions of rights of way where this is really necessary for a land management operation such as tree-felling;

  - Introduce a **new class of restricted byway** to give certainty to users, including carriage drivers, as to their rights;

  - Set a **deadline of 25 years for registering forgotten historic footpaths and bridleways** on the local definitive maps of the rights of way network. This will bring benefits for both landowners and those using the rights of way. Landowners will have certainty as to whether a footpath or bridleway exists on their property; and the existence of a deadline will encourage work to be done more quickly on the identification of forgotten footpaths and, especially, bridleways to the benefit of walkers and horse-riders. We have chosen a deadline that gives enough time to research forgotten rights. We shall provide grants to voluntary associations of an average of £2m per year to help them undertake research to complete definitive maps;

  - We will also provide **resources of up to £19m to local highway authorities** to enable them to carry out their new duties;

- We shall **monitor the performance** of local highway authorities and review the performance plans of those that are making poor progress. Some authorities have an excellent record in fulfilling their duties to define, maintain and signpost rights of way; others do not. The Countryside Agency is undertaking a further survey to record the state of the rights of way network in 2000. We shall use the results of the Countryside Agency survey as a base from which to judge improvements to the system and use the best value procedures now being introduced to ensure that local authorities undertake their rights of way work efficiently and effectively. By 2005 we aim to achieve a 10% improvement in defining, maintaining and publicising the rights of way network.

## 11.3. Recreation for all

### Countryside around towns

**11.3.1.** The countryside around towns has a particular importance as source of recreation for city dwellers. It also creates the environmental setting for a city which will encourage inward investment – as increasingly firms want to locate in places where they know their employees will have easy access to attractive and good quality green areas. Our aim is to improve its amenity value.

Children using access created under Countryside Stewardship, at Great Western Community Forest, Wilts.
Credit: MAFF

- We will continue to protect **green belts** as a means of helping to keep our towns and cities compact and distinct, and for the environmental resource that they provide;

- The Countryside Agency will administer a new fund to provide up to £4.5m over the next three years for schemes to improve the **countryside around towns**;

- The New Opportunities Lottery Fund recently announced a multi-million pound programme of lottery grant aid to transform and upgrade **green spaces in local communities** across the UK. The countryside around towns is extremely well placed to benefit from this programme, which includes nearly £13m for the Countryside Agency to help disadvantaged urban and rural communities create or revive public green spaces. The Agency will be awarding grants of up to £150,000 during this initiative, and we urge local authorities and other key players to help local communities benefit from these grants;

- The Countryside Agency will be issuing guidance on best practice to revitalise the **country parks** around our towns and cities. Over 250 country parks were established around towns, most in the 1970s. Many are now beginning to show their age. Yet they remain potentially a great asset for urban dwellers, providing 'gateways' between town and country. We want to see country parks better maintained and brought up to date to accommodate the activities and sports that people are now interested in, and they will be eligible for help from both lottery funding and the Countryside Agency grant scheme for countryside around towns;

- We will consult on **a revision of our planning policy guidance on sport and recreation (PPG17)** to give local planning authorities a clearer framework to make provision for open spaces in and around our towns;

- **Farming** remains an important activity even in the countryside immediately around towns maintaining attractive landscapes. At the same time, farmers near towns are especially well placed to diversify into the provision of recreational facilities for their urban neighbours. Where appropriate MAFF's Countryside Stewardship scheme can be used to enhance the countryside around towns and to improve opportunities for people to enjoy it;

- **Community forests.** The Countryside Agency and the Forestry Commission, working together with local authorities and others, have helped create 12 community forests on the edges of our larger towns and cities. These woodland areas provide peace and recreation, improving the quality of life of half of England's population. The Government would like to see the approach adopted more widely and will consider how it can be used to assist with the implementation of other regeneration, forestry and community-based initiatives.

**11.3.2.** Many of the other policies described in this paper will help the countryside around towns. The target of 60% of new housing on brownfield sites will help reduce the especially acute pressures for development in the countryside around towns, although there will be a need to develop on some green fields on the urban fringe. Our measures to promote the better planning of development will help ensure that development in these areas reflects the character of the local landscape and helps strengthen the sense of community.

**11.3.3.** The countryside around towns will also be eligible to benefit from the £70.4 million lottery funding for SUSTRANS for *Green Routes Safe Routes*, including green transport corridors to, from and in disadvantaged areas.

### Helping all sections of the community to enjoy the countryside

**11.3.4.** We want the countryside to be a source of enjoyment for all sections of society. We are concerned that most country pursuits such as walking are now largely the preserve of the white, middle-aged, middle-class and able-bodied. Over the next few years we shall be looking for ways to spread the benefits of countryside recreation more equally, while ensuring that this is done in a way which both protects the countryside itself and brings benefits to local communities.

**11.3.5.** The proposed new statutory right of access to open countryside will open up huge new areas of land close to where people live, particularly for those in the conurbations of Northern England. If new national parks are designated in the New Forest and South Downs, millions more people in the conurbations of Southern England will then live close to a national park managed by an authority concerned to promote opportunities for people to enjoy the special qualities of the Parks.

**The Norfolk Broads**
Credit: Countryside Agency, David Woodfall

**11.3.6.** We also want to make it easier for people to benefit from the increased opportunities which will exist for enjoying the countryside. We shall expect local authorities to give priority to links between **town and country** in their rights of way improvement plans and local transport plans. And we shall expect local transport plans to consider town to country journeys for leisure purposes as well as those from the country to town for work, shopping and education. We will also encourage local authorities to develop and promote public transport links for people wishing to go to the countryside.

**11.3.7.** Surveys have shown that many people are inhibited from enjoying countryside recreation fully because of uncertainty about what is available and what they may legitimately do. We shall be improving the **information** available to them.

- The Countryside Agency will publish **Codes of Practice for walkers and for landowners** to accompany the new statutory right of access to open countryside;

- We plan to establish **a National Access Database**. This will be on the internet and will give full up-to-date information about both rights of way and areas open to the public.

**Farthing Down, Surrey**
Credit: Countryside Agency, R M Pilgrim

**11.3.8.** We have asked the Countryside Agency to investigate what more may be done to provide opportunities for disabled people, ethnic minorities, residents of inner city estates, and young people to enjoy countryside recreation. They will be establishing pilot projects in a number of areas. We will also expect local authorities' rights of way improvement plans to include proposals for making improvements for people who do not normally visit the countryside, for instance increasing accessibility for those with sight or mobility problems. We are encouraging local authorities to consider all social groups and the full range of countryside recreation in drawing up their local cultural strategies. But we accept that we need to do more at government level to develop a longer term strategy.

- By 2005, we will carry out a full **diversity review** of how we can encourage more people with disabilities, more people from the ethnic minorities, more people from the inner cities, and more young people to visit the countryside and participate in country activities. Initially we will do this by seeking their views on what they need to enjoy the countryside. Then we will draw up a plan of action.

### Tourism and Transport

In some honeypot areas, tourist numbers can be damaging to the local environment if not properly managed and some rural communities may feel swamped by visitors in the peak seasons. We believe that the main solution to these problems is to develop effective visitor management schemes and a marketing approach which spreads visitors to new attractions in the less visited regions and away from honeypot sites. The main challenge is transport. The majority of tourist visitors to rural areas use private cars rather than public transport, adding to pollution, and traffic congestion. Without action this is likely to become worse over the next decade as the popularity of visits to the country grows. We favour a two-pronged approach:

- Providing realistic alternatives in the form of better **public transport infrastructure** and better access to cycling. Bodies such as the Youth Hostels Association and the National Park Authorities are already developing interesting schemes. For example, the *Moorsbus Network* provided by the North York Moors National Park supplements the network of rail and bus services which serves many of the main towns and villages in the area to allow walkers to plan routes without the need to return to a car. Its aim is to provide recreational access to the National Park at the lowest environmental cost;

- Even with such schemes, a large number of visitors to the countryside are still likely to come by car and we will need to see more use of **toll and car parking schemes.** They will not be possible or appropriate everywhere. But they are likely to have a useful role in managing visitors to particularly popular sites; and toll and parking charges can also help cover the costs of maintaining those sites. An example of how the powers that the Transport Bill will give local authorities to charge for road use could be used is the planned small scheme centred on Derwent Lane, a popular beauty spot in the Peak District National Park. This would tackle congestion and environmental damage by levying vehicle charges at peak times, using the surplus charge revenue to expand public transport provision and provide better facilities for cyclists and walkers.

A better view: more sustainable transport
Credit: The Countryside Agency, Graham Wiltshire

### Sports and other activities

**11.3.9.** Many people go to the countryside to admire the scenery, listen to the sounds of nature and generally feel that they are 'away from it all'. But others (or the same people at other times) value the countryside because it offers the space to enjoy more active pursuits which cannot be undertaken in built-up areas. We are keen that the countryside should offer opportunities for adventure and sport, so long as these do not interfere unduly with the enjoyment of others or with land management work. We believe that by careful planning and management there is a place for all activities. In many instances this will require local authorities, including National Park Authorities, and others to identify the demand for activities in their areas and to see how it can be accommodated. There is a role for central Government in reviewing overall provision and ensuring that local authorities have adequate powers to deal with any problems.

**11.3.10.** Many people would like more freedom to swim and undertake other activities on **waterways, ponds and lakes**. The recent White Paper on Inland Waterways – *Waterways for Tomorrow* describes how the Government wishes to maximise the opportunities for leisure and recreation, tourism and sport on canals. We have also recently revised the *Code of Practice on Conservation, Access and Recreation* giving guidance to bodies with statutory responsibilities – such as the Environment Agency, and water and sewerage companies – on the need to have regard to the provision of recreational facilities.

River Witham, Bassingham, Lincolnshire
Credit: Countryside Agency, Andy Tryner

**11.3.11.** The British Canoe Union has drawn attention to the fact that one million canoeists have access to only 3% of navigable water. The Environment Agency has issued a guide Agreeing Access to Water for Canoeing to encourage the establishment of voluntary agreements on the use of waterways for canoeing. But access for canoeists has to be managed in a way that is compatible with the rights of existing users such as anglers. The extent of the problems over access to water for boating and other water sports is difficult to ascertain, and we feel that we need more information before taking decisions on the best way forward.

- We shall therefore commission research into the extent of **access to water for sport and recreation**, and into the problems which exist, in order to inform our future strategy for optimising the recreational possibilities of water.

**11.3.12. Horse-riding** is an increasing pastime. The British Horse Society has plans for a national bridleway network to provide more safe routes for horseriders. And the support we are providing for research into historic rights of way may well result in the discovery of additional bridleways for use by riders.

**11.3.13. The National Cycle Network** – a Millennium Commission project undertaken by SUSTRANS – will provide continuous traffic-free routes and traffic-calmed minor roads, running right through urban areas and reaching all parts of the UK. It will be a safe, attractive, high quality network for cyclists and a major new amenity for walkers and people with disabilities. The first 5,000 miles were officially opened in June. By 2005 there will be over 8,000 miles.

The Tees Forest Awareness Camp: informal adventure activities and experience of the natural environment coordinated by the Tees Forest and the Admiralty Ecology Group.
Credit: The Tees Forest

## Traditional countryside sports and activities

**11.3.14.** Concern has been voiced about hunting with hounds. The arguments over hunting with hounds have been well rehearsed. To inform the position the Government commissioned the Burns report which covered four key areas in relation to hunting;

- The contribution that hunting makes to employment and the rural economy as well as to social and cultural aspects of life in rural areas;
- Animal welfare issues and matters of population management;
- Whether drag hunting is a viable alternative to hunting with hounds;
- An assessment of the consequences on any ban on hunting, and how a ban might be implemented.

Following that report the Government is to bring before Parliament, for a free vote, proposals on a range of options for the future of hunting with dogs.

**11.3.15.** The Government recognises there has been some concern too over shooting and fishing. We guarantee that we will not ban these countryside sports. We recognise the major role that these sports have in the countryside, not just as a source of recreation and employment, but also as a contributor to the conservation of landscape and wildlife.

Woodland is managed to provide cover for game birds, producing beneficial habitats for other species.
Credit: The Game Conservancy Trust

## Game shooting and wildfowling

These have a far-reaching influence on landscapes, habitats and wildlife. The management of 7.3 million hectares (18 million acres) is influenced by 4,500 professional gamekeepers; 23% of upland Britain and 80% of small woods in England is managed for game. Wildfowling clubs own or manage 18% of the 163 UK estuaries, of which 90% are designated conservation sites; a number are managing National Nature Reserves in agreement with English Nature.

The management practices adopted by those involved in these pursuits make a significant contribution to biodiversity in rural areas. The environmental value of the heather moorlands of northern England has been maintained through the land management regime pursued to raise game birds, and that management produces an important further benefit by providing a habitat conducive to the survival of other bird species, such as curlews and golden plovers.

## Angling and fishing

These remain one of the most popular reasons for visiting the countryside, with over a million anglers a year buying rod licenses from the Environment Agency. The important role that angling and freshwater fishing play in the rural economy and in conservation was confirmed by the Salmon and Freshwater Fisheries Review commissioned by the Government from independent experts in 1998 and published in March 2000.

# Part 3

## a *protected* countryside – objectives and spending

**Objectives:**

- To conserve and enhance rural landscapes and the diversity and abundance of wildlife (including the habitats on which it depends).

- To increase opportunities for people to get enjoyment from the countryside. To open up public access to mountain, heath, moor and down and registered common land by the end of 2005.

| £m | Spending (£ million) | | | |
|---|---|---|---|---|
| | 1996–7 | 2000–01 | Projected for 2003–4 | Projected 2001/2–2003/4 |
| National Parks and Broads Authorities (including new parks) | 17 | 21 | 30 | 77 |
| National Forest Company | 2 | 3 | 4 | 11 |
| Countryside Agency (access and environment) | n/a | 33 | 44 | 117 |
| English Nature | 40 | 51 | 64 | 183 |
| Implementation of measures in Countryside & Rights of Way Bill | – | – | 25 | 58 |
| Countryside around towns | – | – | 2 | 5 |

Note: MAFF and FC expenditure on agri-environment and forestry schemes under ERDP is included in the table at the end of Part 2.

# Part 4

# a *vibrant* countryside

*We want to see a vibrant countryside, which can shape its own future and whose voice is heard by government at all levels*

# local power for
## country towns and villages

## The issues

- Rural communities could play a much bigger part in running their own affairs, influencing and shaping their future development but they often lack opportunities, and support.
- Lack of involvement can result in an adversarial approach to change and less well targeted services.
- There is a need for better partnership between all types of authorities, a greater willingness to work together and deliver locally managed services
- Rural areas often have a strong sense of community and a valuable network of voluntary groups, but these are under threat as ways of life, people and attitudes change.

## The future – what we want to see

- People living in rural areas being fully involved in developing their community, safeguarding its valued features, and shaping the decisions that affect them.
- Flourishing local councils acting as the voice of the local community.
- Strong partnerships between county, district and town and parish councils, supporting and encouraging rural communities on matters which local councils can manage themselves, and working in partnership on wider local services.
- Support for established local voluntary networks in rural areas.

### Summary of measures

- The quality parish – a new role for town and parish councils;
- Town and parish councils working in partnership with counties and districts to deliver more services locally, where this is best value, including Community Information Points;
- Help for over 1,000 rural communities to prepare Town and Village Plans to shape their future;
- Training and support for parish councils;
- Better consultation between counties, districts and town and parish councils;
- Increased support for voluntary groups.

# 12

## Contents

## 12.1. Introduction

**12.1.1.**   People in rural communities care strongly about the places where they live, about the services and activities that hold the community together, the local landscape and its features, and how it is likely to evolve in the future. Every country town and village has its own priorities, local strengths and distinctive features which are special and unique.

**12.1.2.**   We recognise that diversity and local pride. We want to enable rural communities to improve their quality of life and opportunity. We want to give them a bigger say in managing their own affairs and the chance to give everyone in the community a say in how it develops. To achieve this we will:

- Encourage all town and parish councils to reach the standards of the best, to achieve a new status in local government as the voice of their community and enable them to work more closely with their partners;
- Enable larger and efficient towns and parish councils to deliver a wider range of local services in partnership with principal authorities;
- Help all rural communities develop Town, Village and Parish Plans to indicate how they would like their town or village to develop, to identify key facilities and services, to set out the problems that need to be tackled and demonstrate how its distinctive character and features can be preserved;

- Create stronger local partnerships in rural areas through more modern local government, including the Community Strategies prepared by Counties and Districts;
- Help rural communities train and attract volunteers to support local projects.

## 12.2. Strengthening town and parish councils – the most local tier of local government

**An active community meeting in Amebury, Wiltshire**
Credit: Salisbury District Council

**12.2.1.**   We want to give rural communities a bigger chance to run their own affairs. For most country people, the town or village is the defining measure of local identity and the parish or town council, as the most basic unit of local government, is closest to their communities. But there is a large variation in the size, role and vigour of local councils. Some represent a hamlet of 50 people and others a town of 25,000 and it would not be right to seek the same role for all. While some already set an outstanding example in community leadership, a large number could or would like to do more and we will help them achieve that.

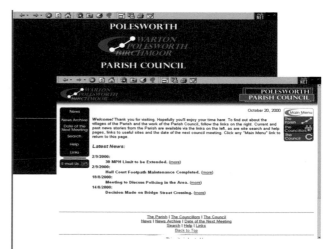

**Polesworth Parish Council's website, providing up-to-date information on the work of the Council, plus links to other useful sites**
Credit: © Adam Craig

## Quality town and parish councils

**12.2.2.** The potential for towns and parishes to take on a stronger role has been highlighted over the last decade but too often the right framework of support from Government or local partners has been missing. We will put this right. We envisage a new concept of a **quality town or parish council** to equip local councils to take on a stronger role and which would be achievable by any parish council, whatever its size or role. We will be consulting widely, including with the Local Government Association in the Central/Local Partnership, on how best to achieve this. We will want to see piloted innovative and imaginative partnerships involving such quality councils, their principal authorities (counties, districts and unitary authorities) and others so as to give rural communities a better deal on local services and a stronger voice in decisions affecting people's day to day lives. A quality parish council will:

- Be representative of all parts of its community;
- Meet a **quality test** – show that it is effectively managed, with audited accounts and a trained clerk (See Box);
- Be committed to work in partnership with principal authorities;
- In proportion to size and its skills, deliver local services for principal authorities;
- Work closely with voluntary groups in the town or village;
- Lead work by the community on the Town or Village Plan;
- Working with its partners, act as an information point for local services.

- **A quality test** would operate through a series of simple criteria which can be easily validated. **We will be consulting further on the details of these but we think they are likely to include**

  - Electoral mandate – for example all parish councillors to have stood for election;

  - Minimum number of meetings in year (greater than the 3 meetings and annual meeting already required to show activity of council);

  - Trained parish clerk (to indicate a basic competence);

  - Published annual report describing its activities;

  - Up-to-date, unqualified and properly audited accounts;

  - For Best Value parish councils the test could include that the annual performance plan had been cleared by the auditor, and that no adverse report following an inspection had been issued;

  - A further test – of minimum size (perhaps based on annual expenditure) – would be used for councils wishing to consider taking on services from district councils. It would be open to smaller parish councils to meet this test through a partnership with a neighbouring parish council. It may be possible to require that councils wishing to qualify as 'quality' parish councils, who are below the best value income threshold (£500,000 pa) but above, say, £100,000 pa, 'opt in' to the best value arrangements and have their compliance certified by the auditor.

---

### How a Quality Parish would work

The first requirement of a quality parish council is that it is representative of its community. To demonstrate that, it will actively engage all its residents, businesses and surrounding landowners and managers in its work through regular meetings and events, newsletters, surveys, working groups, youth councils etc. In conjunction with them it will identify the needs of its community and set out its priorities for action in a readable and widely available parish plan. Working in partnership with principal local authorities (counties, districts and unitary authorities) and other agencies affecting its village, it will be a key part of their local consultation processes – contributing to housing, transport, health and other local plans. Already, those parish councils who are **best value parish councils** (budgeted income in excess of £500,000 a year – see paragraph 12.4.7) will be doing many of these things to fulfil their best value duties.

The quality parish council, working with partners, including the voluntary and community sector, will **undertake services funded from its own resources – looking after the village environment** (litter, bus shelters, village green, cemeteries etc) and provide public facilities such as playgrounds and village halls. It will help to draw up a **town or village plan**, and support local biodiversity action plans. To promote **inclusive communities** it will support community transport schemes and childcare provision; seek suitable sites and projects for affordable housing, and help develop youth activities and services for the elderly. The quality parish council in partnership with its principal authority and others, may wish to **take on the delivery of some services** (eg facilities management, litter collection, street lighting) on behalf of its partners, where this represents best value and gives the local community the best deal.

**Wired up through ICT**, the quality parish council will be an access point for information about local services (bus times, taxis, community transport, concessionary fares, housing applications, council tax rebates/housing benefit, council agendas/minutes, local plan/planning applications etc) and for further advice.

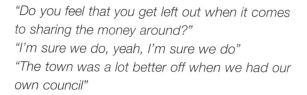

*"Do you feel that you get left out when it comes to sharing the money around?"*
*"I'm sure we do, yeah, I'm sure we do"*
*"The town was a lot better off when we had our own council"*

Standon Parish Information Centre, Hertfordshire, where villagers can access information on jobs, training and use office facilities
Credit: National Association of Local Councils

## Towns and parishes influencing and delivering local services

**12.2.3.** A parish council which meets the quality standard is demonstrating that it is active, competent and representative and, in relation to its size is able to play **an enhanced role in partnership with principal authorities**. We see the key elements of this role as being:

- an integral part of all **consultation** and co-ordination arrangements set up by principal authorities and other service providers on how services are delivered in its area including Community Planning (see paragraphs 12.4.3–5);
- partnership with principal authorities on the discussion, **management and delivery of services** which they, as parishes may carry out and deliver, on their partners' behalf, or using their existing powers, to give best value to local communities;
- quality parishes to work with partners on provision of **access points to information on services of principal authorities** and linked to their IT systems, for example through operation of high street kiosks, information points or a community office which can be used by a range of different services (County, District, Parish and other service providers).

**12.2.4.** In most local areas strong links already exist between parish and town councils and the principal tiers. Following the joint Local Government Association/National Association of Local Councils concordat on relations between the tiers, many local authorities have agreed **local level concordats** and agreements on consultative and other links. These agreements can help parish and town councils, whatever their size, to contribute more effectively to local governance.

- We will set out in **guidance**, which we will publish in draft for consultation, **how a Quality Parish might work**, what tests it should meet, and, building on the LGA/NALC protocol, how principal authorities and town/parish councils can work together in partnership to better meet the needs of their communities. We will include a model 'charter' based on existing Best Practice by Counties and Districts which will enable principal authorities to set out the basis on which well managed parishes could act in partnership with principal authorities and deliver on their behalf neighbourhood services including provision of public information, management of facilities such as car parks, markets, or local amenities and maintenance and cleaning of public space;

- Subject to consultation, we will amend our guidance on Best Value (see paragraphs 12.4.6-7) so that **principal authorities include their terms for partnership with parishes on neighbourhood service delivery** and to enable Town and Parish Councils who wish to do so to put their own proposals on service delivery. To support this process we will also consider changes to bring more Town and Parish Councils into the Best Value regime (as set out in paragraph 12.4.7).

- We expect to see over time a significant increase in the number of **service delivery partnerships between principal authorities and parishes** which meet Best Value principles. These would entail Town and Parish Councils who are able and willing, taking on more of the most basic local functions, such as running the local market, car parks or providing public information, with the support of their partner authorities.

Bramshott and Liphook Parish Council's Information Point, Hampshire, which offers local people access to a Citizen's Advice Bureau, East Hampshire Housing Association, and access to the County Council Information Centre via a free-phone link
Credit: Bramshott and Liphook Parish Council

A lengthsman involved in highways maintenance – one of the duties devolved to parishes under Staffordshire County Council's Parish Council Charter
Credit: Staffordshire County Council

## Case study – Staffordshire Parish Council Charter

The **Staffordshire** Parish Council Charter between Staffordshire County Council and the Staffordshire parish and town councils was agreed in 1995 and reviewed and renewed in 1999. It covers themes such as consultation, service provision, practical support and information and complaints. Under the charter, parishes have agreed to undertake routine highways maintenance (grass cutting, sign cleaning etc); to manage local public footpaths, and to assist in monitoring waste management sites for the county council. The county council has also led a number of training courses for local councils and has agreed the use of its central Print and Design Unit for local council publications and leaflets. The principles of the charter are also carried through into locally agreed charters between district councils and local councils. There is general agreement that the Charter has been a real benefit to improved inter-tier working in the county.

**12.2.5.** Our modernising local government agenda will promote much closer working between authorities – for example through community planning and Best Value. These give principal authorities a strong incentive to work in partnership with parishes among other local partners. And **we want to encourage both parishes and principal authorities to work much more closely together**. Our goal is greater co-operation between all tiers. As part of our consultation on Quality Parishes (as in paragraph 12.2.4) we would welcome ideas on how best to achieve this, including the contribution that conciliation based on local government best practice might make in bringing this about.

## Support and training for parish councils

Students on the residential Level 1 Local Policy Course at Cheltenham and Gloucester College of Higher Education
Credit: Cheltenham & Gloucester College of Higher Education

**12.2.6.** To help parish councils to meet the quality standard we will give them support and assistance. We will making available £2m over the next three years to help:

- A national strategy to provide **training and support** for parish and town councils in partnership with NACC, LGA and IDeA – the local government training organisation;

- The Countryside Agency will equip every town and parish council with access to an **internet linked management** and **best practice toolkit** to help provide simple guidance, learn from experience elsewhere, and make parishes more effective, representative and accountable.

## Funding for parish councils

**12.2.7.** We want to make sure that the financial arrangements for parish councils will help them take on the new quality parish role. We are consulting in our Green Paper *Modernising Local Government Finance* on several reforms including:

- Increasing or removing the limit on the amount that parishes can raise for expenditure that will benefit their area and for which they have no specific powers;
- Strengthening the prevention of 'double taxation' of parish residents – where they pay for a service to be provided in their area by the parish but also have to contribute to the cost of provision of that service elsewhere by the principal authority;
- Simplifying the financial regime for funding capital expenditure by parishes and reducing the auditing requirements for small parishes.

**12.2.8.** The Green Paper also looks at whether different financial regimes should apply to smaller and larger parish councils (including the possibility of the latter having similar controls, freedoms, responsibilities and access to government grants and the business rate as principal authorities; and at how access to such funding could be managed in practice). To ensure that parish councils act with propriety the new ethical framework being introduced by the *Local Government Act 2000* will apply to parish councils and provide a mechanism for upholding their ethical standards.

**12.2.9.** To help parishes do more to support their local communities we have also decided to give parishes more direct access to government funding for parish led **transport schemes** (as set out in chapter 6) and for the development of parish plans (see 12.3.3) and community projects identified in them (set out in chapter 3).

## 12.3. Town and village plans

**12.3.1.** We want to give rural communities the chance to set out what their town or village should look like and to guide its future development. The best decisions on these issues result from giving local people a share in those decisions. That means not only the opportunity to comment on individual proposals, but the ability to set out a vision of what is important, how new development can best be fitted in, the design and quality standards it should meet, how to preserve valued local features and to map out the facilities and services which the community needs to safeguard for the future. This can include the surrounding countryside, for example including Estate Plans and farm diversification.

**12.3.2.** By taking the policies set out in the local Development Plan and setting out their views on how those should be achieved, local communities have a real opportunity to influence the nature and quality of future development. Town and parish councils are well placed to lead this process and providing their Plan is consistent with the local Development Plan, and the relevant national planning guidance, the design and land use aspects can be endorsed by the planning authority as **Supplementary Planning Guidance**. This approach has the potential to reduce the adversarial nature of new proposals and reduce costs for all, but this will only be achieved if everyone in the community has a real opportunity to contribute their views.

Part of the village of Dalton, Lancashire and its Village Design Statement
Credit: Dalton Parish Council. Photo and drawing: J M Goodger

**12.3.3.** Some communities and local authorities have prepared local design guides and some have carried out **parish appraisal and Village Design Statements** but overall less than 2% of rural communities have a plan or appraisal which is specific to their community. Creating such plans takes time, effort, and the commitment to try to achieve a common vision for the future. We will help local communities achieve that:

- We will set up a new £5m programme administered by the Countryside Agency to help **1,000 rural communities prepare their own town or village plan;**

- We will set out in **national planning guidance the role that town or village plans** can play now as Supplementary Planning Guidance. We will also examine whether and how the role of more locally based plans in the planning system might be further developed.

### Case study – Taunton Deane planning scheme

Taunton Deane Borough Council in 1993 initiated a trial scheme devolving minor planning decisions to eight parish councils (with populations ranging from 380 to 1,200). Planning Officers employed by the Borough Council attended and advised meetings of the parish councils discussing applications, at which applicants and members of the public had the right to speak. By the end of 1996, 249 planning applications had been decided by parish councils – in 237 cases the Planning Officer's recommendation had been followed, 10 had been approved against recommendation, and 2 refused against recommendation. No appeals were lodged in the first three years of the scheme's operation and the scheme has been judged very successful.

**12.3.4.** A town or village plan is also about much more than design and land use issues. Developing or safeguarding local services such as shops and leisure facilities and addressing community needs such as the availability of space for playgroups or a meeting room are issues which a comprehensive plan can tackle. The plan is an opportunity to develop community agreement on local priorities and options for addressing them and is an important input to the wider community planning by districts and counties described in paragraphs 12.4.3-6. below.

### Case study – Braintree Quality of Life Plan

**Braintree District Council's Quality of Life Plan 1999** was produced following extensive consultation and opinion polling, including active encouragement for parish and town councils to carry out their own community appraisals. A 'Village Appraisal Fieldworker' was appointed to assist parish and town councils and community groups in carrying out the appraisal process. The 54 parish and town councils with the district have also formed 14 parish cluster groups which provide forums for bottom up feedback to the district council and other service providers on local issues needing action, and an opportunity for neighbouring parishes to discuss issues of common concern.

The Braintree Quality of Life Plan, along with its Annual Report, detailing what the Plan achieved for local people during its first year
Credit: Braintree District Coucil

## 12.4. Modern local government for rural areas

**12.4.1.** Town and Village Plans are an important input to a wider framework. To improve the full range of local services for rural communities needs a broader partnership approach which involves not only counties, districts, towns and parishes but the other key public service providers such as health and police authorities. In many rural areas, particularly those which need regeneration, the Regional Development Agencies will have a key role to play. Progress entails a commitment to working together to the principles of continuous improvement, building on success and best practice, using new technology to improve services and to engage the communities they serve in their decision making.

The Government's e-envoy visited Rutland, to see how Rutnet works
Credit: Rutnet

**12.4.2.** Rural areas will benefit from more modern local government which contributes to a process of democratic renewal by ensuring that councils are accountable, open and responsive to local needs. Key reforms are: the duty to prepare community strategies; the changes to the constitutions of councils; the introduction of the best value regime; and local Public Service Agreements. Each of these is being implemented to reflect rural issues. We are also intending to modernise the local government finance system.

### Case study – LGA Website of the Year 2000

The **Rutnet** (www.rutnet.co.uk) site is a partnership between Rutland County Council and Rutland On Line Ltd to provide an essential virtual community and information resource. The site raises awareness of the potential of the internet and e-commerce for local businesses, enhancing on-line information on lifelong learning opportunities and encouraging village communities to join and contribute to the information network.

## Community strategies and community planning

**12.4.3.** Community leadership is central to the role of modern local government and counties and districts are well placed to provide a clear co-ordinated overview of a community's needs across a wide range of services and to ensure that action is taken to respond to them. We have therefore introduced a new duty on principal councils to produce community strategies which promote the economic, social and environmental well-being of their communities. They will be expected to bring together parish and town councils, other public agencies, the private and voluntary sectors and all sections of the local community, to identify and work towards a long term vision and action for improving the quality of life in their area. The town and village plans set out in Section 12.3 will be an important contributor to the community strategy for the wider local authority.

**12.4.4.** The community planning approach can particularly benefit rural governance because:

- Typically rural areas have three (and four in areas with national park authorities) layers of local government – encouraging joint working and service co-location between these authorities (and others) can therefore be particularly fruitful;
- There may be a perception which a plan can dispel that rural communities and their needs can be overlooked in some more urban dominated local authorities with rural fringe and/or hinterlands within their area;
- Rural communities can be widely dispersed within a local authority area and can have, for various reasons, widely different access to services and different needs and aspirations. The community planning process should help to identify and meet these needs;
- The integrated planning of services in dispersed communities is particularly critical to ensuring reasonable access to services and preventing social exclusion.

**12.4.5.** We believe that local authorities themselves, with the local strategic partnerships they establish and with the active involvement of local people, should determine the process for preparing their community strategies. However, we will:

- Make clear in the **community strategies guidance** that the approach to preparing them should take account of rural circumstances in relevant areas, also setting out the role that effective parish and town councils can play;
- Work with the LGA on the production of companion guidance on good practice for community strategies which will include examples from rural areas.

### Local Strategic Partnerships (LSPs)

We are currently consulting widely on our proposals for Local Strategic Partnerships (LSPs) which have the goal of improving public services by bringing together all service providers at local level, in partnership with their local communities and business sectors. We are not asking authorities to duplicate existing partnership arrangements, but rather to build on the arrangements they have already established. Partnerships set up in line with the guidance on community strategies would, by definition, be LSPs.

*"I just think they need to stop lumping everyone together and think about places as individual rather than looking at one thing overall and saying, 'Well that's good for everybody', 'cos it doesn't work like that, 'cos it's quite unique here – there's not many places that are this far away from anything. I just think it needs to be realised that it is different and needs thinking about in a different way"*

### Case study – New Commitment to Regeneration

The "New Commitment to Regeneration" approach developed by the Local Government Association provides models of how a Local Strategic Partnership can work. The twenty two local authority-led strategic partnerships comprising public, private, voluntary sector and community partners have included a number covering rural areas.

#### Herefordshire

The partners in Herefordshire are committed to the concept of 'One Partnership, One Plan' to provide an overarching framework to link the needs of local people to specific policy agendas and individual organisations' business plans. But although comprehensive it is intended to keep the concept streamlined. The plan will, therefore, serve as a:

- Community Plan;
- Local Agenda 21 Plan;
- Regeneration Strategy;
- Local Performance Plan.

As a rural area, Herefordshire's main need is for the plan to provide for a widely scattered population where poverty and relative prosperity exist in close proximity. Community involvement and consultation is a crucial feature of a Herefordshire approach.

**The South Wiltshire Alliance** (a partnership involving 12 local stakeholders including Wiltshire CC and Salisbury DC) has been developing a joint approach to community planning since June 1998. Community plans have been developed for each of the six identifiable communities in South Wiltshire. Some 32,000 local people have contributed to the area plans which include 'action plans' setting out targets for the local agencies on the priority themes: young people; crime; rural life and services; rural transport; and health and welfare.

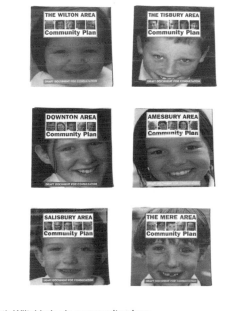

South Wiltshire's six community plans
Credit: Salisbury District Council

### New constitutions for councils – The Local Government Act 2000

**12.4.6.** The *Local Government Act 2000* provides the powers and structures to help every county and district council to meet the needs of local people more effectively. The changes brought about under Part II of this Act will see the implementation of new constitutions for councils which will ensure everyone knows who is in charge of the local council and the services it provides. It gives authorities greater flexibility to adopt systems to suit their area; for example area committees may bring particular benefits to rural areas. Most councils will have the choice of three styles of executive governance: mayor and cabinet; leader and cabinet; and mayor and council manager. In addition to the executive arrangements available to all councils, there is an additional framework based on a modernised committee system with integral overview and scrutiny available to small

district councils in two-tier areas. These options will enable rural councils to develop political management arrangements that will put in place the strong and accountable leadership that is necessary for building thriving rural communities.

### Best Value

**12.4.7.** A central objective for both local and central government service delivery will be to develop clear and published targets for accessibility of all services, and the duty of Best Value (see Box) placed on local authorities sets the framework for this. While this process is still underway and it will take time for the full benefits to feed through, the approach has already helped authorities to improve their services in rural areas. Best value also applies to some 41 larger **town and parish councils** and we will look again at whether it would be helpful to bring more town and parish councils within this regime particularly where it supports partnership arrangements for the delivery of services on behalf of principal authorities by towns/parishes. In the meantime we will amend Best Value guidance to enable town/parish councils to make proposals on service delivery on behalf of principal authorities.

Carrick District Council in West Cornwall held a door-to-door review of the 'community alarm service' as part of its Best Value pilot project. The alarm service allows local residents to remain in the rural home they have often lived in all their lives. An action plan was produced following the review identified the need for closer links to social services, the health authority and CCTV monitoring.
Credit: Carrick District Council

**12.4.8.** We are determined to make sure that Best Value delivers better services for rural communities. To achieve this:

- **The Best Value performance indicators which we are introducing include 'fair access' to services (in terms of ease and equality of access).** 'Fair access' embraces both getting services to the people who need them and providing services to 'hard to get at' groups. In both cases an important feature of the Best Value regime is to ensure that 'fair access' embraces geographic accessibility for dispersed communities and people, for example villages or clusters of villages and market towns;

- We will **amend Best Value guidance** so that principal authorities include the terms on which they would work in partnership with town/parish councils on delivery of neighbourhood services (see paragraph 12.2.4) and ask principal authorities to report on their consideration of town and parish proposals in their Performance Plan. To help parishes who wish to take on a stronger role we will also consider how to bring more town and parish councils within the Best Value regime without creating an unacceptable burden;

- We are supporting the setting up of rural networks for authorities to develop and disseminate best practice within the local government community and promote joined-up and partnership working amongst the various stakeholders;

- We are asking the Audit Commission as well as the Countryside Agency to review and report on how Best Value is promoting greater accessibility to councils' services in the light of experience;

## Funding for local government

**12.4.9.** We will be providing average real increases of 3% a year for local authorities over the next three years. The extra costs for rural authorities in delivering services to a dispersed population are taken account of, along with other factors, in the current system for distributing revenue grant. In 1998 (before the current three-year freeze on grant distribution formula changes was introduced) we made an adjustment for the extra costs to social service departments of delivering domiciliary care (such as home helps) in rural areas.

**12.4.10.** Local authorities in rural areas and elsewhere have been contributing to the review of how grant is distributed to them. We have now issued a Green Paper consulting on proposals to modernise local government finance *Modernising Local Government Finance* and invited responses by Friday 8 December 2000.

---

### Local Public Service Agreements (PSAs)

We are currently working with 20 local authorities to develop and pilot local Public Service Agreements from April 2001. The intention is that individual councils will be able to sign up to challenging targets in about twelve areas of national or local importance. In return, they will receive agreed operational freedoms and flexibilities to help them deliver their services more effectively, some limited financial assistance up-front and rewards for success if they meet their targets. Local PSAs therefore provide an opportunity for direct discussion between central and local government taking into account local circumstances, including the needs of rural areas.

The pilots include a number of counties with large rural areas (Kent, Cambridgeshire, Norfolk, Derbyshire and Warwickshire). We are currently discussing their proposals, which include targets for rural issues such as better rural transport, improved accessibility to services and pupil achievement in rural schools

---

## 12.5. More active rural communities

**12.5.1.** A healthy and active voluntary and community sector is essential to the effective functioning of society – urban and rural. The voluntary sector often steps in to meet local needs and fill gaps in services, and the social networks which link local residents also encourage mutual aid. Activity ranges over a very wide spectrum from organising leisure activities' through relatively informal volunteer-run welfare activities (meals on wheels, community transport schemes, play groups etc), to professionally-run projects by non-profit making organisations. The report by the Social Exclusion Unit Policy Action Team on *Community Self-Help (PAT9)* concluded that community activity needs sensitive, well directed support by local authorities, government agencies, and other public bodies in the form of commitment, training, and the will and capacity to work across organisational boundaries. Women are often at the heart of the social networks which link local residents and encourage mutual support. They play a key role in understanding and responding to the needs of rural communities.

Watton at Stone's local transport information leaflet
Credit: Watton at Stone Parish Council

### Voluntary and community sector

**12.5.2.** In rural areas, the voluntary and community sector is highly varied: individuals and purely local groups; branches or members of national organisations; and local development agencies working to support voluntary action. The 38 county-based Rural Community Councils are an important part of the voluntary sector in rural areas. They work to promote the welfare of local communities through voluntary effort and self-help. They undertake research, collect and disseminate information, provide technical and professional support and represent the voluntary sector.

---

### Case studies – Chillington Village Care Scheme and Benington, Aston and Watton at Stone Transport Survey

**Chillington** village in Bedfordshire is running a Village Care Scheme. Volunteers have given every resident in the village a number which they can call and ask for help with virtually anything from a lift to the shops or changing a light bulb, to filling in a form or picking up a prescription.

The parishes of **Benington, Aston and Watton at Stone** in East Hertfordshire have undertaken transport needs surveys for their communities, identifying journey patterns, modes of transport and volunteers for a voluntary car scheme. A community bus scheme for elderly residents has also been piloted in Aston as a result of the surveys, and local transport timetables showing all modes of transport (including buses, trains, taxis community and voluntary transport) have been produced for each village and distributed to every household.

---

### Case study – Wensleydale Community Office

**Yorkshire Rural Community Council** (YRCC) was involved in setting up a Community Office in Wensleydale. The office is an access point for both district and county services ie housing, planning, social services etc, plus a Job Centre; Citizens' Advice Bureau; a police contact where crime can be reported and documents processed; business advice; trading standards advice; community education; tourist information; and, through links with the local college, training and work placements. They also provide internet access for the public; a laptop computer loan scheme for students; community printing; and paypoints for gas and electricity. Over 10,000 visits are made to the centre each year. The Community Office is the culmination of YRCC work over a long period of time with communities in the Upper Dales area through the Upper Wensleydale Community Partnership consisting of community organisations, businesses and county, district and the parish councils. The office now runs with little YRCC involvement but their role in setting it up was crucial. The office has been so successful that other communities are asking for YRCC's involvement to set up similar offices in other parts of Yorkshire.

**12.5.3.** We have increased support for the rural voluntary sector which now receives it from a wide variety of sources. These include local authorities, National Lottery Charities Board, and funding from the EU Leader Programme (in designated areas). The Countryside Agency provides funding for Rural Community Councils and for the NCVO Rural Unit; and for specific initiatives such as the Local Heritage Initiative, Millennium Greens, and Parish Path Partnerships.

'The Village Hall' by Katie Gresswell
Credit: East Markham Village Design Statement, © Trade Link Publications

### Village halls and community centres

**12.5.4.** A key part of the infrastructure for much local voluntary activity is an adequate community centre – both as a place for meeting and to host activities. Rural communities will generally not have the access to the range of public buildings which voluntary groups in some urban areas will have but will depend on a village or church hall or other community centre. Current availability of such facilities is quite good (70% of parishes have access to some kind of facility) although the size may be limited and quality is very variable. Increasingly village halls are being used as access points for a wider range of services and other activities and we are encouraging this.

### Case study – Mickleton Village Hall

Mickleton Village Hall (Teesdale, County Durham) provides a range of facilities for its local community including art, needlework, dance and women's self-defence classes. The hall is also used for badminton, a youth club, playgroup, film showings, theatre performances and a day club for older people. The Hall has its own website, courtesy of www.teesdalehalls.co.uk, detailing exactly what and when events are taking place, and people are encouraged to come along to the hall's monthly management committee meeting to offer any ideas or views they may have.

Mickleton Village Hall, Tynedale – a multi-function activity centre for the local community
Credit: Mickleton Village Hall Association

### Supporting voluntary activity in rural communities

**12.5.5.** To strengthen the rural voluntary and community sector we will be taking the following steps

- **Making sure new government voluntary and community sector initiatives are accessible to rural communities.** For example the two new Home Office funding projects for small community groups (the Community Resource Fund and the Community Development Learning Fund) which arose from recommendations in the *PAT 9 report* are both being piloted in rural as well as urban areas;

- We will continue to support through the Countryside Agency the infrastructure for the voluntary sector in rural areas (the Rural Community Councils) including support for village halls. We are providing additional funds for community development work on social exclusion (see 4.4.14) and for community projects (see 3.2.5)

# thinking rural

## The issues

- The impact of government policies on rural people, businesses, and the countryside has not always been properly considered, and they have not always been adjusted to take account of specific rural problems.
- A lack of co-ordination of government policies and activity in rural areas has meant that programmes are not best managed to resolve conflicts and get the results everyone wants.
- Rural people feel that they are not sufficiently listened to.

## The future – what we want to see

- Systematic assessment of the rural dimension of all government policies as they are developed and implemented – nationally, regionally and locally.
- Programmes targeted on management of the countryside, for aims which have been agreed with local communities and businesses, co-ordinated to maximise their impact and avoid duplication and conflict.
- Better arrangements to ensure that government knows what rural communities want, and that the communities themselves are involved in the implementation of policy.

**Summary of measures**

- Annual report by the Countryside Agency on the rural aspects of government policies, as well as their annual *State of the Countryside* report;

- A rural 'check-list' for Government Departments to ensure that they take account of the rural dimension in developing policy;

- Better regional co-ordination of Government activities, with MAFF regional strategy staff joining Government Offices;

- Establishment of National and Regional Rural Sounding Boards.

# 13

## Contents

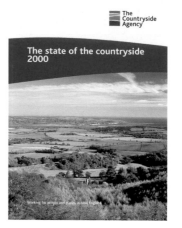

The Countryside Agency State of the Countryside Report 2000 – monitoring and evaluating the state of the rural areas, and advising Government accordingly, is an important part of the Agency's work

## 13.1. Introduction

**13.1.1.** Our consultation with people in preparing this White Paper revealed some clear messages about the way that Government deals with rural issues:

- That the government often appears not to 'think rural' when developing and implementing its policies. We have been urged to make sure all our policies are 'rural-proofed';

- It was emphasised that the need for 'joined-up' government is particularly important in rural areas. The gain from working together can be very great. The use of a village outlet, such as a Post Office, by many different services, can mean the difference between viability or closure;

- Made clear they felt that rural communities are not always listened to, and that they need to be more directly involved themselves.

**13.1.2.** Our aim is therefore to:

- Ensure that our policies take account of specific rural needs;
- Encourage better coordinated programmes and projects both locally and regionally;
- Strengthen the ways in which we listen to the rural voice

## 13.2. Rural proofing

> **What does rural proofing mean?**
> Rural proofing means that as policy is developed and implemented policy makers should systematically:
> - Think about whether there will be any significant differential impacts in rural areas;
> - If there are such impacts assess what these might be;
> - Consider what adjustments/compensations might be made to fit rural circumstances.

### At the national level

**13.2.1.** The Prime Minister has already set up the Cabinet Committee on Rural Affairs to coordinate our policies for rural areas and to consider major rural policy issues. We need to build on this. As announced in *Spending Review 2000*, we will now be underpinning the work of the Cabinet Committee through a number of measures:

- We are providing for a fuller role for the **Countryside Agency, the Government's statutory adviser on rural issues.** We established the Agency in April 1999 as a rural champion. It will be advising Government and its partners across the range of rural issues, conducting research and highlighting, piloting and spreading best practice. The Agency is establishing a rural-proofing studies unit to look at particular service areas;

- The Agency will make annual reports on the rural aspects of the Government's policies. This will be published, and considered by the Cabinet Committee on Rural Affairs and the **Rural Sounding Board** along with the Agency's annual *State of the Countryside* report (see 13.4.1.);

- The Agency is preparing a **rural checklist** to help policy makers take account of the rural dimension as policy is developed. Our Cabinet Office guidance on better policy making (being developed in the light of the Cabinet Office's report on improved policy making in government *Professional policy making for the 21st century*) will identify rural impact as an issue to be routinely considered, and will give contacts for further advice and assistance;

- **Each Government Department will make an annual report to the Cabinet Committee on Rural Affairs on how their policies have been rural proofed.** A central rural contact point within each department will be established to co-ordinate their rural proofing of policy. This will include periodic meetings with Countryside Agency on current policy development and research programmes. Where appropriate, departments will undertake rural pilots of programmes and policies and develop targets and monitoring systems for key programmes that identify rural impacts;

- **We will equip policy makers with rural policy skills and awareness.** Staff training and development, with help from the Centre for Management and Policy Studies (the main civil service training organisation), will include training on rural policy issues. We will also promote secondments between Government Departments, the Countryside Agency and rural bodies so as to develop wider experience and perspectives on rural issues.

### Case study – rural proofing in practice: Sure Start

The Sure Start national unit in the Department for Education and Employment has worked with the Countryside Agency to make Sure Start (see box at 4.4.12) work effectively in rural areas.

Changes to the Sure Start catchment model will make it more suitable for rural areas where children living in poverty are dispersed over a wide geographical area. This follows research carried out by the Countryside Agency earlier this year which suggested changes to the Sure Start criteria to help rural areas participate. The key ones: were greater flexibility over numbers; a broader understanding of the term 'coherent neighbourhood'; an appreciation of the higher per capita cost of providing services for dispersed rural populations; and a recognition of the low existing service base on which to create new services and facilities.

A small number of programmes among the third wave of Sure Start programmes will try out new models in rural areas with a view to developing further guidance. The new models are likely to include proposals for small villages targeting individual families and working out from a small town into a small rural area.

### Regional level

**13.2.2.** It is also important that Government takes full account of the rural dimension regionally. The nine Government Offices act as the voice of central government in the regions, managing regional programmes on behalf of departments and facilitating effective linkages between local partners and programmes. There is already a network of rural contact points within each regional Government Office. These meet periodically and also have meetings with central government Departments. Similarly the Regional Development Agencies have a rural network. **The Government Offices** have a crucial role to play in taking forward our rural agenda. To ensure that they play this role effectively:

- Government Offices' annual reports to central Government will in future include an explicit rural report and will report collectively on the regional implications of national rural policy developments;

- We will encourage secondments and exchanges of staff between organisations with a rural remit so as to broaden their rural expertise;

- The Countryside Agency's regional offices will advise and assist other regional organisations in taking forward the rural dimension of their work.

## 13.3. Better co-ordination of policies in rural areas

### Better regional co-ordination by government

**13.3.1.** The PIU report *Reaching Out* on the role of Government at the regional and local level found that, while there was a great deal of good work going on at regional level, the regional networks of Government Departments were fragmented, with no part of Government responsible for co-ordinated action in the regions. The clear message was that Government would need drastically to improve the way it develops and implements policy affecting regional and local areas. To follow up the PIU report:

- We have set up a new cross-departmental **Regional Co-ordination Unit (RCU)** to modernise the way Government works at regional and local level. Through the RCU we will improve the delivery of public services by overhauling the way in which we identify priorities and develop policies which affect the regions. This will involve changing the way we work both in Whitehall and the regions;

- We are strengthening the presence of key Government Departments in the regional offices. From 1 April 2001, **MAFF will participate fully in the work of the Government Offices for the Regions** by providing a senior member of its staff (with support) to join each office. This will strengthen MAFF's contribution to developing and implementing policy in the regions and building relationships with regional stakeholders.

**13.3.2.** The Government Offices will work in partnership with the Regional Development Agencies, the Countryside Agency, English Nature and others in delivering our rural policies and programmes.

- **We will encourage more co-ordinated rural data collection and sharing of information** at the regional level between different Government Departments and other organisations, for instance through joint commissioning of research and sharing the results from research programmes.

**13.3.3.** The preparation of the regional chapters of the England Rural Development Programme (ERDP) has already been a major step forward in a more integrated approach to rural development bringing together agricultural and forestry organisations with those with an interest in the environmental, social and wider economic issues to develop the strategy for the Programme. The mid-term review of the ERDP in 2003 will consider whether further integration of the regional delivery activities within the Government Office framework would be appropriate.

- We will build on the skills of staff in the Farming and Rural Conservation Agency and MAFF's Regional Service Centres **to create a new delivery service for the England Rural Development Programme;**

- **We will create a new CAP payments agency,** merging the functions of MAFF's nine Regional Service Centres and the Intervention Board to provide top quality customer service using modern electronic systems.

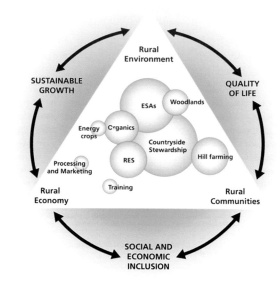

The England Rural Development Programme
Credit: MAFF

### Budget co-ordination

**13.3.4.** One obstacle to joined up delivery is that budgets for complementary activities are held by separate organisations. At a local level, local authorities already have considerable budgetary flexibility. We have increased the scope for flexibility through:

- **The new power for local authorities to take any action they consider necessary to promote or improve the economic, social, and/or environmental well-being of their local area and communities,** introduced by the Local Government Act 2000;

- **The new power for Health Authorities to fund non-health functions** introduced by the *Health Act 1999*. The Health Act also from April 2000 gave NHS bodies and local governments wider powers to develop joint funding and delivery of services where they wish to do so.

**13.3.5.** We will continue the development of a **joint countryside planning process** which will entail co-ordinating the use of resources for rural areas at regional level across a range of bodies including MAFF, DETR, English Nature, the Countryside Agency, English Heritage and Regional Development Agencies. This will make sure that the best value is obtained from the interaction of these programmes and that local activity such as one-stop shops can be facilitated.

Willow weaving at the Burnley Forest, an initiative funded by the **East Lancashire Partnership**
Credit: East Lancashire Partnership

**13.3.6.** We wish to see more co-ordination of funds from different agencies to support an integrated plan for a local area, to achieve a specific local objective or to deliver joint service plans for particular communities or joint initiatives to tackle social exclusion. We are proposing a more co-ordinated approach in market towns (see chapter 7). We are already developing land management initiatives with a more 'one-stop' approach such as the MAFF Uplands Experiments (see box in section 8.2). The Countryside Agency's study into restoration of the South Downs and English Nature's proposals for Lifescapes (see section 10.3) will also develop more co-ordinated approaches.

**13.3.7.** The Local Government Association is piloting an initiative, Urban/Rural Compacts, to look at how to make a reality of an integrated approach and the urban-rural connections.

## 13.4. Listening to the rural voice

### Listening nationally

**13.4.1.** It is important that Ministers should be fully informed of the state of the countryside and should have have regular and direct contact with the main rural groups so that they know what is going on and what countryside people think.

- **We will create the new role of Rural Advocate to argue the case on countryside issues and for rural people at the highest levels in government and outside.** The Rural Advocate will have direct access to the Prime Minister and his Ministers and will attend the Cabinet Committee on Rural Affairs, providing a voice at the heart of government for rural concerns. Together with the Countryside Agency, the Government's statutory advisor on the countryside, the Rural Advocate will play a key part in rural proofing policy decisions and implementation. The Rural Advocate will be a member of the National Rural Sounding Board, bringing to it expertise and an authoritative voice, and taking away from it messages based on the wide range of rural advice and experience available there. The advocate role will be taken on by the Chair of the Countryside Agency as an addition to his other responsibilities.

- **The Countryside Agency will submit to Government on an annual basis its** *Report on the State of the Countryside* in addition to its annual 'rural-proofing' report on the rural aspects of Government policy.

- **We will establish a National Rural Sounding Board, as set out in** *Spending Review 2000.* It will meet at least once a year. It will be chaired jointly by Ministers from DETR and MAFF, and will bring together Ministers from Government Departments with a wide variety of organisations and individuals with an interest in rural policy. It will be informed by the Countryside Agency's assessment of the Government's performance in its 'rural-proofing' report.

### Listening locally

**13.4.2.** We want to do more to ensure that local people are directly involved in public sector activities so that their voice can be heard, and their knowledge and experience can be fully used. One way that this can be done is by the establishment of consultative groups so that those making and implementing policy locally can hear local concerns at first hand. Many regions have already established rural forums to address rural issues.

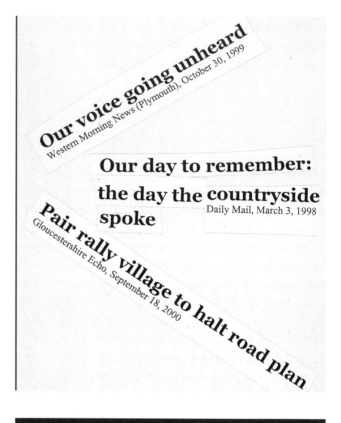

Our voice going unheard
*Western Morning News (Plymouth), October 30, 1999*

**Our day to remember: the day the countryside spoke**
Daily Mail, March 3, 1998

Pair rally village to halt road plan
*Gloucestershire Echo, September 18, 2000*

### Case study – The Rural Forum for the North West of England

Established in May 1998 by the Government Office for the North West and MAFF, the Rural Forum for the North West of England aims to facilitate a 'rural voice' which can quickly respond to challenges in times of change, and advise regional decision makers and central government on rural policy issues. The Forum enables the exchange of information between rural interest groups including central government.

Since 1998, the Forum has agreed a programme of work and now has 230 members. It has been able to co-ordinate a coherent rural response on emerging issues such as the Regional Strategy, and Regional Planning Guidance Review and the ERDP.

More recently, the Forum has set-up a Social Inclusion Sub-Group to consider the issues of rural poverty and deprivation and to search out examples of best practice which can be propagated throughout the region. It also plans to organise a sub-group to monitor rural cross-regional border issues that range from land-use planning through to the stewardship of biodiversity in transitional areas.

**13.4.3.** But more can be done:

- **We will establish Regional Rural Sounding Boards** bringing together rural stakeholders within regions to inform and monitor the regional and local delivery of policy in rural areas. These will build on existing Rural Forum arrangements in each region, taking account of further developments in community involvement;

- We will set up a **Rural Sub-Group of the Central-Local Partnership**. This partnership brings together Ministers from relevant Departments with Councillors from the Local Government Association. The aim is to ensure that central government works more closely with the local government players who are close to their local communities. The sub-group will begin immediately to assist the implementation of this White Paper.

**13.4.4.** We also want the voice of local people to be heard and heeded by giving them more direct involvement in local policies. For instance, well integrated affordable housing for local people will best be achieved where the community has a say over its siting and design, and chapter 12 describes the encouragement we are giving to village appraisals and Village Design Statements.

**13.4.5.** Another example is the NHS Plan which will put **more responsibility in the hands of local professionals and local people**, to allow them choice in deciding the best way for their area to meet the national standards of care. Resources and greater responsibility have already been devolved to local groups of doctors and nurses working together with patient and community representation, in **Primary Care Trusts** and their precursor **Primary Care Groups.** At October 2000 43 Primary Care Trusts have been established to take direct responsibility for over 80% of the local healthcare budget and spend it in the best way to meet local needs. Some of these already cover rural populations where they have sought to ensure rural representation and the NHS Plan envisages 100% coverage by 2004.

**13.4.6.** Following the 1999 Health Act, NHS bodies such as PCTs and PCGs already have the discretionary power to work with local authorities to pool funds to enable more closely integrated services (see case study on Somerset Joint Commissioning Board). We now propose to make it possible for health and social services authorities to take the extra step to establish new multi-purpose legal bodies, to be known as Care Trusts, to be responsible for all health and social care. The first wave of Care Trusts could be in place next year.

### Case study – Herefordshire Primary Care Trust

Herefordshire is one of the smallest mainland Health Authorities in Britain in terms of population but one of the largest in terms of area covered. From October, its new Primary Care Trust will among other things:
- Devolve decision making and resources to local primary care professionals;
- Implement the second wave Personal Medical Service and Personal Dental Service pilots, improving health for the travelling community and enhancing dental services.

## Overall

**14.4.2.** We have set targets for indicators five, twelve, and thirteen as part of the Public Service and Service Delivery Agreements; and we have national targets which are relevant to indicators three, six, and seven, which refer to rural areas only. Where specific targets do not exist, **our aim is for the indicators to move in the right direction over time**. We will review progress and set further targets for specific outcomes in line with the commitments set out in this paper.

### Table 14.1: Headline Rural Indicators

| What we want to see | How we will know |
| --- | --- |
| Themes and objectives | Indicator(s) |
| **A Living Countryside** | |
| 1 Equitable access to services | Geographical availability of key services in rural areas: % of households within x km of food shops, post offices, cash points, child nurseries, primary schools, GP surgeries[6] |
| 2 Tackling poverty and social exclusion | Low income: % of people in rural wards in low income bands[5] |
| 3 Better education for all | Qualifications of young people in rural areas[5] |
| 4 An affordable home | Proportion of rural population disadvantaged in access to housing |
| 5 Better rural transport | Proportion of households in rural areas within about 10 minutes walk of at least hourly bus service[1] |
| 6 Safer communities | Recorded crime levels and fear of crime in rural areas[5] |
| **A Working Countryside** | |
| 7 High, stable levels of employment | Employment activity rates in rural areas[5], unemployment rates in rural areas[5] |
| 8 Prosperous market towns | Proportions of market towns that are thriving, stable or declining (based on service provision, business activity and employment) |
| 9 Thriving rural economies | Business health: new business start ups and turnover of businesses in rural areas[5] |
| 10 A new future for farming | Total Income from farming and off farm Income[2]<br>Agricultural employment (full-time, part-time and seasonal)[2] |
| **A Restored Countryside** | |
| 11 Protecting and enhancing the countryside | Change in countryside quality including biodiversity, tranquillity, heritage, and landscape character[6] |
| 12 Restoring and maintaining wildlife diversity | Populations of farmland birds[4,7]<br>Condition of Sites of Special Scientific Interest[3,4] |
| 13 Protection of natural resources | Rivers of good or fair quality[4]<br>Air quality (low level ozone) in rural areas[5] |
| 14 Increase enjoyment of the countryside | Numbers of people using the countryside and types of visit; kind of transport; and level and type of spend[6] |
| **A Vibrant Countryside** | |
| 15 Community involvement and activity | Community vibrancy: % of parishes in four categories (vibrant, active, barely active, sleeping) assessed on numbers of meeting places, voluntary and cultural activities, contested parish elections |

Notes to Table

A. This set of indicators will be derived largely from the existing sources of information and indicators referred to above (para 14.2.1. ). It comprises existing national indicators that are particularly relevant to rural areas (eg populations of farmland birds); indicators looking at the rural part of a national indicator (eg employment levels); and some specific to largely rural issues (eg health of market towns). The Countryside Agency plans to report on most of the indicators in April 2001 but numbers 4, 8, 11 and 15 are still under development.

B. What is taken as the meaning of 'rural' is currently decided separately for each policy heading. This causes difficulty for clear reporting, and for rural proofing. To tackle this, the Performance and Innovation Unit report on Rural Economies recommended that the Countryside Agency, ONS, DETR and MAFF should agree and promote a small set of rural definitions. We are now taking this work forward for both rural and urban definitions and will conclude it by the summer of 2001.

| | | | | | |
| --- | --- | --- | --- | --- | --- |
| 1 | DETR Service Delivery Agreement target | 4 | 'Quality of Life Counts' Indicator | 7 | MAFF Public Service Agreement Target |
| 2 | From MAFF's pilot set of Sustainable Agriculture Indicators A6 and A9 | 5 | Rural 'cut' of 'Quality of Life Counts' Indicator | | |
| 3 | DETR Public Service Agreement Target | 6 | Development of 'Quality of Life Counts' Indicator | | |

# Conclusion

**15.1.** Many of the measures set out in this White Paper mark the start of a process and it will take time, partnership and initiative to realise the potential of the policies we have set out. We want to see:

- a step change in improving access to, and the quality of, the essential services which rural people need;
- an economy in rural areas which can respond to the challenges of remoteness and lack of scale and which builds on the strengths and needs of small country towns and the land based sector, including farming; skills and employment levels as good in deprived rural areas as in the region as a whole;
- a protected countryside, rich in biodiversity and accessible to all, with less development pressure on greenfield sites;
- flourishing local communities taking an active part in influencing and managing the services they need, and in shaping their future.

**15.2.** Our countryside is vital – vital to those who live and work in it, vital for those who use and value what it produces, vital for all of us as a precious national asset. Tradition and change go hand-in-hand, as they always have. But the challenge of change in country areas is particularly pressing now. While people locally will in many cases provide the best responses to these challenges, there is a broader national perspective. Government has a responsibility to set the best possible framework in which our countryside can survive and thrive.

**15.3.** An integrated approach to urban and rural areas is essential. Rural and urban areas are different, with different perspectives on issues, and on the difficulties that they face. But they are also interdependent, Policies which promote development on brownfield sites will not only benefit our urban areas. But by easing pressures on rural development, they will also help to secure the future of our countryside.

**15.4.** The proposals put forward here offer a real way forward for the countryside. We believe in a living, working, protected and vibrant countryside, thriving rural communities, access for all to high quality public services, a diverse rural economy including farming, and a protected and sustainable rural environment which everyone can enjoy. It means a countryside which is listened to by government at all levels, and a countryside which can shape its own future. That is our vision. The measures detailed here will help put that vision into practice. They concentrate on people, and on the issues which matter most to people, in rural as in urban areas: jobs, a healthy economy, a stable and safe society, and better services. A countryside which offers opportunity for all. A countryside for people who live and work there. But a countryside, too, for everyone.

# annex:
## helping rural business to succeed – sources of funding and advice

This Annex aims to guide those already running and those starting up a business in a rural area through the many sources of available advice. It focuses initially on key organisations within the public sector:

## Small Business Service

The new **Small Business Service (SBS)** was set up by DTI this year to focus Government's support for small businesses. Its business support strategy is built on a detailed understanding of small business needs, particularly those of start-ups, micro-businesses (0-9 employees) and the self employed, which are particularly significant in rural areas.

Its business support strategy is being built on the **Information and Advisory Service** which, when fully operational in April 2001, will provide existing and prospective business people with wide-ranging, independent and impartial advice on matters such as finance, marketing, and regulation. It will particularly benefit those in remote locations through advice accessible by Internet and telephone.

The SBS has now contracted with a **new network of 45 Business Links**, business-led organisations which, starting in April 2001, will tailor their services to the needs of all groups in their areas. All rural communities will have access to high-quality support services provided through their new local Business Link. Until then, the existing Business Links remain in place. These are run by partnerships which include DTI, Chambers of Commerce, Training and Enterprise Councils, local authorities, enterprise agencies, local businesses and others.

> www.sbs.gov.uk
> www.businessadviceonline.org

## Department of Trade and Industry

DTI promotes enterprise, innovation and increased productivity across the economy as a whole. It encourages successful business start-ups through the SBS and through initiatives such as the National Campaign for Enterprise, which will help to change attitudes to entrepreneurship, develop entrepreneurial skills and encourage the growth of successful businesses. It implements a regional policy which is aimed at improving the economic performance of all regions (working with other Government Departments and Regional Development Agencies), focusing support for business on the best opportunities for sustainable investment and employment and supporting effective use of EU structural funds. It is also involved through UK Online for Business in helping small businesses connect to the digital marketplace. DTI also works to develop a fair and effective legal and regulatory framework, by ensuring that it encourages enterprise and avoids unnecessary burdens on business, while providing a fair deal for consumers.

> www.dti.gov.uk

## Learning and Skills Councils

From April 2001 the national and local Learning and Skills Councils (LSCs) comes into being to streamline the delivery of post-16 education and training. The national LSC will involve all the national training organisations, including LANTRA, the land-based sector organisation. Funding for local LSCs covering rural areas will recognise the additional needs that may arise, eg for on-line learning.

LSCs must ensure that the strategic needs of local employers are met and that rural learners have full access to good-quality post-16 learning opportunities.

These functions are currently carried out by Training and Enterprise Councils (TECs), operating at county level, are responsible for the delivery of training and business support under the direction of a board including representatives from local industry. The

**Consortium of Rural Training and Enterprise Councils (CORT)** brings together all TECs with substantial rural interests.

www.tec.co.uk
www.cort.org.uk
www.lantra.co.uk

## European Structural Funds

have been and will continue to be a major source of funds for rural areas. During the 1994/99 programming period English Objective 5b areas (rural areas in need of development and structural adjustment) received around £364 million.

The Structural Funds comprise:

- European Regional Development Fund (ERDF);
- European Social Fund (ESF);
- guidance section of the European Agricultural Guidance and Guarantee Fund (EAGGF);
- Financial Instrument for Fisheries Guidance (FIFG).

These funds make grants towards the costs of a variety of measures including regional and local infrastructure, training, business support and diversification of farming and other economic activity in rural and coastal areas facing difficulty.

For 2000–2006, Structural Funds support for rural areas will come through Objective 1 (areas most in need) and through the rural strand of Objective 2 (industrial, rural, urban and fisheries areas in structural difficulty). The Objective 1 and 2 allocations for England are respectively just under and just over £2bn. Cornwall has been classified as an Objective 1 area, and will be receiving some £310m from Structural Funds between 2000 and 2006. The proportion of total Objective 2 funding made available to rural areas will differ between English regions, but it is expected to total nearly £300m.

Many fishing communities make a substantial contribution to the economy of coastal rural areas, but the sea fishing industry has to meet the challenges arising from reduced fish stocks and changes in the way fish is marketed. FIFG will provide support totalling £11 million over the period 2001-03.

All rural areas are now able to seek funding from the LEADER+ programme, a European Community Initiative specifically aimed at smaller rural communities. LEADER+ aims to complement the mainstream structural programmes by promoting innovative schemes conceived and implemented by active partnerships operating at the local level. The aim is to encourage and help rural communities to think about the longer-term potential of their area, and encourage the implementation of integrated, high-quality, original strategies for sustainable development. For 2000-2006 the English LEADER+ programme will receive around £35 million.

www.europa.eu.int
see also Government Offices for the Regions below

## Food From Britain (FFB)

FFB, supported by MAFF, works to help the regional and speciality food sector. Work includes:

- funding regional food groups (for example, 'A Taste of the West', 'North West Fine Foods') who provide trade development services for their producer members;
- developing an e-commerce site to enable speciality businesses to trade over the internet.
www.foodfrombritain.com

## Ministry of Agriculture, Fisheries and Food

MAFF currently implements a variety of common agriculture policy (CAP), ERDP and other schemes through nine Regional Service Centres. Plans are currently being made for a radical change in the ways CAP schemes in particular are delivered and MAFF is also planning to join the Government Offices for the Regions (see below) next year. Full details of the new arrangements will be made available in due course.

www.maff.gov.uk

## Government Offices for the Regions

The 9 GOs bring together the regional activities of DETR, DfEE and DTI and provide a focus for a coherent approach to competitiveness and regeneration. They distribute and manage a number of major public expenditure regimes, including EU regional funds.

NE www.go-ne.gov.uk
NW www.go-nw.gov.uk
Y&TH www.goyh.gov.uk
WM www.go-wm.gov.uk
EM www.go-em.gov.uk
E of E www.go-east.gov.uk
SW www.gosw.gov.uk
SE www.go-se.gov.k
LON www.open.gov.uk/glondon

## Regional Development Agencies

RDAs were established in 1999 to help further economic growth and prosperity and to improve the quality of life in urban and rural communities. They offer a range of support measures to rural businesses, including the Rural Development Programme, the Redundant Building Grant Scheme and other initiatives covering business start-up, expanding or relocating from overseas.

www.onenortheast.co.uk
www.nwda.co.uk
www.yorkshire-forward.com
www.advantage-westmidlands.co.uk
www.emda.co.uk
www.eeda.org.uk
www.southwestengland.co.uk
www.seeda.co.uk

## Countryside Agency

The Countryside Agency is the statutory body charged with conserving and enhancing the countryside and promoting social equity and economic opportunity for people who live there. It specifically runs two schemes to improve the performance of village shops and village pubs.

www.countryside.gov.uk

## English Nature

English Nature is the statutory body that champions the conservation and enhancement of the wildlife and natural features of England. It advises on nature conservation and regulates activities affecting designated sites in England, enables others to manage land for nature conservation, through grants, projects and information, and advocates biodiversity for all as a key test of sustainable development.

www.english-nature.org.uk

## Local Authorities

Many local authorities provide dedicated economic development services. www.open.gov.uk/index/orgindex provides an index of all local authority websites.

## Local Enterprise Agencies

England's 150 LEAs are companies set up in partnership between the private sector and local authorities, with some support from central government. Their key purpose is to promote economic regeneration through supporting small firms. Work at a national level is undertaken by the National Federation of Enterprise Agencies (NFEA)

www.nfea.com

**There are many other non-governmental organisations active in helping business in rural areas. The following is necessarily a selected list of those operating most widely in rural England:**

## National Farmers Union

The NFU's central objective is to promote successful and socially responsible agriculture and horticulture, while ensuring the long-term viability of rural communities by providing advice and support to growers.

www.nfu.org.uk

## Country Landowners' Association

The CLA provides advice to its members, owners of agricultural and other countryside land and other rural businesses.

www.cla.org.uk

## National Rural Enterprise Centre

NREC, a division of the Royal Agricultural Society of England, promotes a living and working countryside by helping communities improve their local economies. It is particularly interested in how ICT can help rural businesses and communities.

www.ruralnet.org.uk

## Rural Business Network

RBN is a joint venture between ADAS, the CLA and the NFU. It is an on-line business service designed to help all areas of rural and farming industries.

www.rbnet.co.uk

## Partners In The Countryside

PITC operates at a national and local level to accelerate the regeneration of rural Britain by promoting self-help in rural communities.

www.pitc.org.uk (in preparation)

## Development Trust Association

The DTA is the national body for development trusts and community enterprise, encouraging and advising on the creation of new development trusts.

www.dta.org.uk

## British Chambers of Commerce

Through a national network of Approved Chambers of Commerce the BCC represents local businesses in all sectors of the economy, of all sizes.

www.britishchambers.org.uk

## Federation of Small Businesses

FSB is a membership organisation working to promote the interests of the self-employed and small business sector.

www.fsb.org.uk

## Association of Convenience Stores

ACS is the trade association for convenience and small store retailing.

www.acs.org.uk

## Business in the Community

an association of some 400 major companies, aims to inspire business to increase the quality and extent of their contribution to social and economic regeneration by making corporate social responsibility an essential part of business excellence.

www.bitc.org.uk

# bibliography

## Chapter 1

**Rural spaces and urban jams,** by Christie, I and Jarvis, L: In British social attitudes: the 16th report. Who shares New Labour Values? Edited by Jowell, R, Curtice, J, Park, A, Thomson, K, Jarvis, L, Bromley, C and Stratford, N. Ashgate, 1999.

**Countryside and Right of Way Bill.** The Stationery Office, 2000.

Rural Economies, Cabinet Office Performance and Innovation Unit. The Stationery Office, 1999. Also available at www.cabinet-office.gov.uk/innovation

**Spending Review 2000 – Public Service Agreements 2001-2004.** HM Treasury, July 2000. Cm 4808. Also available at www.hm-treasury.gov.uk/sr2000/psa/index

**DETR SR2000 Service Delivery Agreement.** DETR, November 2000. Available at www.detr.gov.uk/sr2000/index

**Cross Departmental Review of Rural and Countryside Programmes.** Spending Review 2000 – New Public Spending Plans 2001-2004, Chapter 23. HM Treasury, July 2000. Cm 4807. Also available at www.hm-treasury.gov.uk/sr2000/index

**Rural England: a discussion document.** DETR, 1999. Also available at www.wildlife-countryside.detr.gov.uk

**Environment Transport and Regional Affairs Select Committee Seventh Report: Rural White Paper.** The Stationery Office, 2000. Also available at www.parliament.uk/commons/selcom/etrahome

**The Government's Response to the Environment, Transport and Regional Affairs Committee's Seventh Report: Rural White Paper.** DETR, November 2000. Cm 4910. Also available at www.wildlife-countryside.detr.gov.uk

## Chapter 2

**Better Care, Higher Standards: A charter for long term care** DH/DETR, 1999. Available at www.doh.gov.uk/longtermcare

## Chapter 3

**The Changing Village.** National Federation of Women's Institutes, 1999. ISBN 0 947990 87 9

**1997 Survey of Rural Services.** Rural Development Commission, 1998. ISBN 1 869964 62 4

**Modernising Local Government Finance:** Green Paper. September 2000. Also at www.local.detr.gov.uk.greenpap/index (closing date for comments 8 December 2000).

**Counter Revolution: Modernising the Post Office Network.** Cabinet Office Performance and Innovation Unit, 2000. Also available at www.cabinet-office.gov.uk/innovation

**Raising standards, opening doors – developing links between schools and their communities.** DfEE January 2000. Also available at www.dfee.gov.uk/opendoor

**National Childcare Strategy** was first set out in DfEE Green Paper Meeting the Childcare Challenge. The Stationery Office, May 1988. Also available at www.dfee.gov.uk/eydcp/index

## Chapter 4

**The NHS Plan: A plan for investment, A plan for reform.** The Stationery Office, July 2000. Also available at www.nhs.uk/nationalplan

**Pharmacy in the Future: Implementing the NHS Plan.** DH, September 2000. Available at www.doh.gov.uk/medicines

**National Service Framework for Coronary Heart Disease.** DH, 2000. Available at www.doh.gov.uk/nsf/coronary

**National Service Framework for Mental Health.** DH, 2000. Available at www.doh.gov.uk/nsf/mentalhealth

National Cancer Plan. DH, 2000. Available at
www.doh.gov.uk/cancer

Modernising NHS Dentistry – Implementing the NHS Plan.
DH, September 2000. Available at
www.doh.gov.uk/dental/strategy

Care in the Country: Inspection of community care in rural
communities, Social Services Inspectorate (by D Brown).
Department of Health, 1999. Available at
www.doh.gov.uk/scg/poltrng

Cross-Departmental Review of Government Intervention in
Deprived Areas (GIDA). Spending Review 2000 – New
Public Spending Plans 2001-2004, Chapter 23. HM Treasury,
July 2000. Cm 4807. Also available at
www.hm-treasury.gov.uk/sr2000/index

Indices of Deprivation 2000: summary report and
forthcoming final report give full details of the indicators and
domains, methodology, presentation of the results and
guidance with interpretation of the indices as well as
comparison of the changes since the 1998 ILD. The summary
can be downloaded from www.regeneration.detr.gov.uk
together with Excel files containing the indices and a report
which considers issues raised in consultation.

A Sporting Future for All. DCMS, April 2000. Also available at
www.culture.gov.uk/sport/index.html

The British Crime Survey England and Wales 2000.
Available at www.homeoffice.gov.uk/rds

Best Value and Audit Commission Performance Indicators
for 2000/2001, DETR, 1999, are described at
www.local-regions.detr.gov.uk/bestvalue

Challenging Racism in the Rural Idyll Project Report.
Available from Home Office Race Equality Unit, 0207 273 3839

## Chapter 5

Local Housing Needs Assessment: A Guide to Good
Practice. DETR, 2000. Available from DETR Priced
Publications

Developing Housing Strategies in Rural Areas: A Good
Practice Guide (by T Brown, H Hay, R Hunt & B Line).
Chartered Institute of Housing, The Countryside Agency & The
Housing Corporation, 2000. ISBN 1 900396 84 X

Housing Green Paper Quality and Choice: a decent home
for all. DETR, 2000. Also available at
www.housing.detr.gov.uk.

Planning Policy Guidance (PPG) 3: Housing, The Stationery
Office March 2000 (ISBN 0 11 753546). Also available at
www.planning.detr.gov.uk/ppg3

Guide to Good Practice, Affordable Housing for Rural
Communities: Sussex Rural Community Council and the
Housing Corporation – September 1998.

Housing in England: a report of the 1998/99 survey of
English housing. DETR, 2000. The Stationery Office £3.50.
ISBN 0 116213655

Wasted Rural Homes – a Blueprint for Action, Empty
Homes Agency, 1999. Available from 195-197 Victoria Street,
London SW1 or www.emptyhomes.com

By Design – Urban Design in the Planning System:
Towards Better Practice. DETR and the Commission for
Architecture and the Built Environment May 2000. ISBN 0
7277 2937 3. Available from Thomas Telford Publishing, Book
Sales Department, 1 Heron Quay, London E14 4JD.
Tel: 020 7665 2464. www.t-telford.co.uk

## Chapter 6

A New Deal for Transport: Better for Everyone. DETR,
1998. ISBN 0101395027. Available from The Stationery Office.
Also available at www.detr.gov.uk/itwp

Transport 2010: The 10 Year Plan, DETR, July 2000.
Also available at www.detr.gov.uk.trans2010

Transport 2010: The Background Analysis, DETR, July
2000. Also available at www.detr.gov.trans2010

Transport Bill. The Stationery Office, 2000

Study into Secondary Rail Lines. Shadow Strategic Rail
Authority June 2000. Also available at
www.sra.gov.uk/Publications/Consultation_Docs/ruralrailreport
1_content

Guidance on Full Local Transport Plans. DETR, March
2000. Also available at www.local-transport.detr.gov.uk/fulltp

Tomorrow's roads – safer for everyone: the Government's
safety strategy and casualty reduction targets for 2010.
DETR, March 2000. Also available at
www.roads.detr.gov.uk/roadsafety/strategy

Traffic Calming on major roads. DETR Guidance on traffic
calming measures in villages: DETR Traffic Advisory Leaflet
1/00. Also available at www.roads.detr.gov.uk/roadnetwork

## Chapter 7

Rural Economies, Cabinet Office Performance and Innovation
Unit. The Stationery Office, 2000. Also available at
www.cabinet-office.gov.uk/innovation

Planning Policy Guidance (PPG) 6: Town Centres and
Retail Development. The Stationery Office, June 1996
(ISBN 0 11 753294 0)

The Secretary of State's Proposed Changes to Draft
Regional Planning Guidance for East Anglia published in
March 2000 is an example of where, in line with the policy in
paragraph 7.2.5, the role of market towns is recognised.

**Planning Policy Guidance (PPG) 11: Regional Planning,** The Stationery Office, October 2000. Also available at www.planning.detr.gov.uk/ppg3

**Planning Policy Guidance (PPG) 13: Transport.** HMSO, March 1994. PPG 13 is being revised.

**Modernising Local Government Finance: Green Paper.** September 2000. Also at www.local.detr.gov.uk.greenpap/index (Closing date for comments 8 December 2000).

**Regional Strategies.** RDAs, October 1999. Regional strategies are available on RDAs' websites:

> www.onenortheast.co.uk
> www.nwda.co.uk
> www.yorkshire-forward.com
> www.advantage-westmidlands.co.uk
> www.emda.co.uk
> www.eeda.org.uk
> www.southwestengland.co.uk
> www.seeda.co.uk

**Waterways for Tomorrow.** DETR, June 2000

**Tomorrow's Tourism.** DCMS, 1999. Also available at www.culture.gov.uk/tourism

**Planning Policy Guidance (PPG) 17: Sport and Recreation.** HMSO, September 1991 (ISBN 0 11 752520 0). A consultation document on revisions to PPG 17 is about to be published.

## Chapter 8

**A New Direction for Agriculture.** MAFF, December 1999

**Action Plan for farming.** MAFF, March 2000. Also available at www.maff.gov.uk/farm/farmindex

**England Rural Development Programme.** A summary is available free of charge from MAFF Publications Admail 6000, London SW1A 2XX. Tel: 089459 556000. Also available at www.maff.gov.uk/erdp

**England Rural Development Programme.** The full programme and an executive summary will be published in November 2000 and can be ordered from MAFF Publications (as above) or viewed at MAFF regional offices. Will be available at www.maff.gov.uk/erdp

**Planning Policy Guidance (PPG) 7 The Countryside – Environmental Quality and Economic and Social Development.** The Stationery Office, February 1997

**Planning Policy Guidance (PPG) 13: Transport.** HMSO, March 1994. PPG 13 is being revised.

**Action Plan for Farming Bulletin No 1.** MAFF, July 2000. Also available at www.maff.gov.uk/farm/farmindex

**The NHS Plan: A plan for investment, A plan for reform.** The Stationery Office, July 2000. Also available at www.nhs.uk/nationalplan

**Planning and rural businesses:** a joint statement from the Regional Development Agencies and the Countryside Agency. 6 September 2000. East of England Development Agency Press Release; Countryside Agency Press Release 50/2000.

## Chapter 9

**Rural Economies,** Cabinet Office Performance and Innovation Unit. The Stationery Office, 2000. Also available at www.cabinet-office.gov.uk/innovation/2000/reports

**Stronger Planning Protection for AONBs:** Parliamentary answer by Nick Raynsford MP to a question from Dr Alan Whitehead MP (Southampton, Test), 13 June 2000, Hansard Col. 555W.

**Countryside and Right of Way Bill.** The Stationery Office, 2000.

**Greater Protection and Better Management of Common Land in England and Wales.** DETR, January 2000. Also available at www.wildlife-countryside.detr.gov.uk/consult/common

**A New Focus for England's Woodlands – Strategic Priorities and Programmes.** Forestry Commission, December 1998. ISBN 0 85538 539 3

## Chapter 10

**Biodiversity: The UK Biodiversity Action Plan.** HMSO 1994. ISBN 0 10 124282 4

**Local Government Act 2000.** The Stationery Office, 2000

**Wildlife and Countryside Act 1981.** HMSO, 1981

**A New Direction for Agriculture.** MAFF, December 1999

**A Better Quality of Life: A Strategy for Sustainable Development in the United Kingdom.** The Stationery Office, May 1999. ISBN 0 10 143529. Summary available at www.detr.gov.uk/environment/sustainable/factsheets/summary

**Local Environment Action Plans.** Environment Agency. Available through Environment Agency Customer Contact Teams in relevant Regional Head Office, or the Public Enquiries Unit at Rio House, Waterside Drive, Aztec West, Almondsbury, Bristol. Tel: 01454 624507.

**Making Biodiversity Happen: Green Ministers Biodiversity check list.** DETR, March 2000

**Climate change and UK Nature Conservation:** a review of the impact of climate change on UK species and habitat conservation policy, published 26 October as part of the UK Climate Impacts Programme funded by DETR.

## Chapter 11

**Countryside and Right of Way Bill.** The Stationery Office, 2000.

**Walks on Ministry of Defence Lands.** Defence Estates, June 1996. Obtainable from ATL Focal Point, Defence Estates, HQ Land Command, Hill Block, Erskine Barracks, Wilton, Salisbury, Wilts SP2 0AG. Also available at www.defence-estates.mod.uk

**In Trust and on time – the Strategy for the Defence Estates.** The Stationery Office, 2000. ISBN 0117729396

**Planning Policy Guidance (PPG) 17: Sport and Recreation.** HMSO, September 1991. ISBN 0 11 752520 0 A consultation document on revisions to PPG 17 is expected to be published.

**Waterways for Tomorrow.** DETR, June 2000

**Code of Practice on Conservation, Access and recreation.** DETR, June 2000

**Agreeing access to water for canoeing.** Environment Agency, 1999. Available from Environment Agency Recreation and Navigation, Rio House, Waterside Drive, Aztec West, Almondsbury, Bristol. 01454 624507.

**The Final Report of the Committee of Inquiry into Hunting with Dogs in England and Wales.** HMSO, 2000. Also available at www.huntinginquiry.gov.uk

**Salmon and Freshwater Fisheries review.** MAFF, February 2000. Also available at www.maff.gov.uk

## Chapter 12

**Best Value Guidance** is available at www.local-regions.detr.gov.uk/bestvalue

**Modernising Local Government Finance: Green Paper.** September 2000. Also at www.local.detr.gov.uk.greenpap/index (Closing date for comments 8 December 2000).

**Local Government Act 2000.** The Stationery Office, 2000.

**Rural regeneration – progress in the rural New Commitment to Regeneration pathfinders.** Local Government Association Research Report No 10. LGA, 2000. Available from IDeA Publication Sales, 020 7296 6600, quoting reference SR013

**Community Self-Help Social Exclusion Unit Policy Action Team (PAT9) Report.** Home Office, 2000. Available at www.cabinet-office.gov.uk/seu/2000/compendium

## Chapter 13

**Professional Policy Making for the Twenty First Century.** Report by Strategic Policy Making Team. Cabinet Office 2000. Available at www.cabinet-office.gov.uk/moderngov/policy/index

**Reaching Out: The Role of Central Government at regional and Local Level.** Cabinet Office Performance and Innovation Unit. The Stationery Office, 2000. Also available at www.cabinet-office.gov.uk/innovation

**England Rural Development Programme.** A summary is available free of charge from MAFF Publications Admail 6000, London SW1A 2XX. Tel: 089459 556000. Also available at www.maff.gov.uk/erd

**England Rural Development Programme.** The full programme and an executive summary will be published in November 2000 and can be ordered from MAFF Publications (as above) or viewed at MAFF regional offices. Will be available at www.maff.gov.uk/erdp

**Local Government Act 2000.** The Stationery Office, 2000.

**Health Act 1999.** The Stationery Office, 1999

**Spending Review 2000 – New Public Spending Plans 2001–2004.** HM Treasury, July 2000. Also available at www.hm-treasury.gov.uk/sr2000/index

**The NHS Plan: A plan for investment, A plan for reform.** The Stationery Office, July 2000. Also available at www.nhs.uk/nationalplan

## Chapter 14

**Spending Review 2000 – Public Service Agreements 2001-2004.** HM Treasury, July 2000. Cm 4808. Also available at www.hm-treasury.gov.uk/sr2000/psa/index

**A Better Quality of Life: A Strategy for Sustainable Development in the United Kingdom.** The Stationery Office, May 1999. ISBN 0 10 143529. Summary available at www.detr.gov.uk/environment/sustainable/factsheets/summary

**Towards Sustainable Agriculture – A Pilot Set of Indicators.** MAFF, February 2000.

**The State of the Countryside 2000.** Countryside Agency, April 2000. Distributed by Countryside Agency Publications. Po Box 125, Wetherby, West Yorkshire LS23 7EP.

### Notes

DETR priced publications are available from: DETR Publications Sales Centre, Unit 21, Goldthorpe Industrial Estate, Goldthorpe, Rotherham S63 9BL. Telephone: 01709 891318, Fax: 01709 881673.

DETR unpriced publications are available from: DETR Free Literature, PO Box 236, Wetherby, LS23 7NB. Telephone: 0870 1226 236, Fax: 0870 1226 237

Printed in the UK for The Stationery Office Limited
On behalf of the Controller of Her Majesty's Stationery Office
Dd 5069528   11/00   19585   TJ2994